RELIGIOUS OFFENCE AND CENSORSHIP OF PUBLICATIONS

This book analyzes the role of laws and the judiciary in the process of censorship in India. It examines the rationales and observations produced by the judiciary when demands for censorship are directed against publications that allegedly offend religious sentiments. Focusing on a micro-level analysis of censorship of publications, it presents a hard case to understand the limitations of freedom of expression and the role played by the judiciary in defining its boundaries. The volume traces the evolution of laws governing freedom of expression since the colonial period and the context in which these laws were amended after Independence. It also explicates how the legal process – the structural and functional aspects of working of judiciary – affects the fate of freedom of expression in India. Employing comparative legal analysis, it tries to understand and situate the Indian case within the larger discourse of censorship and freedom of expression around the world, thereby marking its similarities and differences. In unravelling the politics of censorship, the author also examines the interaction among different stakeholders like government, non-state actors and the judiciary.

A tract for our times, this book will be of great interest to scholars and researchers of law, especially constitutional law and fundamental rights, politics, especially political theory and Indian politics, modern India and South Asian studies.

Nishant Kumar teaches Political Science at Dyal Singh College, University of Delhi, India. After finishing his undergraduate studies from Hindu College (DU) and postgraduate studies from the Centre from Political Studies (JNU), he completed his PhD from King's College London, UK, as Commonwealth Scholar. His areas of interest include political theory, constitutional law in South Asia and intellectual history. He is currently also the coordinator of IHRG (Intellectual History Research Group), an international group of scholars working in the field of the history of ideas in India.

RELIGIOUS OFFENCE AND CENSORSHIP OF PUBLICATIONS

An Enquiry through the Prism of Indian Laws and the Judiciary

Nishant Kumar

Routledge
Taylor & Francis Group
LONDON AND NEW YORK

First published 2023
by Routledge
4 Park Square, Milton Park, Abingdon, Oxon OX14 4RN

and by Routledge
605 Third Avenue, New York, NY 10158

Routledge is an imprint of the Taylor & Francis Group, an informa business

British Library Cataloguing-in-Publication Data
A catalogue record for this book is available from the British Library

ISBN: 978-1-032-38499-3 (hbk)
ISBN: 978-1-032-43892-4 (pbk)
ISBN: 978-1-003-36925-7 (ebk)

DOI: 10.4324/9781003369257

Typeset in Sabon
by SPi Technologies India Pvt Ltd (Straive)

Dedicated to *Naima*

CONTENTS

ACKNOWLEDGEMENTS

Writing this book was the most beautiful and adventurous journey I have ever undertaken. It therefore becomes imminent to express my gratitude towards all individuals and institutions, which in different roles, either became co-travellers or facilitators in this journey. I wish to first thank Commonwealth Scholarship Agency for providing me the required funding as Commonwealth Scholar to undertake this research in London. I would also like to thank my PhD supervisors, Sunil Khilnani and Christophe Jaffrelot, and my examiners, Bhikhu Parekh and Rochana Bajpai, without whom this project would not have seen the light of the day. Words are not enough to express my gratitude for the office staff at various institutions: King's College London, SOAS, LSE, British Library, Nehru Memorial Museum and Library, and National Archives of India, who graciously offered all help possible to locate archival sources and other materials for research. There are some, without whom this journey would not have even started. Smita for being such a wonderful life partner, and my parents for doing whatever they could to make me whatever I am today. Last, but not the least, I would like to acknowledge the contribution of Naima, who in several undefined ways, remained a constant source of strength and motivation. My special thanks to the entire Routledge team, including the reviewers and editorial board, for making this dream come true.

LIST OF ABBREVIATIONS

AIMF	All India Minority Forum
AIR	All India Reporter
CAD	Constituent Assembly Debates
CPI (M)	Communist Party of India (Marxist)
CriJL	Criminal Law Journal
CrPC	Code of Criminal Procedure
CSDS	Centre for the Study of Developing Societies
DMK	Dravida Munnetra Kazhagam
ECHR	European Convention on Human Rights
ECtHR	European Court of Human Rights
ICCPR	International Covenant on Civil and Political Rights
IPC	Indian Penal Code
LSD	Lok Sabha Debates
MIM	Majlis-e-Ittehadul Muslimeen
NMML	Nehru Memorial Museum and Library, Delhi
PUCL	People's Union for Civil Liberties
RSD	Rajya Sabha Debates
RSS	Rashtriya Swayamsevak Sangh
SAHMAT	Safdar Hashmi Memorial Trust
SCC	Supreme Court Case
SCR	Supreme Court Reporter

LIST OF CASES

Arun Ghosh v. State of West Bengal, (1969) 1970 3 SCR 288.

Baba Khalil Ahamad v. State, A.I.R. 1960 All. 715.

Baragur Ramachandrappa & Ors. v. State of Karnataka & Anr., (1998) CriJL 3639.

Beauharnais v. Illinois, (1952) 343 U.S. 250.

Bhagwati Charan Shukla v. Provincial Government, (1947) A.I.R. 1947, Nagpur 1.

Brij Bhushan v. State of Delhi, (1950) AIR 37 SC 129.

Chaplinsky v. New Hampshire, (1942) 315 U.S. 568.

Choudhury v. United Kingdom, (1991) Application No. 17439/90, ECommHR.

Devi Sharan Sharma and another v. King Emperor, (1927) 14 AIR 594 (Lahore).

Devidas Ramachandra Tuljapurkar v. State of Maharashtra & Ors., (2015) (Criminal Appeal No. 1179 of 2010).

Dr. Ram Manohar Lohia v. State of Bihar and others, (1965) 1966 AIR 740.

Gopal Vinayak Godse v. Union of India and others, (1971) AIR BOM 56.

Harnam Das v. State of Uttar Pradesh, (1961) A.I.R 1662.

I.A. v Turkey, (December 13, 2005) Appl. No. 42571/98).

Kasem Said Ahmad and Asmaa Abdol-hamid v. Denmark, (18 April 2008) Communication no. 1487/2006, CCPR.

M/S Prakash Jha Productions vs. Union of India, Writ Petition (Civil) No. 345 of 2011.

Manzar Sayeed Khan v. State of Maharashtra (2009) 12 S.C.C. 157

Maqbool Fida Hussain v. Raj Kumar Pandey, (2008) Crl. Revision Petition No. 114/2007.

Master Amanpreet Singh and Others v. Government of India and others, (1996), AIR PH 284.

Mohammad Khalid v. The Chief Commissioner, Delhi, (1967) A.I.R. 1968 Delhi 13.

N. Veerabrahmam v. State of Andhra Pradesh, A.I.R. 1959 A.P. 572.

Nand Kishore Singh v. State of Bihar, AIR 1986 Pat 98.

National Socialist Party of America v. Village of Skokie, (1977) 432 U.S. 43.

New York Times Co. v. Sullivan, (1964) 376 U.S. 254.
Police Dept of Chicago v. Mosley, (1972) 408 US 92 96.
Public Prosecutor v. P. Ramasamy Nadar, Case Number - Crl. App. No. 125 of 1962.
R. V. Bhasin v. 2 Marine Drive Police Station, (2010) Criminal Application No. 1421 of 2007.
R. v. Chief Metropolitan Stipendiary Magistrate, ex p. Choudhury (Queen's Bench Division) (1991), 1 QB 429 (1990)
R.A.V. v. City of St. Paul, (1992) 505 U.S. 377.
Raj Pal v. King Emperor (1927) 14 AIR 590 (Lahore)
Ram Manohar Lohia v. State of Bihar, (1966) AIR SC 740.
Ramji Lal Modi v. State of Uttar Pradesh, (1957) AIR 620.
Ramlal Puri vs. State of Madhya Pradesh (1970) AIR 1971 MP 152
Ranjit Udeshi v. *State of Maharashtra*, (1965) A.I.R. 881.
Rigsadvokaten (Director of Public Prosecutions), (2006) J. Nr. RA-2006-41-0151.
Romesh Thapar v. State of Madras, (1950) AIR 37 SC 124.
S. Rangrajan v. P. Jagjivan Ram, (1989) 2 SCC 574.
S. Tamilselvan and other v. The Government of Tamil Nadu and others, (W.P. No. 1215 of 2015).
Shiv Ram Dass Udasin v. The Punjab State, (1954) A.I.R. 1955 P H 28.
Shreya Singhal v. Union of India, Writ Petition (Criminal) No. 167 of 2012.
Sri Baragur Ramachandrappa & Ors. v. State of Karnataka & Anr, (2007) 5 S.C.C.11.
State of Bihar v. Shailabal Devi (1952) AIR 329 SCR 654
State of Gujarat v. Mirzapur Moti Kureshi Kassab Janat (2005) 8 SCC 534, 567
State of Maharashtra & Ors. v. Sanghraj Damodar Rupawate & Ors. (2010) Civil Appeal of 2010 (Arising out of S.L.P. (C) No. 8931 of 2007)
State of Uttar Pradesh v. Lalai Singh Yadav (1976) 1977 AIR 202
Sujato Bhadra v. State of West Bengal (2006) 39 A.I.C. 239
Superintendent, Central Prison, Fatehgarh v. Ram Manohar Lohia (1960), 2 SCR 84
The State of Madras v. V. G. Row (1952) AIR 196 SCR 597
The State of Mysore vs. Henry Rodrigues And Anr. (1961) 1962 CriLJ 564
The Trustees of Safdar Hashmi Memorial Trust v. Govt. Of NCT of Delhi (2001) CriLJ 3689
Virendra v. State of Punjab (1957) AIR 896 SCR 308
Whitehouse v. Lemon (1977) (1979) 2 WLR 281
Zac Poonen v. Hidden Treasure Literature (2001) 2002 CriLJ 481

INTRODUCTION

"The writer Perumal Murugan is dead."

This announcement was made by Perumal Murugan, a Tamil writer, in his Facebook post on 12 January 2015 (*The Indian Express*, 15 January 2015). It reflected the state of the writer's mind after one of his popular novels, *Madhorubagan* (One Part Woman), first published in December 2010 and a recipient of several prizes and accolades, suddenly became the subject of controversy in 2015. *Madhorubagan* was set in a village near Tiruchengode (Namakkal district) during the colonial period, and it told of the social stigma faced by a childless couple.[1] The controversy over Murugan's novel erupted when, in December 2014, some pages of the novel were photocopied and distributed along with a handbill that accused the author of demeaning women belonging to the Kongu Vellala community (also called Gounders) and of vilifying an old tradition attached to the village temple. The accusation took a dramatic turn after around 40 different caste-based outfits, mobilized by the local leaders, decided to launch an agitation against the author for presenting in poor light the character of Gounder women and the old temple ritual, which, they held, brought a bad name to Tiruchengode. The town was shut down in protest, and the author received threats to his life from the local community. Though no formal ban was placed on the book, the attitude of the district administration created a sense of forced censorship. On 12 January the District Revenue Officer, V. R. Subbulakshmi, who also served as Additional District Magistrate, convened a 'peace committee meeting', to which Murugan along with his lawyer were also invited. However, in the meeting, Murugan and his lawyer were not allowed to present his case, nor was he allowed to meet the protesting groups. Rather, authorities ordered him to sign a statement, as had been demanded by the protesting groups. It stated that the author wished to apologize unconditionally, agreed to recall all copies of the book, change controversial references and paragraphs, and never in the future to write anything connected with Tiruchengode. In order to buy peace, the district administration had sacrificed, it would seem, the freedom of speech and

DOI: 10.4324/9781003369257-1

expression of P. Murugan. Murugan's subsequent Facebook post claiming his death as a writer was a reaction to these events, which he claimed had left him 'insecure and disgusted'.[2]

This episode is just one among many that illuminate forms of censorship that are operational in Indian society. The case of Murugan also exposed different layers involved in the process of censorship. Let me highlight some of the important issues involved in this case. First, when the book was originally published in the local language (Tamil) more than four years before the incident, there was no protest against the content of the book. In fact, it became a bestseller, with the publisher selling more than 5,000 copies before the controversy began.[3] The gap between the time of publication and the claims about hurt sentiments suggest other intervening factors at play. Second, the attitude of the government authorities of Tamil Nadu was open to question. The district administration claimed that its action was best to control a potentially disruptive law-and-order situation in the town. In the 'peace-meeting', the administration brokered a one-sided deal which not only legitimized the claims of hurt by the protestors, but also ensured that their demands were met. Neither did the administration investigate who was responsible for the circulation of photocopies of selective portions from the book that had incited the harassment of Murugan, nor did the police try to find out the people who had threatened Murugan and his family members. The message was clear: the district administration wanted to avoid public-order problems, and it was convinced that the freedom of expression of the author was a small price to be paid to secure that.

The third important aspect related to the case, which has often been ignored by analysts and commentators, was the role of the court. After Murugan was forced to sign a compromise letter by district authorities, several organizations including the People's Union for Civil Liberties (PUCL) filed writ petitions in the Madras High Court highlighting two issues: first, continuous harassment of Murugan by 'caste and religion based groups'[4] and, second, the role of state authorities in pressuring Murugan to sign the agreement. Based on these grounds, the court was requested to hold the agreement 'illegal, unconstitutional, and not being enforceable'. The first petition in this regard was filed on 26 January 2015 in the High Court. Petitions were also filed by the protesting groups, requesting the court to order the government to ban the book and bring criminal proceedings against Murugan for vilifying religious practices and disturbing communal harmony. Within a month, Murugan submitted his reply in the form of an affidavit, where he spoke out about his experiences as well as his discomfort with the attitude of the state authorities. However, it took more than one-and-a-half years for the court to pronounce its final judgement on the subject.[5] Such delays in judgements create uncertainty as far as the issue of legality is concerned and have proved detrimental to the defender's right to freedom of expression. Scholars and commentators on free speech have held that cases like that of Murugan have a tendency to produce a 'chilling effect' that acts as an informal mode of censoring freedom of expression.[6] Further, it exposed a looming complexity in the response of the Indian state when claims of religious offence are directed against freedom of speech and expression.

Such incidents, however, are not new for Indian society. A survey of case laws and archives of newspapers and periodicals suggests that a fundamental right to freedom of speech and expression has routinely faced challenges. When the constitution of independent India was being drafted and the provisions concerning fundamental rights were being discussed, the constitution makers assigned a special role to the judiciary: that of safeguarding citizens' fundamental rights from encroachment by individuals, groups or the executive. It was assumed that in case of contradictions and controversies, the judiciary would act to protect the rights of citizens. But how far has the judiciary succeeded in upholding this expectation of the constitution makers? In the present work, I examine this aspect through an analysis of the role that law and the legal process have played when freedom of expression is threatened by the claims of religious offence or hurt sentiments. Central to this is the judiciary's role as the interpreter of the constitutional provisions that guarantee freedom of speech and expression and the laws that allow for its restrictions.

As the field of freedom of speech and expression is too broad, the scope of this study has been confined specifically to censorship of publications. Focus is on those publications which invoked religious issues and became contentious as they were claimed to be 'offensive' to religious sensibilities by socio-religious groups. Commentators on censorship in India have claimed that since Independence there have been many publications that became party to such controversies, and were either banned or censored by authorities citing reasons like a threat to public order or the hurt caused to the religious sentiments of different communities (Dhavan 2008; Kumar 1997). Censorship of publications becomes a representative case to analyze and understand the scope of freedom of speech and expression due to various reasons. First, in India, where the average literacy rate is low, it is striking to note how a publication could generate controversy over hurt caused by the publication's content. Moreover, most books that attracted controversy were not even aimed at public consumption. The price of the book and the specificity of the subject (especially in cases of academic publications) should have acted as hurdles to broader public reception or awareness. Therefore, the chances of publications being a cause of hurt sentiments are much less than in cases of other modes of expression. It is easier, for example, in the case of visual representation, like films and cartoons, to reach a wider audience and attract opposition if it is controversial. However, it is often seen that in controversies related to publications, rumours and hearsay play important roles in spreading the content and its interpretation. The fact remains that publications, like any other visual forms of expression, are equally vulnerable to the claims of hurt sentiments and they are indicative of the scope of freedom of expression. Second, censorship of publications also helps to clarify the legal boundaries of freedom of speech and expression. Section 295(A) of the Indian Penal Code (IPC), related to hurting religious sentiments, and section 153(A), related to promoting enmity between two classes of citizens, have been routinely used by government authorities as well as non-state actors in their efforts to censor different forms of expression. In 2001, authorities in Delhi used the provisions under section 153(A) and 295(A) of IPC to disallow a public exhibition arranged by the Safdar Hashmi Memorial Trust (SAHMAT) group.[7] Similarly, in case of the artist M. F. Hussain, the petitioners filed criminal charges against the painter under the same statutory laws.[8] Third, controversies related to censorship of publications also explicate the interplay of power relations between important stakeholders – government agencies, courts and non-state actors. Hurt caused to religious sensibilities has been one of the most potent reasons invoked for censoring and banning publications in India. Although government authorities have also exercised their legal powers against publications that were adjudged to be against national interest, defamatory of individuals or obscene, the contentions based on religious subjects have been vital. One important reason for this is the fact that claimants of hurt sentiments have often used the logic of another fundamental right – that is, the right to freely profess, practice and propagate their religion, guaranteed by article 25 of the constitution.[9] So, focus on the subject also enables a broad understanding of how legal processes in India deal with situations where two different fundamental rights are in contention – freedom of speech and expression guaranteed under article 19(1)(a) and freedom of religious practice guaranteed under article 25.

Freedom of Speech and Expression and Legal Intervention: A Comparative Perspective

Freedom of speech and expression has always enjoyed a special value within liberalism. On the one hand, almost everyone seems to agree that freedom of speech and expression is important, and it ought to enjoy special legal protection that does not extend to any other class of acts in society; on the other hand, there is no real agreement amongst philosophers, lawyers, legislators and citizens as to why such freedom is important and how much freedom might be too much freedom. Historically, the primary justifications put forward in favour of freedom of speech fall in one of these four categories – (1) for the purpose of promotion of truth (or the marketplace of ideas theory) (Emerson 1966; Mill 1978); (2) its benefits to democracy and self-government (Meiklejohn 1966); (3) its role in promotion of other virtues that survive society (Bollinger 1988); and (4) its contribution to individual's self-realization and self-determination (the autonomy-based defence of free speech) (Baker 1989). Interestingly, none of the advocates dismisses the need for state intervention. For example, though J. S. Mill (1978) advocated that freedom of speech was important to produce a marketplace of ideas which could get us closer to truth, he also devised the 'harm principle' and argued that government interventions could be valid if they aimed to neutralize speech acts that had high potential to cause harm to others. With respect to state intervention, however, most advocates of freedom of speech and expression suggest that the principles of 'neutrality' be followed – both 'content-neutrality' and 'viewpoint neutrality'. It is claimed that state action should neither be based on the content of the speech acts nor on the viewpoint that the speech acts represented. Similarly, there remains scepticism about the nature and scope of the state's interventions. For example, there is wide acceptance that 'child pornography' should be banned, but there are continuing debates about whether the state is justified in making laws to regulate adult pornography, blasphemy and forms of speech which are widely referred to as hate speech. Regardless of the theoretical debates on the subject, most governments across the world have provisions in law to restrict free speech in some form or other.

International law, which appears to vociferously defend the right to free speech, also recognizes the need to allow some liberty to member states to legislate in order to balance free speech against its harms. For example, article 19(2) of the International Covenant on Civil and Political Rights (ICCPR) of the United Nations provides for the right to freedom of expression. However, it also allows the member states to restrict free speech by law under clause 3 of the same article, if such restrictions are meant to protect the 'rights' or 'reputations' of others or for national security, public order or public health and morals. It is further specified under article 20(2) that 'any advocacy of national, racial or religious hatred that constitutes incitement to discrimination, hostility or violence shall be prohibited'. Similarly, article 10 of the European Convention on Human Rights (ECHR) protects freedom of speech subject to certain restrictions that the member states could by law deem necessary

> in the interests of national security, territorial integrity or public safety, for the prevention of disorder or crime, for the protection of health or morals, for the protection of the reputation or rights of others, for preventing the disclosure of information received in confidence, or for maintaining the authority and impartiality of the judiciary.

It is evident that even international organizations like the UN and the EU observe the rights of its member states to restrict free speech on some important grounds.

If we look at the legal provisions devised by individual countries to control the harms of free speech, we find a wide disparity. At one end of the spectrum stands the US legislation under the First Amendment, which allows strong protection to freedom of speech, and at the other end appear laws devised under the German system, where article 130 of the Strafgesetzbuch

(German Criminal Code) adopted in 1960 prohibits attack on human dignity, which includes: (1) inciting hatred against a certain part of the population, (2) inciting to violent or arbitrary acts against such part of the population, or (3) insulting, maliciously ridiculing or defaming such part. Bhikhu Parekh has rightly pointed to the diversity of issues that have prompted legal restrictions in different countries:

> Britain bans abusive, insulting, and threatening speech. Denmark and Canada prohibit speech that is insulting and degrading; and India and Israel ban speech that incites racial and religious hatred and is likely to stir up hostility between groups. In the Netherlands, it is a criminal offence to express publicly views insulting to groups of persons. Australia prohibits speech that offends, insults, humiliates, or intimidates individuals or groups, and some of its states have laws banning racial vilification. Germany goes further, banning speech defining and diminishing hate speech that violates the dignity of an individual, implies that he or she is an inferior being, or maliciously degrades or defames a group.
>
> (2012: 37)

Case laws in different countries appear to define the scope for government regulation based on the challenges and potential threats that extreme defence of free speech could pose in that society. For example, in the US case, Samuel Walker (1994) argues that the Supreme Court has shown a significant shift in its position from the early 20th century to the 1940s, and then from the 1950s to the 1980s. This shift could occur because the civil rights movement in the US recognized that free speech was the only resource available for the powerless and the excluded, and so always stood in its favour, as it served broad social and political needs in the struggle for racial equality (Walker 1994: 160). One can definitely locate a shift in the courts' position from the early 20th century, when hate crimes of the white supremacist group the Ku Klux Klan were widely reported, to the post–Second World War period of ideological opposition to communist and fascist ideologies. A shift in the judiciary's attitude is clearly visible from cases like *Chaplinsky* (1942) and *Beauharnais* (1952), where it upheld laws against group libel and argued that not all speech is protected by the First Amendment, to cases like *Sullivan* (1964), *Mosley* (1972) and more prominently in the *Skokie* (1977) and *R. A. V* (1992). The debate seems to have taken a further turn with the challenge of 'campus hate speech' that became prominent from the 1980s onwards. This phase is also marked by the rapid expansion of feminist theory, critical race theory and other alternative discourses, all of which attacked mainstream and official speech as inherently oppressive and white-male-dominated discourse and argued for pluralization and fragmentation of discourse (Rosenfeld 2012: 255). As the judgements in different cases show, the court has set very high standards for free speech, and its regulation is possible only in exceptional circumstances, even in cases concerned with hate speech. However, at the same time if we look at the cases that appear in the European courts, especially, in the European Court of Human Rights (ECtHR), it appears that the court has upheld the right of the member states to use legal sanctions against the claims of free speech in a wide range of cases. For example, in *Otto-Preminger-Institut* (1994), the court held the forfeiture and seizure of the anti-religious film *Das Liebenskonsil* (Council in Heaven) did not contravene article 10 of ECtHR since it was aimed at the protection of the religious right of the majority, in that case the Christians of Austria. Similarly, in *I.A.* (2005), the court held that the case of blasphemous libel of a publisher was justified for printing a fictional work by Abdullah Riza Erguven entitled *Forbidden Verses* in which a character makes disparaging comments about Islam. It argued that the conviction was intended to protect Muslims against offensive attacks on matters regarded as sacred by the community.

These readings of the legal provisions and case laws show that there is no uniformity in the way questions surrounding the scope and limitations to free speech are handled around the world. In this respect, the case of India is no different. In India, though freedom of speech and expression is a guaranteed constitutional right, it in no way enjoys any primacy or prior preference over other rights. The Constituent Assembly Debates (CAD) clearly show the tension between different aspects of rights and the way the constitution makers tried to balance them along with the possible threats emanating from freedom of speech and expression by providing certain restrictions under article 19(2). This article, as it stands today, imposes reasonable restrictions 'in the interests of the sovereignty and integrity of India, the security of the State, friendly relations with foreign States, public order, decency or morality or in relation to contempt of court, defamation or incitement to an offence'. However, India's difference from the Western democracies is also clearly visible if we examine major legislation designed to regulate free speech, and try to identify the reasons for prosecution specified in these laws. For example, even if we argue that 'incitement to an offence' and concern for 'public order', as present in article 19(2), may reflect the debates in the West, how do we account for restrictions based on 'decency', 'morality' or 'defamation'? The broad latitude of restrictions to free speech that India allows can further be gauged from the language used to define the statutory laws. For example, section 153(A) of the IPC criminalizes the promotion of 'enmity between different groups on grounds of religion, race, place of birth, residence, language etc' or engagement in 'acts prejudicial to maintenance of harmony'. The broad scope of section 153(A) is further buttressed by section 153(B), which prohibits 'imputations and assertions prejudicial to national-integration'. The section criminalizes the use of 'words either spoken or written', signs 'or by visible representations or otherwise'. Similarly, there are other provisions like:

- Section 295, which prohibits 'injuring or defiling [any] place of worship with intent to insult the religion of any class';
- Section 295(A), which prohibits 'deliberate and malicious acts, intended to outrage religious feelings or any class by insulting its religion or religious beliefs';
- Section 298, which prohibits 'uttering words, etc, with deliberate intent to wound religious feelings';
- Section 505(1), which prohibits 'statements conducive to public mischief'; and,
- Section 505(2), which prohibits 'statements creating or promoting enmity, hatred or ill-will between classes'.

These legal provisions, unlike most European provisions, use terms like 'injury', 'insult', 'malicious act', 'outrage feelings', 'wound', 'promoting enmity' and 'ill-will', which have much wider, normative and practical connotations. These legal provisions and the historical background in which they emerged indicate that the right to freedom of speech and expression is treated differently in India. This obviously stands in contradistinction to the expectations of those advocates of free speech who assume there can be any right way to establish free speech through abstract principles, which could then be applied anywhere, regardless of local conditions. Charles Taylor (1989) has rightly questioned such assumptions based on two reasons: (1) Any regime of freedom of expression, he opined, required some broad consensus. It cannot just be imposed by law, because, if its principles are too distant from mass sensibilities, it will be rendered nugatory by all sorts of extra-legal pressures; and (2) Any regime of free expression has limits which are justified by the possibility of harm inflicted on others. This is an issue which is sensitive to cultural differences.

In the case of India, though one may disagree with the kind of regulative and restrictive mechanism allowed to be placed in the hands of government, one cannot deny that the regulations were included in a particular social and historical context. The complexities of inter-communal relationships, marred by the memory of partition, and the challenges facing the post-colonial Indian state, particularly that of national integration and nation-building, became reasons for such extensive provisions for restricting free speech in India. So as the European nations argued for regulation of hate speech in the context of the Holocaust and, later, under the pressure exerted by the 'multi-cultural' nature of the European society, and in the US in the context of racism and anti-communism, India had its own complex reality to deal with. The impact of context on legal regulation of free speech is very well reflected by Parekh in his discussion about hate speech. As he puts it:

> Western societies have several mechanisms to cope with hate speech and its consequences, such as an open and competitive economy, a vibrant civil society, a reasonably cohesive and integrated society,

> a varied media representing a wide spectrum of views, and a plural and self-limiting public culture. They can therefore afford to assign law a relatively limited role.... So far as the developing countries are concerned, the situation could not be more different. Most of them are composed of ethnic, religious, and racial groups with little experience of working together and a long legacy of mistrust, ignorance, misunderstanding, and hostility. Rumours, jokes, inflammatory or ill-conceived remarks by politicians seeking short-term gains, and even reasoned criticisms made in the course of an uninhabited exercise of free speech can arouse deep-seated fear, trigger unrest, and undo years of good work in nation building.
>
> (2012: 55)

Many scholars and legal practitioners have made critical assessments of the nature and scope of laws in India that govern free speech. One line of criticisms pertains to the continuance of laws that had colonial roots. It is argued that such laws have lost their relevance in the present era and should therefore be scrapped (Ghosh 2004; Kumar 1990; Liang 2004). This idea echoes the concern that many lawmakers had also raised on the floor of the Constituent Assembly, when the restrictions enshrined under article 19(2) of the constitution were being debated. Another set of scholars highlight how these laws do not prove effective in achieving the goal they were meant to achieve – preventing hate speech or protecting hurt to religious sentiments of the people. There are two primary apprehensions raised by scholars in this regard – the first is with respect to the way in which these laws, rather than preventing hate speech which could hurt sentiments, allow for mobilization in the name of hurt sentiments (Liang 2004); the second apprehension is about the 'slippery slope' effect of laws, concerning the misuse of laws by state agencies in promoting or enforcing a legal sanction that might create hurdles for free exercise of the right to freedom of speech and expression (Ghosh 2004; Liang 2004). Highlighting the inefficacy of the Indian statutory laws in dealing with the subject of hate speech, these scholars cast doubts about the need and presence of such laws.

Contrary to these views are the arguments of those who believe that given the nature of Indian society, where political power structures favour religious majorities, and where caste and gender inequalities render large numbers of citizens vulnerable and exposed to the threat of hate speech based on their caste, religious or gender identity, the state needs to intervene for their protection. Scholars like A. G. Noorani (1999), Rajeev Dhavan (2008), Iqbal Ansari (2008) and Rajeev Bhargava (2012) represent this view, and they constantly highlight the importance of 'reasonable restrictions' as enshrined in the constitution. However, they are cautious to suggest that the state machinery should understand that it is the fundamental right of speech and expression that is 'sacred' and not the restrictions themselves. Reports on riots in India show that most of the instances of communal violence were preceded by altercations often incited by pamphlets, booklets or other publications or even hate speech targeting the vulnerable religious group of the region, which included threats or vilification of their religious beliefs or practices. Studies such as those by Paul Brass (2003) and Steven Wilkinson (2005) support such explanations. These facts are used by human rights activists, such as Teesta Setalvad, to argue that hate-speech laws are integral to the protection of the plural and secular nature of multi-religious Indian society. In the absence of hate speech laws, Setalvad (2011) holds that the instances of hate crimes against minorities could rise.

The present study does not intend to judge whether the presence of legal provisions against free speech is a good thing or not. Rather, it tries to understand what the presence of these laws means to the discourse of freedom of speech and expression in India. Therefore, one of the focus areas is the genesis of these laws – the context in which such laws were devised and the major actors who were involved in their formulation. It includes a study of the circumstances that led to the formation of the provisions under the constitution and statutory laws as well as the amendments introduced at later stages. The legislative debates shall help us to contemplate the attitude of lawmakers towards freedom of speech and expression, both under colonial rule as well as after independence. The legal apparatus to control freedom of speech and expression was historically handed down by the British, who took it upon themselves to codify criminal and civil laws in India. They devised far-reaching laws that were considered relevant according to the needs of the colonial context. Some laws were promulgated to maintain British control over the means of free expression, especially the press, and other laws were devised to legitimize the authority of the British as neutral arbiters of diverse cultural and religious interests that communities in India represented. A study of legislative proceedings of the period reveals that some Indian representatives had raised issues with regard to British attempts to curb freedom of expression. But, as argued in Chapter 1 of this work, concerns like maintenance of public order and protecting religious sentimentalities of different communities from hurt formed the bedrock on which the edifice for the legal regime to control free speech was constructed. After independence, though the nature of Indian state and its character changed significantly, the concerns regarding probable harm of free speech remained similar as they did during the colonial period. Challenges like partition and other events that marked the birth of India as a free nation warranted a fresh consideration of the legal aspects in order to avoid crisis at the level of internal security and prevent public-order issues. The new set of challenges forced amendments to the constitution, most significantly to those articles that dealt with freedom of speech and expression, in order to strengthen the executive's control. The justification forwarded, as discussed in Chapter 2 of this book, was that the citizens of a free nation should entrust confidence in its democratic government to protect and promote the interests of its citizens. This paternal attitude is explicitly reflected in the debates of the Parliament when amendments were introduced to the constitutional provisions as well as the statutory laws.

Censorship and the Role of the Courts

Censorship is a form of suppression whereby speech considered harmful, objectionable, sensitive or inconvenient is controlled. There can be several forms of this control and several agents that might perform this act. Traditionally it was understood to be under the power of some legitimate authority, mostly the state, to decide about censorship, but the nature and forms of censorship have changed drastically in recent decades. More recently, censorship has come to be understood as a power relation operating at different nodal points in social relationships. While histories of censorship used to chronicle official legal suppression of speech, Foucault's work invited us to 'escape from the limited field of juridical sovereignty and state institutions, and instead base our analysis of power on the study of techniques and tactics of domination' (Post 1998). A set of scholars have used the Foucauldian method to develop a framework to view this power relationship, which is popularly called 'new censorship'.[10] These scholars point at the change in the practice of censorship with the growth of new power centres, sometimes visible, at other times imperceptible. So, a range of new vocabularies have entered the discourse like 'self-censorship', 'market censorship', 'social censorship' and others. All these present different notions of censorship based on the difference in the location of power. The assumption is that threats to free speech come from all directions, not just from government. To this extent, censorship has been privatized, taken out of the hands of the state and located in other sources of power (Lee 1990).

Commentators on censorship in India have primarily focussed on the role of the state in the process. Concepts like 'market censorship' and 'self-censorship' are fairly new entrants into this scholarship. It is not to say that other forms of censorship did not exist in the Indian context, it is just that the field is heavily under-researched. Moreover, the state in India still plays a dominant role as censor. The only other form of censorship that appears prominently in the literature on censorship in India is 'social censorship', or what Noorani (1995) calls 'informal censorship'. Some scholars believe that the issue of social censorship has still not acquired centrality in the discourse of free speech, even though it has greater ramifications than the traditional form of censorship practiced by the state institutions (Dhavan 2008; Kumar 1997). If this is true, what happens to the traditionally defined role of the state as the legitimate authority to take decisions regarding censorship?

The demand for censoring or banning a publication on a religious subject can be based on different grounds: feeling of offence, hate, vilification, discrimination or threat experienced by individuals belonging to the target religious groups, or the feeling of any disruption or interruption in the enjoyment of the constitutionally guaranteed freedom of religion. In such controversies it is expected that the state shall act according to rational judgement, thereby providing a balance to contradictory claims. If any party is dissatisfied with the response of the state, he or she can approach the judiciary requesting legal scrutiny of executive's action.

The pragmatic vision of the lawmakers capacitated the judiciary to review executive decisions regarding important fundamental rights and, at the same time, to adjudicate the scope and relevance of the laws with changing times. Constitutionally, the first amendment to the constitution added the clause of 'reasonability' in relation to restrictions placed on freedom of speech and expression under article 19(2) of the constitution.[11] This 'reasonability' test provided courts with a tool to keep a check on the arbitrary actions of the government and thereby to protect individual rights to free speech from regulation even in the name of public order or protecting socio-cultural rights. Other than this, as the custodian of fundamental rights, the judiciary is also empowered by the constitution to review, strike down or sit on any law that appears to be contravening provisions of fundamental rights. Further, the power to adjudicate on cases of freedom of expression also draws from the provisions of statutory laws. For example, Section 96 of the Code of Criminal Procedure (CrPC) allows for any interested person to challenge the decision of forfeiture or ban of any publication by the government in the respective High Courts. This wide-ranging space for intervention by the judiciary ensured that after Independence, courtrooms became sites for struggles to define the scope and boundaries of freedom of speech and expression.

As guardian of fundamental rights, courts enjoy considerable respect and legitimacy in the eyes of the people. For such reasons, advocates of free speech also look towards the courts with high expectations. However, the history of free speech jurisprudence in India reflects a complex dynamic emerging from a balance based on respect for group identities and individual rights (Bhargava 1999: 26–59). The balance is not fixed, and there is always a scope for its shift of prioritizing one over the other. In the context of fundamental rights, the challenge of balancing was clearly reflected in the concerns of the constitution makers. Although the constitution guaranteed individual political rights and civil liberties, all these were severely circumscribed in the name of either national interests or the need to protect interests of cultural communities (Mahajan 1998: 155–158). The same is reflected in the approach of the judiciary. For example, unlike the US judiciary, which has largely dealt with the question of 'hate speech' by means of 'fighting words' and 'clear and present danger' doctrines, the Supreme Court in India takes a wider cognizance of the test for 'reasonableness' of restrictions imposed by the state machinery by treating each case differently from the substantive as well as procedural standpoints. Although one can easily locate references to US free-speech case laws in their judgements, judges in India have consistently maintained that the context and nature of society being different, the principles and positions that the courts in other countries take may not be reproduced in India. For example, free speech scholar Daniel Hantman (2014) invokes a comparison between Indian and US Supreme Courts' approach to freedom of expression and argues that Indian courts show a higher degree of tolerance for restricting socially offensive and emotionally harmful speech. He concludes that this has been made possible due to the persisting tension present between India's Western governing system and indigenous communal social structure.

Regardless of the centrality of the judiciary in free speech discourse in India, it has (until recently) largely remained an under-studied area. Most literature available on the subject is about press freedom (S. Bhatia 1997; Sorabjee 1976). Other than this, the subjects of censorship of books, art, films or obscenity find space in journalistic writings and are primarily in the context of specific acts of censorship. Works on censorship such as Bhowmik's on film censorship (2009), Girja Kumar's on book censorship (1997), Brinda Bose's on gender and censorship (2006) and Kaur and Mazzarella's edited volume on censorship in South Asia (2009) have all avoided critical engagement with case laws. Though they use judicial pronouncements in their work, one can find only a selective use of case laws aimed to buttress their arguments. Recently some serious engagement with the topic can be seen in the works of legal scholars like Rajeev Dhavan, Gautam Bhatia, Siddharth Narrain and political scientist Pratap Bhanu Mehta. Dhavan (2008) shows that courts in India, especially higher courts, have tried to provide a strong defence to freedom of speech. However, the legal process is so exhaustive and painful that the process itself becomes a form of punishment. This point has been reiterated by Narrain in his study of hate-speech laws in India (2016a). However, with reference to case laws, Narrain has highlighted the ambiguities that exist even at the level of Supreme Court judgements, and hence he shows that the judgements even from courts at the highest level are not immune to contradictions, which makes the fundamental right to speech and expression more vulnerable in the Indian context. The issue of ambiguity in free speech–related judgements is also pointed to by Pratap Bhanu Mehta (2008), who believes that one of the reasons for such ambiguity is the concern for and the tilt of the courts towards communitarian values, especially when a fundamental right such as that of speech is posed in contention with freedom ofreligion. An approach based on values of individualism, according to Mehta, could help the courts overcome their bias against the right to freedom of speech and expression. Bhatia (2016) presents a set of contradictory streams that appear as foundational to the judiciary's position on free speech. He argues that the judges have either favoured a 'moral-paternalistic vision' or a 'liberal-autonomous vision'. The 'moral-paternalistic vision' holds that since human beings are corruptible, they may not be entrusted with extreme freedoms, and it is therefore the duty of public institutions to prevent any harm to the citizens. The 'liberal-autonomous vision', according to Bhatia, is based on the immanent faith on human judgement and choices, and any form of interference with that is seen as unwarranted. Where on the one hand, the 'moral-paternalistic' attitude limits the scope of free speech, therefore allowing wider interference from the state, on the other hand, the 'liberal-autonomous' attitude favours the claims of free speech. Bhatia argues that, based on these approaches, the courts decide the fate of free speech cases. These recent works on the subject have contributed significantly to the discourse. Such scholarship helps to grasp the multiple ways in which the role of the judiciary can be viewed. Taking cues from each of the above-mentioned scholarships, this book presents a detailed study of courts role vis-à-vis the claims of religious offence against publications. A detailed study of courts' approach towards free speech, as well as the laws and legal process that define the boundaries of free speech, reveals that there are many variables that impact the fate of the case laws. For example, the courts' generous consideration of the public-order situation and the emphasis on protecting the secular and plural credentials of Indian society has prompted moves to limit free speech. Similarly, the ambiguity in the court's decisions, as well as the operative constraints like delay in judgements, has increased the vulnerability of freedom of speech and expression in the Indian context. At such a juncture, the philosophical considerations that scholars like Bhatia impose on the judiciary might not represent the actual complexity. Mehta's opinion about an individualism-based approach might be fruitful, but the judiciary does not actually enjoy that liberty as it is guided by the constitution, where freedom of expression is not the only value that needs protection. The courts are under a lot of pressure to balance this fundamental right with others like freedom of religion, and in the process, even if the courts fail the expectations of libertarians who argue for extreme freedom of expression, it appears prepared to do that. For its justification of curbing free speech, the courts easily invoke article 19(2) of the constitution, which defines the limits to freedom of speech and expression. In the present work, I critically engage with all these scholars through the prism of case laws. However, the study is limited not only to an analysis of case laws. It also looks at the structural and operative aspects of courts' functioning, which have been overlooked by both Bhatia and Mehta. This helps to develop a broader understanding about the role of the courts in the debates over freedom of expression. For example, the duration of the time taken by the courts in India to pronounce judgements in cases related to publications claimed to be offensive shows that it usually takes long for the courts to adjudicate in the matter. This creates conditions whereby authors/publishers try to evade the legal process and agree to out-of-court settlement with the complainants, even if it hampers their free exercise of freedom of expression. Further, I also look at cases where government, non-state actors and the judiciary interact. This helps to examine the consequences of such interactions, and also to understand how courts view the role of non-state actors in censorship, an issue largely overlooked in earlier studies.

Notes

1 The novel highlights the plight of Kali and Ponna, the protagonist couple, and while discussing their attempts to conceive, it also refers to an age-old local custom of the community which, according to temple laws, allowed consensual union among consenting adults outside of marriage during the village festival to overcome the problem of childlessness. More than 5,000 copies of the novel had been sold and on popular demand a translated version with the title *One Part Woman* was published by Penguin in 2013. Two sequels to the novel have also been published.

2 Murugan expressed his anguish in an affidavit that was submitted to Madras High Court on his behalf, where a plea to dismiss the undertaking had come up (W.P. No. 2668 of 2015). Ilangovan Rajasekaran, 'Writer Speaks Out', *Frontline*, 20 March 2015, Available at http://www.frontline.in/the-nation/writer-speaks-out/article6955375.ece (accessed on 30 April 2017).

3 This is a part of the information provided by S. R. Sundaram as the publisher of Murugan's book in a counter-affidavit filed in the case *S. Tamilselvan and other v. The Government of Tamil Nadu and Others* (2015) W.P. No. 1215 of 2015.

4 The petition was filed by S. Balamurugan, General Secretary of PUCL in Tamil Nadu and appeared as *S. Balamurugan v. The Government of Tamil Nadu and others* (2015) W.P. No. 2668 of 2015.

5 The Madras High Court finally pronounced its judgement in the case on 5 July 2016, almost one and half years after the petition had first appeared in the court.

6 A chilling effect applies to cases where the state might not directly censor free speech, but its role produces conditions that lead to self-censorship. It may either be due to uncertainty in legal sanctions or an unfriendly attitude of administration or any such reasons. See LaMarche (1991: 56–58).

7 The case appeared in Delhi High Court as *The Trustees of Safdar Hashmi Memorial Trust v. Govt. of NCT of Delhi*, (2001) CriLJ3689. SAHMAT is a left-oriented cultural organization that includes academicians, artists and others, and it claims to promote the values of pluralism and secularism in Indian society.

8 The case was dealt by the Delhi High Court as *Maqbool Fida Hussain v. Raj Kumar Pandey* (2008) Crl. Revision Petition No. 114/2007.

9 Article 25 provides for freedom of conscience and free profession, practice and propagation of religion. Clause 1 of the article is most important; it reads: 'Subject to public order, morality and health and to the other provisions of this Part, all persons are equally entitled to freedom of conscience and the right freely to profess, practise and propagate religion'.

10 Advocates of this new approach include Richard Burt (1994), Sue Curry Jansen (1991) and Michael Holquist (1994), among others. However, this approach has also received severe criticism from scholars like Beate Muller (2004) and Robert Post (1998). For example, Robert Post criticises the new scholarship on censorship by arguing that it has 'flattened distinctions among kinds of power, implicitly equating suppression of speech caused by state legal action with that caused by the market, or by the dominance of a particular discourse, or by the institution of criticism itself'. This invariably makes it difficult to formulate a pointed criticism of censorship itself because it gets so difficult to locate the point of origination.

11 Article 19(2) of the constitution allows the validity of existing laws and empowers the government to make new laws vis-à-vis free speech, only if the laws impose 'reasonable restrictions' and are 'in the interests of the sovereignty and integrity of India, the security of the State, friendly relations with foreign States, public order, decency or morality or in relation to contempt of court, defamation or incitement to an offence'.

1

CENSORSHIP OF PUBLICATIONS IN COLONIAL INDIA

The Genesis of a Legal Idea

The ideas and institutions of colonial modernity were brought to India from outside – that is, by the agents of European, especially British, imperialism. This was in sharp contrast to primarily internal or indigenous processes through which Europe itself had launched its project of enlightenment and modernity (Mehta & Pantham 2006; Kaviraj 2010). The claim of monopoly and expertise over modernity was used as justification by the colonial powers to fulfil its imperial ambitions. For many, British India was a contradictory political formation. In Henry Maine's words, it was a 'most extraordinary experiment' involving 'the virtually despotic government of a dependency by a free people' (Maine 1876: 233). The colonial rule reflected dichotomies at two different levels. Firstly, liberty, which was held to be the most sacred and universal value of the enlightenment project, was being curtailed through the processes of colonialism and creation of subject peoples – another product of the same enlightenment project. Further, the same argument of modernity used to enlarge civil liberties in the West was being used to deny basic rights to the colonial masses. This contradiction was sharply reflected in the case of freedom of expression. The people who celebrated and claimed freedom of expression and the press as sacred in their own societies became, under the garb of imperial rulers, its ardent opponents in the colonies, restricting both free expression and freedom of the press for their own benefits. These dichotomies produced a new context through the interaction of 'East' and 'West', which is clearly reflected in the translation and understanding of freedom of speech and expression in India.

The power relationship operating in colonial India can be deduced, as Guha (1977) argues, by deriving a relation between dominance and subordination. The British tried to establish their hegemony by inducing changes in the institutional structures. The introduction of Western education was an important part of this strategy, with an aim to produce a rationalist intelligentsia, who could ensure a relay of ideological justification for their activities (Kaviraj 2010: 61–66). Though the class of new intelligentsia largely remained loyal to this cause, the liberal ideas based on values of rights and liberty encouraged a section of the same intelligentsia to question the

DOI: 10.4324/9781003369257-2

rationale of the colonial rule in India. The press became an effective tool to expose and criticize the British. Such interventions frustrated the attempt to generate legitimacy, which meant that the British rule had to extensively depend on coercion as the primary mode of dominance. They responded by enacting several laws to curb the freedom of the press. This was just the beginning of a series of censorship laws initiated by the British that also witnessed a parallel struggle for the demand of freedom of speech and expression by the native Indians.

Press Censorship and Its Opposition in the Early Nineteenth Century

The formal debate over freedom of speech and expression in India began to take shape from the early 19th century, which, according to C. A. Bayly, was the period of the advent of 'constitutional liberalism' in India. This development, according to him, shared some connection with the great expansion of the press and the idea of association across the world, beginning in the 1780s (2012: 28–34). The first newspaper in India was also started during this period. However, James Augustus Hickey's *Bengal Gazette* or *The Calcutta General Advertiser*, which took off in 1780, was stopped only two years after its inception as its exposure of the private lives of company servants did not go well with the British authorities (Chaudhuri 1955: 291). In 1799, the idea of press censorship became more explicit and official with the Censorship of Press Act introduced by Lord Wellesley. It brought all the newspapers under government scrutiny before their publication. Later, in 1807, it was extended to cover all kinds of press publications – newspapers, magazines, books and pamphlets. The act was revoked by Lord Hastings in 1818. However, the abolition was initiated on the terms that the editors would take responsibility to exclude matters likely to affect the authority of government or be injurious to the public interest.

During this period, Raja Rammohan Roy arose as the undisputed representative of the Indians in the struggle for freedom of speech and expression. Roy's aim was to build an Indian 'public' from the ground up, so that within a generation Indians would begin to share in power and legislative authority (Bayly 2010: 27). His concern for freedom of speech and expression is reflected in his opposition to the arbitrary deportation of editors and formal press censorship. Along with other Indian liberals of his time, like D. N. Tagore, G. C. Bonnerjee and others, Roy wrote a memorial to the Supreme Court against the ordinance initiated by the then acting Governor General John Adam in December 1823, popularly known as the Licensing Regulation Act. When the Supreme Court did not pay heed to the request and went on to register the regulation, he pursued the case further and wrote another memorial, this time addressed to King George IV in London (Roy 1925). These memorials are often cited as evidence of his undaunted love and concern for freedom of speech and expression. The comparison of this document with Milton's *Areopagiticia* seems to be valid not only because it was the first comprehensive appeal in defence of the free press in India as Milton's *Areopagiticia* was in Britain, but also because of the similarity of arguments in both documents. Although it was one of the pioneering tracts in the field, it, like Milton's, cannot be considered a strong argument for liberty per se, but a strategic response to the context in which it was written.

The memorial makes it explicit that Roy was not in support of unbridled freedom, nor was he opposed to already existing laws that limited such freedom, like laws against libel, among others. In fact, he argued that if there were objectionable or seditious publications, the judicial system should render a 'writer or publisher culpable and amenable to punishment' (Roy 1925: 60). Further, he also ensured that should the limitation of the liberty of the press become necessary if it was (1) for the sake of 'greater security and to preserve the union existing between England and this country' or (2) against a seditious attempt to excite hostility with neighbouring or friendly states, the colonial subjects would be perfectly willing to submit to additional penalties to be legally inflicted (1925: 71–72).

Rammohan Roy was sure that an Indian public could come into existence only through the expansion of public knowledge, and the press as an organ of education could play an important role in this. Importantly, there was yet another point raised in defence of a free press that is significant. It was about the role of a free press in religion. The first printing press in India was brought by the Jesuit missionaries from Portugal to Goa in 1556. The publishing of books and pamphlets helped the missionaries to promote and spread their religious viewpoints. Though the British government was largely suspicious of missionary activities, during this period liberal concessions were allowed for papers published by them. For example, the papers published by Seerampore missionaries were never targeted even after the ordinance by John Adam came into effect, whereas the government came down heavily on editors like J. S. Buckingham[1] and C. J. Fair,[2] who were deported for their activities. In the memorandum, Rammohan mentioned the presence of the ideological clash between different religions and how the free press was being used by the native religions to defend themselves from the onslaught of English missionaries, through debates and discussions. He writes:

> After a body of English missionaries have been labouring for about twenty five years by preaching and distributing publications in the native languages in all parts of Bengal, to bring the prevailing system of religion into disrepute, no alarm whatever prevails, because your Majesty's faithful subjects possess the power of defending their religion by the same means that are employed against it, and many of them have exercised the freedom of the press to combat the writings of English missionaries, and think no other protection

> necessary to the maintenance of their faith. While the teachers of Christianity use only reason and persuasion to propagate their religion, your majesty's faithful subjects are content to defend theirs by the same weapons.
>
> (Roy 1925: 60)

This, according to Roy, was a significant contribution of the free press in India, which allowed for debates over key tenets of belief and faith in a non-violent and discursive environment. It is evident that Roy and others did not contemplate that in the future the press could be used to incite communal violence. Though such concerns did not find a place in Milton's *Areopagiticia*, the fact that both were pleas against the Licence Act of their times (in the case of Milton it was to the legislature and in the case of Rammohan to the king) to reconsider the law, and return to the pre-licence phase (thereby status quo) makes them similar in many senses. But similarly in both cases, the defence of freedom of speech and expression was a weak one. It would not be wrong to say that though the Indian liberals of this phase stressed the importance of a free press, they did not include deep concern for an individual's freedom of speech and expression, nor was it seen as a necessary philosophical defence of the former. If anything, the argument for a free press was teleological and not concerned with the value of free speech as a good-in-itself. It prioritized the benefits a free press could have for society, both for the governors as well as the governed. So, the demand for a free press, it can be argued, was not a claim but a plea based on the shared notion of values that it served. Further, a need was seen to reasonably restrict this freedom under laws such as those against libel and sedition. However, Roy's memorial received no response and the act remained in place till it was abolished by Charles Metcalfe, another acting governor general, on persuasion by Lord Macaulay.

British Attitudes towards Free Expression in Colonial India

From the beginning of press culture in India, the British authorities wanted to ensure that press freedom did not pose a threat to their rule. So, though some freedom was allowed, it was always subjected to conditions that determined its scope. The legislation introduced during this period reflects this approach. In the process, the basic tenets of liberalism were modified to develop a creative logic in support of imperial control. The most important advocates of liberalism and free speech, like J. S. Mill, were also engaged in justifying the control over free speech of the colonial subjects (U. Mehta 1999; Parekh 1994: 11–13). One of the important figures who contributed in this redefinition was Thomas Macaulay, who spearheaded the formulation of the IPC.

Regulating Free Speech through Law: The Indian Penal Code (IPC) and Legal Provisions

In 1833, Thomas Macaulay was appointed India's First Law Member and Head of its first Law Commission. The legal system in India, which he inherited, was complex, pluralistic and in many respects unmanageable as it suffered from what James Fitzjames Stephen would later call 'vices of vagueness'.[3] The reference point for Macaulay was his predecessors like James Mill and Charles Grant, who claimed to have exposed the instability, injury and ignorance inherent in the Indian society and believed it to be the duty of the British to assimilate them into the civilizational umbrella and try to improve their condition. Macaulay also envisioned the British Empire as 'an enlightened and paternal despotism', morally obligated to the reform of Indian society. But such moral achievement was not the only driving force. Macaulay's vision was also guided by the material aims of the Raj. 'To trade with civilized men is infinitely more profitable than to govern savages', he maintained (Macaulay 1898: 583). To achieve such aims, Macaulay held it necessary that the language of the laws should be clear, unequivocal and concise.

The lawmaking process of this period was dominated by the Utilitarians, in particular the followers of Jeremy Bentham (Smith 1988; Stokes 1959). Macaulay tried to introduce an attitude that has been described as a 'fusion of utilitarian clarity and rigour with Burkean pragmatism' (Collini, Winch & Burrow 1984: 198). Certainty and clarity were two aspects of Benthamite tradition that remained central for Macaulay. For him, laws should resonate 'uniformity where you can have it; diversity where you must have it; but in all cases certainty' (Macaulay 1898: 578). This was also necessary to 'limit the power which the courts of justice possess of putting their own sense on the laws', rendering them uncertain and contradictory (1898: 424). The codification of penal laws in India was an attempt in this direction. The formulation of the IPC reflected not only the productive engagement of Macaulay in creating 'a concise, lucid and comprehensive code that aimed to minimize discretion, differences in legal status and concessions to local circumstances' (Wright 2011: 19) but also, as K. J. M. Smith (1989: 145) observes, it represented an important episode in the development of criminal jurisprudence and 19th-century intellectual history.

Chapter XXII of the code, entitled *Of Criminal Intimidation, Insult and Annoyance*, is entirely devoted to forms of offensive language not previously criminalized. He introduced various doctrinal innovations in this section to suit the need of the context. For example, he expanded the term 'defamation' to cover libel and slander as well.[4] Together with this, he also rejected the notion that a strict division between speech and acts could be made. He argued that offensive and insulting language should be conceived as speech acts and ought to be a subject to criminal jurisprudence (Macaulay 1898: 121–123). In many ways his idea of 'performative' speech was prescient to the contemporary understandings as reflected in Mackinnon (1996) and

Butler (1997). He proposed that defamatory spoken words should be considered an offence irrespective of whether they actually caused a breach of peace, on the ground that the mental pain they inflict is a sufficient basis for action. The reason for this proposition was also based on his reading of Indian society. He maintained, 'There is perhaps no country in which more cruel suffering is inflicted, and more deadly resentment called forth, by injuries which affect only the mental feelings' (as quoted in Ahmed 2009: 130).

He was particularly concerned about religious insults and devoted a whole chapter entitled *On Offence relating to Religion and Caste* (chapter XV). In the *Notes* he argues that in contexts such as India's, where the relationship between different religions is volatile, dangers 'can only be averted by a firm adherence to the true principle of toleration'.[5] He also emphasized that the penal codes provided an opportunity to inculcate such values in the society by including strict laws against violation. So, laws like section 298 were inserted into the IPC.[6] This understanding of toleration seems to be aimed at making religious beliefs immune to any criticism. He argued that even if the contents of any religion may be wrong, the 'pain which such insults give to the professors of that religion is real'. It cannot be dismissed that such posture was another attempt by the colonial state to boast about its capacity to impartially regulate and administer a multiplicity of particularistic communities through the rule of law, and thereby to justify its imperial mission. However, in the process, Macaulay introduced some unprecedented interventions in the discourse of free speech in India: (1) the 'volatile' context of India and the 'intolerant' public culture were used as reasons to legally limit the scope of free speech; (2) they made space for prosecution against 'mental injury' or feeling of 'offence'; and (3) at least indirectly, they made religions immune to any criticism or questioning, thereby generating a sense of autonomy which had potential to promote orthodoxy. This completely changed the nature of debate about free speech in India, and the burden of legal limitations has guided the discourse since then, which also made it very different from the West.

The legal experts of the time like John Dawson Mayne (1862) and Sir Lawrence Peel (1848) were very critical of Macaulay's approach. They believed that making wounded sentiments a cause for action was a recipe for disaster and should only be subject to sanction when it led a public disorder. Another person who criticized such an approach was James Fitzjames Stephen. Though he lauded the nature of the Codes and their success, he was particularly suspicious of the scope of such provisions like section 298 (Stephen 1883: 322). Section 298 rendered everyone liable to a year's imprisonment who,

> with the deliberate intention of wounding the religious feelings of any person, utters any word or makes any sound in the hearing of that person, or makes any gesture in the sight of that person, or places any object in the sight of that person.

Stephen believed that it would end the possibility to convince any person that his religious beliefs were untrue.

> It is impossible to convince anyone that he is in error upon religious subject without causing him great pain if he really believes in his creed, and the act of addressing cogent and earnest arguments to him on the subject must of necessity involve a deliberate intention of wounding his feelings.
>
> (1883: 312–313)

Though he believed that the intention of the lawmakers was not this and in the hands of the English magistrates it would be interpreted to apply only to wanton insults, Stephen was suspicious that in future if the power came to the hands of Hindu or Muslim government and judges it could cause havoc as it was too easy to make accusations (1883: 312–313).

Stephen was convinced that strong laws and a proactive state were required to maintain peace and order against ever-present threats of inter-communal conflict in societies like India (as quoted in O'Dowd 2013: 271). This understanding of the Indian context became the basis of his criticism of John Stuart Mill's *On Liberty*, expressed by Stephen in his seminal *Liberty, Equality, Fraternity* (1967, written during his voyage back from India. If one compares the attitudes of Stephen and Mill towards imperial policy in India, though there were great overlaps, they also exhibited significant differences. Stephen's advocacy for coercion was a universal and fundamental aspect of his political thought, unlike Mill, who considered it apt only for societies who were still in early stages of civilization (Mill 1978: 10–11).

Stephen was a firm believer that power preceded liberty and 'that liberty from the very nature of things is dependent on power; and that it is only under the protection of a powerful, well organized government that any liberty can exist at all' (Stephen 1967: 183). As far as his understanding about liberty as a value was concerned, he believed that whether liberty was good or bad depended on the particular context, time, place and circumstances. In certain cases, he believed, the curtailment of liberty was pertinent for the larger benefit of the society and cites the example of British coercion in India. He argued that coercion was extremely necessary in the British efforts to direct moral and religious changes in the Indian society in order to civilize it. Stephen notes that important coercive measures in India had proved very fruitful, and that such changes were necessary in the progress towards civilization. As such, he also claimed, coercion helped in the larger cause of human progress. On similar account, praising the British policies in India, he comments:

> 1) They have forced upon the people, utterly against the will of many of them, the principle that people of different religion are to live at peace with each other, that there is to be no fighting and no oppression as between Mahommedans and Hindoos, or different sects of Mahommedans.

2) They have also forced upon the people the principle that change of religion is not to involve civil disabilities. The Act by which this rule was laid down utterly changed the legal position of one of the oldest and most widespread religions of the world. It deprived Brahminism of its principle coercive sanction
3) They have set up a system of education all over the country which assumes the falsehood of the creed of the Hindoos and – less pointedly, but not less effectually – of the Mahommedans.
4) Whenever religious practices violate European ideas of public morality up to a certain point, they have, as in the case of suttee and human sacrifice, been punished as crimes.
5) They compel the natives to permit the presence among them of missionaries whose one object is to substitute their own for the native religion, and who do, in fact, greatly weaken the native religion.

(1967: 89)

Stephen's attitude towards the state's role in freedom of speech and expression also becomes evident when he questioned Mill's assumption that compulsion was justifiable until the time 'when mankind have become capable of being improved by free and equal discussion' (Mill 1978: 10–11). He believed that in the absence of the heavy hand of the state, no society can fruitfully value its liberties, and therefore insisted that compulsion was a necessary component of any transformation, and it could never be completely replaced by discussion in any society at any time (Stephen 1967: 70). Stephen's engagement with Mill had particular relevance for India as he had been Law Member of the government of India and had introduced measures to control the press, which Indian liberals regarded as authoritarian (Bayly 2012: 11). Most significant among his contributions was the Special Act No. XXVII of 1870, which inserted section 124(A) in the IPC, and which was at par with the sedition law in England.

The period between Macaulay as Law Commissioner and Stephen as Law Member of the Council of the Viceroy (1838–1869) witnessed important shifts in the approach of the British administration – both in terms of attitude and policy imperatives. The revolt of 1857 and the transfer of powers from the East India Company to the Crown in London marked an important moment in this shift. The earlier emphasis on the universalist project of civilization based on the assumption that non-Western societies were politically dysfunctional was replaced by an aim to understand the logic of native society. There seemed to have appeared a consensus in the post-mutiny context to 'curtail the transformative ambition implied in the civilizing mission and reconstitute the imperial order on a more conservative basis, in line with the "traditional" imperatives of native society' (Mantena 2009: 5). According to D. A. Low (1973: 39–82), this initiated in India a more authoritarian insistence on efficiency and stability as the watchwords of imperial policy, and also a reversal of liberal efforts at civilizing and creative reform in favour of protecting and conserving native society. This approach was manifest when the religious causes of the revolt became evident and Queen Victoria's Proclamation made the principle of non-interference into native religious beliefs and customs the cornerstone of the post-mutiny imperial policy. The proclamation said:

> We declare it to be our royal will and pleasure that none be in anywise favoured, none molested or disquieted, by reason of their religious faith or observances, but that all shall alike enjoy the equal and impartial protection of the law; and we do strictly charge to enjoin all those who may be in authority under us that they abstain from all interference with the religious belief or worship of any of our subjects on pain of our highest displeasure.
>
> (As quoted in Philips, Singh and Pandey 1962: 11)

The most important representative of this shift was Henry Maine, who advocated the idea of 'indirect rule'[7] based on his study of Indian society. Significant change in the understanding about law – its utility, its goal and more importantly its scope – can also be marked as a direct product of such a shift.[8] Though Warren Hastings had introduced, back in 1772, the colonial distinction between private and public laws – where 'public' applied to property and commerce and personal law pertained to the 'private' realm of women, family, religion and tradition – such classification got a new definition and importance during this period. This classification formed two different spheres of law based on the socio-cultural understanding of Indian society: on the one hand, the British administered universal law in the public sphere; on the other hand, a separate sphere was left for the administration of Hindu and Muslim 'personal law'. As Thomas Metcalf explained: 'The legal system of colonial India thus accommodated both, the assimilative ideals of liberalism, which found a home in the codes of procedure, and insistence upon Indian difference in a personal law defined by membership in a religious community' (1994: 38).

The colonial lawmakers like Maine argued that crime was universally understood, whereas the civil laws touched upon what he called 'the local peculiarity of the country', and hence it was assumed that the reform of the criminal law would meet with the least social resistance. It was not surprising that the Indian Penal Code (1860), the Code of Civil Procedure (1859) and the Code of Criminal Procedure (1861) were the first three codes enacted by the government. It can be argued that for the British Raj, it was an effective tool to manage its firm control over the administrative aspects of the society and still maintain a certain level of legitimacy. But such bifurcation also had the capacity to sanction a higher degree of autonomy to religious groups and make their internal system more closed. Non-interference in religious matters could also establish a freedom to profess and popularize one's religion, which could later be used to criticize and attack other faiths and belief systems.

The British Raj and 'Selective Censorship'

Just after the revolts of 1857, the English language press, largely owned by members of the European community, came down heavily upon the authorities for being too soft and indecisive in punishing the rebels. Lord Canning was at the centre of the wrath, and he reacted by announcing gag orders against the press that remained in force for around a year. A decade later in 1867, an Act for the Regulation of Printing Presses and Newspapers was passed to replace the Metcalfe Act from 1835. This act later came to be known as The Press and Registration of Books Act. After several modifications and amendments in 1890, 1914, 1952 and 1953, this formed a part of the formal law in post-independent India. However, the biggest and most strategic threat to the idea of free press came in 1878 in the form of the Vernacular Press Act, enacted to give better control over newspapers published in Indian languages. It appeared during the Second Anglo-Afghan War (1878–1880) in order to prevent the vernacular press from expressing criticism of British policies. It was only four years later, in 1882, that Lord Ripon repealed the act. One significant feature of the Vernacular Press Act was that it made an explicit distinction between the English language press and the vernacular press (Seal 1968: 143). The distinction was a product of two long-term developments – on the one hand, public opinion in India was largely being defined by the state as the opinions of the 'non-official' European community, which was mostly represented by the English-speaking press; on the other hand, the vernacular press was held responsible not only for supporting developments that led up to 1857 but also for engaging in statements in the years after. For example, Ashley Eden, the Bengal governor, defended the English-speaking press by 'non-official Europeans' and argued that it should be kept outside the impact of the Vernacular Press Act. He said:

> On the whole the English press of India, whether conducted by Europeans or natives, bears evidence of being influenced by a proper sense of responsibility and by a general desire to discuss public events in a moderate and responsible spirit. There is no occasion to subject that press to restraint, and therefore, naturally enough, it is exempted. It would be a sign of great weakness on the part of government to bring it within the scope of this measure merely to meet a possible charge of partiality.
>
> (As quoted in Buckland 1976: 716–717)

The nationalist movement after 1885 gave a new impetus to the development of the press in India; in fact, the press played a significant role in the movements that followed. By the 1890s, when the issues of sedition became more prominent, government geared for new laws. Most significant was the amendment of section 124(A) of the IPC, which was restructured in

1898 to include 'hatred' and 'contempt' along with 'disaffection towards the government' as being worthy of prosecution. This further limited the space for criticism of the administration. The need for the amendment was justified by the authorities in the name of judicial arguments during sedition trials, including Tilak's, which had raised questions about the validity and the scope of the impugned law (Donough 1911: 42–59). When the amendment was being discussed in the Legislative Assembly, it was proposed that promotion of religious enmity should also be included as an offence against the state under section 124(A),[9] as this period also witnessed communal violence between Hindus and Muslims in several parts of the country. However, after deliberations, the Select Committee recommended the inclusion of a separate section within the IPC to deal with such cases. This led to the formation of section 153(A), which punished anyone who with words, either spoken or written, promoted or attempted to promote feelings of enmity or ill will between different classes of subjects, based on religion, race or other factors (Donough 1911: 60–70).

Each important event in local or international politics that had the potential to engage and mobilize public opinion against the British administration was greeted with heavy censorship of the press in India. Although the press in India was never completely free, special tools were used during crisis periods. For example, the Press Act of 1910 and the Defence of India Act 1939 were promulgated against the background of the two World Wars, respectively. Similarly, the Press Emergency Act during the Salt Satyagraha (1931) and the gag orders during the Quit India Movement (1942) were evidence of this approach of the British government. The understanding of 'crisis' was political and instrumental. It lacked objective assessment and was defined primarily based on the interests of the administrators. For example, when the Cow Protection Movement peaked and took violent forms in 1893, the vernacular press in the hands of both communities – Hindus and Muslims – played an important role in sowing distrust and enmity. Yet on this occasion, the government did not respond to the situation with a sense of urgency to prevent communal clashes. A communication between Lord Lansdowne and the Earl of Kimberley, in 1893, indicates that the authorities were well aware how the communal frenzy was spreading so fast all across the country. On a question about 'why … disturbances are becoming more frequent than in past years', Lansdowne responded:

> One of the causes to which this is due [is] in our opinion, beyond all doubt, the greater frequency of communication and the interchange of news by post and telegraph between different parts of the country.… This rapid dissemination of news and increasing activity of controversy, carried on through the Press, by public meetings, and by the addresses of itinerant preachers, is in some respects a new feature in Indian life, and is one which is likely to grow and add considerably to the difficulties of administration.[10]

Further, he also gives a detailed account of how it was happening:

> In addition to the inflammatory harangues delivered to meetings of Hindus, [wandering ascetics] have distributed throughout the country pictures of the cow, of a kind calculated to appeal strongly to the religious sentiment of the people. One of them, for instance, depicts a cow in the act of being slaughtered by three Muhammadan butchers, and is headed 'the present state'. Another exhibits a cow, in every part of whose body groups of Hindu deities and holy persons are shown, being assailed by a monster with a drawn sword entitled the 'KaliYug' but which has been largely understood as typifying the Muhammadan community.

However, no action was taken to prevent dissemination of such controversial material. Similarly, in the chromolithograph *Chaurasi Devata Auvali Gay*, published by Ravi Verma Press in 1915, which represented a cow with depictions of different Hindu gods in its body and a demon drawing its sword to sacrifice it, the demon was interpreted to be Muslim, and it led to riots in different parts of north India.[11] Such situations were further fuelled by the actions of the authorities. As one of the officers wrote,

> The whole anti-kine-killing movement is, of course, antagonistic to European and Muhammadans. That is inevitable. Therefore it may be said that the picture reflects upon these races, which is true; but *we tolerate the agitation as long as it does not become too violent*, and I should not describe the picture as a particularly violent manifestation of it.[12]

The government did not proscribe this broadside due to the fear that it would be charged of being pro-Muslim (Barrier 1974: 61).

Though the administration had such precise details, very little was done to prevent such circulations in different parts of the country. Even when some kind of censorship was imposed to prevent communal tensions, it was always on the pretext of appeals from local officers, who in most cases were natives. This prevented the British authorities from taking direct responsibility for such acts, and in many cases it led to further uproar as it was assumed that the presiding officer was supporting the cause of his own religious brethren in an indirect way. The case of Munshi Inderman of Moradabad in 1879 illustrates how the spread of print was sharpening existing cleavages and exposing new kinds of social tensions. Inderman, who was a follower/member of the Arya Samaj, had been writing and publishing extensively against Islam and practices of the Muslim community. The Muslim groups, through their press, had been continuously urging the district administration to take steps to prevent such offensive publications, but in vain.[13] Later the magistrate imposed a fine on Inderman and ordered destruction of all the copies of the objectionable books he had published. It was found that the magistrate's orders were based on evidence provided by the Deputy Collector, who happened to be a Muslim. This incident was given a communal colour and popularized to demonstrate that now Muslims in public offices were practicing 'oppression and tyranny upon the Hindus'.[14] The Lahore Hindi weekly *Mittra Vilas* regretted that a 'distinguished disciple' of Dayananda Saraswati should be treated so severely when many offensive Christian Missionary publications went unpunished (Jalal 2000: 82). Attempt was made to mobilize public opinion against both enemies simultaneously – the colonial state as well as the Muslims. In the context of the Arya Samaj movement, this strategy helped further polarization.

Commenting on the attitude of the government vis-à-vis censorship during this period, N. G. Barrier (1974) opines that it barred any title strongly critical of Western civilization or Christianity and was also very strict against any publication against the government and left no stone unturned to charge the offenders under the laws of sedition. Even the courtrooms, in cases of writings against the administration, were used only as signifiers of government's faith in the legal system and its inherent respect for freedom of the press, but in reality the government used all the possibilities at hand to punish such offenders (1974: 63). However, in the case of religious vilification and insult among Hindus and Muslims, even after being well aware of the propaganda, the colonial rulers took calculated steps, exhibiting 'selective censorship'. Robert Darnton (2001, 2002) also notes that government freely used all available means to ensure that those guilty of generating public opinion against the government's policies or actions could not escape the web of law. They had developed strict literary surveillance on the publications in India, and if anything was found to be against their liking, it was deterred and repressed, but such urgency was never visible in issues related to religious insults and offence (Darnton 2001).

It is evident from the above discussion that, on the one hand, the British authorities were not averse to the idea of framing new laws to control what they held to be misuse of freedom of speech and expression. However, they were selective in the use of these laws, especially when it involved the subject of religion, as on the one hand they wanted to project their non-interference on religious matters of the colonial subjects, and on the other hand, they feared that if they acted against members of one community, they would be blamed for favouring the other. So, unlike the political subjects, the government acted in the controversies over religion selectively, considering all the risks and benefits involved.

The Indian Nationalists' Position on the Question of Freedom of Expression

The post-mutiny period witnessed major socio-political changes within the internal structure of Indian society. In politics, a significant development was the formation of the Indian National Congress in 1885, which later led the nationalist response to British colonial rule. Similarly, in the field of religion, this phase saw a wide range of experimental explorations initiated by reformers and revivalists. There were reformers who were using liberal vocabularies to challenge the conservatives (Bayly 2012: 11). Contrarily, it also gave rise to sections of orthodox fundamentalists within each religion, who opposed any kind of attempts to revive or reform. Such conservatives sought to guard the inner citadel of their religions against any form of external intervention or interrogations. Evidently, there was a rise of new forms of communal consciousness, which by the 1880s and 1890s became an all-India phenomenon (Chandra 1990; Sarkar 1983). For example, Christophe Jaffrelot (1999: 11–12) argues that this was when Hindu nationalism was constructed as an ideology and derived from the socio-religious movements initiated by high-caste Hindus, such as the Arya Samaj. The printing press became an important site in the process of cultural self-definition, and also the realm in which 19th-century communalism developed. The early nationalists like Rammohan Roy, who argued that the freedom of the press was important for a non-violent clash of religious ideologies, had not contemplated that the same freedom would be used in the future to incite violence in the name of religion. It was obvious, therefore, that the attitude of Indians of this period towards freedom of speech and expression was different than that of Roy.

Communal Consciousness during the 1870s and the Role of Freedom of Speech and Expression

Historians have held that in India, two ideologies – nationalism and communalism – had simultaneous and parallel growth trajectories (Chandra 1990; Jaffrelot 1999; Sarkar 1983). The British policy of non-interference in the internal matters of religion further allowed a space for cultivation of communal ideologies. Sandra Freitag (1989) has shown how public arena activities like religious ceremonies among the Hindu and Muslim groups helped in consolidating communal consciousness and also became the breeding ground for violent clashes as witnessed during language controversies over Hindi-Urdu or the Cow Protection Movement. The same movements also produced local leaders who carried the baton of the nationalist response to colonial rule.

Partha Chatterjee has claimed that in the wake of colonial modernity, the 'spiritual' or 'inner' domain of culture, such as language, or religion, or the elements of personal and family life, was central to nationalists, and the

> more nationalism engaged in its contest with the colonial power in the outer domain of politics the more it insisted in displaying the marks of "essential" cultural difference so as to keep out the colonizer from that inner domain of national life and to proclaim its sovereignty over it.
>
> (1993: 26)

So, on the one hand, nationalists fought relentlessly to eradicate 'colonial difference' in the outer domain, but on the other hand, they struggled to protect their inner/spiritual domain, thereby retaining its difference. In this way Chatterjee responds to the claims of Benedict Anderson (1983) and Edward Said (1978), who suggested that the colonized people confronted their domination and imagined their nationalism through the discourses made available by the West. In his work, Chatterjee explored one of the ways in which the active and creative process of self-fashioning happened in the colonial context. But as Ayesha Jalal (2000) and Neeladri Bhattacharya (2005), among others, have demonstrated, Chatterjee's assumptions seem to be based on his study of Bengal's middle-class Hindu society. In their respective works, these scholars have shown that there were alternative strategies which were utilized by different sections of the population to counter the threat of cultural invasion. In this context, Jalal (2000) talks about the process of identity formation among Muslims and the way they had to negotiate their space in the nationalist discourse, which was overwhelmingly dominated by Hindu majoritarianism. Bhattacharya (2005) discusses the constant interaction between the 'private' and the 'public' sphere (especially between religion and law) through which the colonial subject defined itself.

Furthermore, the categories Chatterjee uses (of 'inner' and 'outer' sphere) do not seem to engage with the fact that though the 'inner' domain of the colonized was different from the colonizer, it was not homogeneous. The insistence of essential difference between the 'inner' spheres raised possibilities for a multiplicity of subjectivities which consolidated in different forms of available spaces. Hence the forms of consciousness found in this 'inner' domain took multiple forms, motivated by divergent interests – religion, caste, language, among others. Even within religious consciousness, there were several strands/layers – some dominated by the orthodox sections and the other by the revivalists and reformists. The use of modern statistical tools like the census and mapping by the British further added to this process of consolidation. So, even if it was a strategy by the nationalist elites to counter the impact of imperialism in their 'inner' or 'spiritual' domain, it made way for further disintegration and increasing differences among themselves. Also, 'private' and 'public' spheres often intermingled in multiple ways. So there were situations where components of public sphere interacted with the private and vice versa, and such interactions had the capacity to reconstitute and redefine the other sphere. Consider, for example, the sphere of religion. According to Chatterjee, it would form a part of the 'inner' or 'spiritual' domain, and this sphere was guarded by freedom of belief and faith. Similarly, freedom of speech and expression was something of 'public' or 'outer' domain as it was situated in the realm of law, and there was a constant demand to grant such equal rights as enjoyed by the European inhabitants. If the 'inner' and 'outer' spheres existed as autonomous, how do we understand the phenomenon wherein such freedom was also used by different socio-religious groups to not only profess and popularize one's own religion but in the process vilify other beliefs and encourage conversion? The role of the vernacular press, tracts and pamphlets published in the period are evidence of such strategy. In a way, it can be argued that the freedom in the 'external' domain was being used to impact belief and faith, which constituted the 'inner' domain. This form of interaction between the private and public spheres also became a problem for the British administrators, as they were not sure whether to intrude in certain domains. So, though the realm of the communal press remained embedded in the structure of colonial rules, it was relatively autonomous of the direct patronage of the colonial state (Gilmartin 1998). The communal consciousness that occurred under the effect of print during this period did not give rise to a 'public sphere' as understood by Habermas (1992) in a European context, but rather made the public space itself a site of multiple contestations and differences. 'Lay leaders'[15] played a prominent role, utilizing the new techniques of journalism, public preaching and debates, tracts and book writing to promote and profess their ideology. This process also included the invocation of 'history' to define and distinguish different communities.[16]

Initially the printing press was used by Indians to expose the role of Christian missionaries.[17] But soon these same critical tools were directed by Hindu and Muslim groups against each other, exposing the fissures in the religious organization of Indian society. The opposition in this politics was constituted through an imagination of the 'other', which changed according to the context of the clashes. So for example, in Punjab when the activities of the Arya Samaj became prominent, they were challenged by the growth of two different streams – the Sanatanis from within the Hindus and the Singh Sabhas from the Sikhs. However, when the Cow Protection Movement became popular, the natural 'other' was found in the Muslims, and on many occasions, one could see tacit understanding among the Arya Samajists, the Sanatanis and the members of Sikh Sabhas to fight against the common enemy, in this case the Muslims (Barrier 1992; Metcalf 1992).[18]

Though the literate population was still very small, one did not need to be a literate to be aware of such struggles, which often were fuelled by rumours that were transmitted by the spoken word (Bayly 2009; Guha 2009). The contents of newspapers and pamphlets were also disseminated through word of mouth at bazaars and local fairs to rouse communitarian emotions (Jalal 2000). Various newspapers and pamphlets of this period also voiced their resentment and questioned the colonial government's proclaimed policy of impartiality in the domain of religion. Some of the newspapers urged the government to ban all publications intended to inflame religious passions, but in vain. They equally opposed the virus of conversion that was infecting social peace and urged the state to take steps in this regard.[19] The demand for censorship had started to emerge from among the Indians, and it was mainly based on the logic of preventing the misuse of the freedom of press and publication to vilify and denigrate religious symbols and personage, which led to the incitement of communal hatred among different religious communities. However, such demands were largely overlooked by the British authorities.

By the beginning of the 20th century, clashing communitarian narratives, ostensibly emanating from the 'private' domain, flowed in unrestrained form into a public arena of informal politics (Jalal 2000). Freitag (1989) discusses in her work how the public arena became the site of new forms of communal consciousness that contributed both in the project of nationalism as well as communal self-definition. Many of the nationalists during this period were also deeply religious, and often the political use of religious categories blurred the line between nationalism and communalism (Metcalf & Metcalf 2012: 150). This process had two-way repercussions. On one side, the creative energy generated by such consciousness was used in the service of nationalism. For example, Tilak used Ganesh Puja as a public event to facilitate community participation and build a new grassroots unity between Brahmins and non-Brahmins, which contributed significantly to the nationalist project, especially in western India (Kaur 2003; Metcalf & Metcalf 2012). At the same time, such communal consciousness also inflamed fundamental differences and gave rise to new forms of inter-community conflicts that often took the shape of violent riots. As Barbara Metcalf (1992) notes, unlike the European experience, where national loyalty dominated, in the colonial areas, communal divisions were decisive. In India, according to her, this happened due to two significant developments. Firstly, 'representation' and 'communalism' were linked. The British had created a 'form of government structured on representation, in which leaders to be effective had to claim to speak for the interests of communities' (1992: 231). This meant that it was not individuals but communities defined by religious identities that engaged with the colonial state. This led to, as Freitag (1996) has also shown, politicization of religious identities. Secondly, Metcalf also points out that 'the colonial appropriation of public and civic institutions encouraged a kind of retreat to domestic and religious space as sites where cultural values could be reworked and renewed' (1992: 231). In this process, religious vocabulary attained the role of legitimate expression against the colonial rule. Not only this, even when spaces within civic and public institutions were later created for representation of Indian interests, these were so limited in scope that the issues of religion dominated the debates within these spaces. For example, in Allahabad, the electoral rivalry between Motilal Nehru and Madan Mohan Malviya during 1920s revolved around the question of 'who was a better Hindu?' and was dominated by issues like beef eating, organizing the Ram Lila procession and so on (Jaffrelot 2010: 350–353). This suggests how electoral mobilization, even when it involved such avowedly secular leaders as Motilal Nehru, tended to be assimilated into debates defined by communal consciousness during this period.

The practice of surveillance and control on different forms of expression by the British authorities also contributed to the process of communal consciousness. It led to a new tendency among the nationalists to use religious idioms in order to articulate their political aspirations (Pinney 2009).[20] Freitag (1989) argues that because the 'British viewed "political" activities as discrete from "religious" or cultural ones', such attempts were less susceptible to strict censorship. This gave an alternative way to convey the same idea in a covert way. However, the use of religious aspects in national consciousness also opened the dangers of misinterpretations and communal polarization as most of these new experiments used references from Hindu mythologies and tried to portray the superiority of the Hindu race. Take, for example, the religious idioms used in plays written by Indians in the late-19th century. In 1876, the government passed the Dramatic Performances Act to 'prohibit dramatic performances' that were 'seditious or obscene, or otherwise prejudicial to the public interests', 'likely to excite feelings of disaffection to the government established by law in British India', or 'likely to deprave and corrupt persons present at the performance' (Bhatia 2010: 191). The immediate reason for such legislation was the popularity and impact in Bengal of plays like Dinnabandhu Mitra's *Nil Darpan* (1860), Dakshina Charan Chattopadhayay's *Chakar Darpan* (1875), Upendra Nath Das's *Surendra-Binodini* (1875), *Ganjananda and the Prince* (1876) and *Police of Pig and Sheep* (1876). Through these performances, the playwright not only explicitly showcased the atrocities of the government, but also appealed for unity to overthrow the Raj. However, under strict censorship initiated by the new law, the writers had to change the plots and characters. So, plays were now based on mythologies, and the British characters, which were earlier at the centre of criticism, were replaced by the anglicized Indian character carved by imperial rule (Pamment 2009). This antagonized the new middle-class intelligentsia, who along with some from the Brahmin sections had even earlier objected to the plays on grounds of obscenity, to misrepresentation of women subjects and even to the stage performances by women. Further, being based on Hindu mythologies, these plays also lacked appeal to the Muslims: indeed, if anything, the call to Hindu pride put Muslims off. There is evidence that some of these plays were being used with multiple purposes – on the one hand, to expose the British and the other to counter the Muslims claims, especially during the Cow Protection Movement and the Hindi-Urdu controversy (King 1992).

The examples cited above indicate the way that religious symbols were used to speak simultaneously the language of communalism and nationalism. But such symbolism often contained communal overtones, and in the backdrop of multiple moments of religious violence and a culture of vilification of the other religion, the religious differences became more prominent. The situation worsened in the 1920s, and with the extreme political polarization of religious identities, government had to come up with new regulations, in the form of 295(A), which followed the famous *Rangila Rasul* (The Merry Prophet) case in 1927. The most significant aspect of this legislation, however, was that the demand for a law to curtail freedom of expression had emanated from Indians themselves and was passed by the

Central Legislature, which contained a reasonable number of Indian representatives. Though such demands were not new, in the charged political climate, they took on a completely new dimension.

The Rangila Rasul *Controversy and the Making of Section 295(A)*

The *Rangila Rasul* controversy was shaped and propelled in the context of 1920s Punjab. The Non-cooperation-Khilafat phase of Indian politics (1919–1921) represented an unprecedented scale of collaboration between the two largest religious communities of India – the Hindus and the Muslims. However, by 1922, after a sudden call-off of the movement by Gandhiji following the mass violence at Chauri Chaura, things began to change. The void created by the nationalistic politics was overtaken by competing religious sentiments. This was further fuelled by the Shudhi (purification) and Sangathan (organization) movement launched by the Arya Samajists in North India. This was equally and strongly reciprocated by the Muslims. The printing press again became a significant means for propaganda setting, and very soon the reports of communal clashes replaced the news about the nationalist movement as headlines of most major dailies. It turned into a bitter war of tracts and pamphlets which involved not only criticism of each other's faith but went as far as to vilify prominent figures of the other religion. It was in this context that the pamphlet *Rangila Rasul* first appeared.

The tract was published and distributed by Raj Pal, an Arya Samaj polemicist, and it was aimed to denigrate the image of the Prophet Mohammad by primarily mocking his marriages and sex life.[21] The publication appeared in response to another Urdu tract entitled *Unisveen Sadi ka Maharishi* (The Great Sage of the Nineteenth Century), penned by a Muslim fanatic to counter the alleged criticism and misrepresentation of the Prophet and Islam in Satyarth Prakash, the most revered book of the Arya Samajists. When the demand for the banning of the tract *Unisveen aid ka Maharishi* was raised, the government rejected it, citing the absence of 'any general public feeling', 'lack of any public motive' and no formal complaint, unlike *Rangila Rasul*, which 'attracted immediate attention' and received 'wide publicity and was condemned by certain Hindu as well as Muhammadan papers' (as quoted in Kumar 1997: 51). Consequently, Raj Pal was arrested under section 153(A) of the IPC. Though Raj Pal was convicted and sentenced by the lower courts, he was eventually acquitted by the Lahore High Court.[22]

The Case in the Lahore High Court

The final appeal in the case was directed to the High Court at Lahore, where Justice Dalip Singh heard it and handed down the judgement on 4 May 1927 (case details present as *Raj Pal, AIR 590 [Lahore]*). After extensive examination of the evidence and contents of the pamphlet, he concluded that the pamphlet was 'undoubtedly… a scurrilous satire on the founder of the Muslim religion'. In strong words, he maintained that it was a ridiculous piece of writing, liable to 'arouse the contempt of all decent persons of whatever community'. However, he insisted that he could not find anything that showed 'it was meant to attack the Mohammedan religion as such or to hold up Mohammedans as objects worthy of enmity and hatred'. So, he very 'reluctantly' acquitted the petitioner as he believed that the subject in question – malicious satire on the personal life of a religious teacher – was outside the purview of section 153(A). He further suggested that if such writings were to be convicted, there was a need for passage of a law to amend the code 'by which the publication of pamphlets published with the intention of wounding the religious feelings of any person or of insulting the religion of any person might be made criminal'. But because he had to base his judgement in the case upon existing law, he ordered acquittal of the appellant.

The judgement received polarized reactions. It was proclaimed as the victory of Hindu religion by the Arya Samajists. On the other hand, protest meetings were held by Muslims all over India, the one in Lahore being attended by around 10,000 Muslims. It was held that the court had failed in protecting the honour of the Prophet. This caused a serious law-and-order crisis in Punjab. Discussing the situation, Punjab governor Hailey commented:

> There was really a very serious danger of disorder, for an attack on the Prophet was a concrete offence against Islam that stung them to the quick, and they could not bear the thought that Hindus could repeat it with impunity.
>
> (Hailey to Vincent, August 11, 1927, in *Hailey MSS* [Eur. C. 152], IOL/R)

On 11 June, due to the rising fear for the law-and-order situation, Hailey moved beyond the set protocol and met a Muslim deputation.[23] He admitted to them that the judgement had left the government 'much concerned'. He said that he sympathized with those Muslims who felt 'justifiably offended' by the pamphlet, and if required, the government would also seek amendment of the law in order to extend its application as suggested by Justice Dalip Singh. Though the liberal Muslims were convinced by Hailey's promises, according to the popular press reports, these voices were silenced by the strong feeling of betrayal and sense of victimhood felt by the agitated popular Muslim response.[24]

In Punjab, a demand for the resignation of Justice Dalip Singh and reversal of the judgement delivered by him was growing. A radical opinion was expressed under the title 'Resign' in *Muslim Outlook* of 14 June 1927, in which both – the judgement in the *Rangila Rasul* case and Justice Dalip

Singh – were abusively criticized. It included grave allegations against impartiality, justice and the integrity of Justice Singh (Barrier 1974: 100).[25] The demand for his resignation was further echoed by other newspapers. Responding to the situation, government arrested D. S. Bukhari, the editor of the daily, and its printer, Nur-ul-haq, on the charges of contempt of court.[26]

The situation worsened with these arrests. Though Bukhari and Nur-ul-haq were punished under the charges of contempt of court, it was widely perceived differently in connection with the *Rangila Rasul* case. The general feeling among the Muslims was that the government had been vigilant and interested in punishing for the offence of contempt of court but was casual on the issue of the contempt of their Prophet. The sense of anger was rooted in what was seen as a case of bias in favor of Hindus and victimization of the Muslims. The news and the interpretations of the cases spread rapidly all over the country, and the press reported reactions in the form of protest meetings, *hartals* (strikes) and Hindu boycotts from different regions.

The community antagonism was at its peak, and the government was under pressure to restore the faith of protesting Muslims in the justice system. Within a few months, in another similar case involving Devi Sharan Sharma, who published a similar tract entitled *Sair-i-Dozakh* (Passage to Hell) in *Risala Vartman*, the publisher was held guilty and punished. In this case the judges argued against the logic of Dalip Singh and held that any kind of 'promotion of feeling of hatred' in any form was prohibited. Justice Broadway stated that 'any criticism of a religious leader, whether dead or alive, falls within the ambit of section 153(A) of IPC' (*Devi Sharan Sharma and another v. King Emperor* [1927] 14 AIR 594 [Lahore]). The importance the government attached to this particular case can be gleaned from the fact that Justice Broadway, then on vacation, was especially asked to return to Punjab for the court hearing in the hope that he would reverse the earlier decision.[27]

Broadway's judgement delivered what the government was expecting. But it could do nothing to improve the law-and-order situation in the country. The harsh punishment pronounced in the case was enough to alienate the Hindus, especially in United Province and elsewhere. It was argued that in each case of religious vilification it was Hindus who were prosecuted, and no action was initiated against Muslim authors who wrote similar tracts against Hindu deities. It was further held that the harsh punishment delivered in the *Vartman* case was only because of the hysteria created by Muslims after the *Rangila Rasul* case, and the government had buckled under their pressure. Mass meetings were organized all over the United Provinces to condemn and protest against the attitude of Muslims and of government officials.[28]

The Bill in the Legislature

Though the *Vartman* case went as desired by the government, it was thought that uncertainty should be avoided. There was a looming fear of a judgement like *Rangila Rasul* coming up in the future, especially, with the kind of uncertainty it had generated vis-à-vis section 153(A). The doubt over such judicial issues needed to be clarified, and the only way of doing it was by introducing a revision of the law. It was also believed to be helpful in winning back the lost confidence and goodwill among the Muslims. Unlike the popular Muslim demand for legislation, particularly against such vilification of the Prophet, Hailey recommended drafting a general section which could prohibit attack upon any sacred symbol of all religions. Hailey believed that a general law of this nature could find support both among the Muslims and the Hindus, who had been equally vocal in their criticism when the matter came to discussion in the Punjab Legislative Council.[29] The decision to legislate the Religious Insult Bill to amend the required sections of IPC was approved by the Viceroy, and the bill was put on the table for discussion in the August session of the Central Legislative Assembly.

From the time of introduction of the bill to its way through the Select Committee and its final passage, there were several dissenting voices. Most of the dissenters felt that the legislation was being pushed through hurriedly. B. P. Naidu called it a 'panicky legislation' and along with others reiterated the request for a wide circulation of the bill so that responses could be sought from all sections whose interests were at stake.[30] Some members also charged the government of appeasement by acting so hastily on the demands raised by a set of Muslims in north India.[31] Amar Nath Dutt termed it as the 'favourite wife policy'.[32] A large section of the dissenters also believed that there already existed enough such laws, and if the government truly wanted to maintain peace and order in society, it did not need an additional law.

However, the most serious questions were raised about the scope of the bill – about its aims, the fear of misuse and its failure to address the real issues. Though it was recognized that the bill that appeared after the Select Committee stage was much better than what was initially proposed, it did not end all worries. There was a general feeling among dissenters that the bill would not be able to achieve its aims as it did nothing to address the real problem – the causes of Hindu-Muslim tension – since the scurrilous writings were only a product of such tension.[33]

Significantly, there was another issue that received shared concerns from most members across religious and other affiliations. Lajpat Rai, Jinnah, Kunzru and Madan Mohan Malviya were all in support of legitimate criticism of religion or religious reform, especially if made in works of historical importance.[34] Largely it was a concern that the freedom of speech and expression should not be restrained to such an extent that it lost its meaning and true value. Though most of these members were worried about the fate of freedom of expression, the presence of contingent situations forced them to compromise. Freedom of speech and expression in the colonial context, after all, was just a desired claim and not a legal or fundamental right. The lawmakers considered it more important to counter the temporary threat that it was having on public order and tranquillity. There was also a suggestion in the form of amendment that the law be made applicable only for a limited duration, and this was widely supported by the likes of Lajpat Rai and S. Iyengar, but it lost by a close margin.[35] Section 295(A) as finally adopted said:

> Whoever with deliberate and malicious intention of outraging the religious feelings of any class of His Majesty's subjects, by words, either spoken or written, or by visible representations, insults or attempts to insult the religion or the religious belief of that class, shall be punished with imprisonment of either description for a term which may extend to two years, or with fine, or with both.
> (*The Gazette of India*, 24 September 1927)

The case further reflected what I have earlier referred to as an attitude towards using the law for 'selective censorship'. The government did not ban earlier pamphlets like *Unisveen Sadi ka Maharishi* on the pretext that 'no serious threat was visible', whereas it was evident that *Rangila Rasul* was written in reaction of those tracts. If the government would have acted earlier, it is possible that the incumbent situation could have been avoided. Such inaction encouraged aberrants like Raj Pal and raised several issues about the intentions of the government, which were also reflected in the debates in the Assembly.[36] At the same time, it can be seen as a conscious and calculated move to assert the capacity of the state to act as a neutral arbitrator of 'supposedly endemic and inevitable religious conflicts' (Ahmed 2009: 173). In this regard, one should not overlook the fact that section 295(A) was structured in the form of a law for public order and aimed at preventing vilification of religious belief and personalities of all sections. At least in this sense it was projected as a secular law, thereby also upholding its promise of neutrality on religious matters.[37] So, without direct intervention on religious matters, the British could claim to have developed a law that protected the interests of all religious communities.

But how does one understand the role of native Indian representatives in the legislature during the making of section 295(A)? Neeti Nair has argued that in the context of 'competitive communalism', this moment should be seen as a case of 'legislative pragmatism', where leaders from opposition parties came together to stop wanton attacks on religious figures and create an atmosphere for dialogue between the two communities (2013: 329). A close analysis of the Assembly debate suggests that this analysis is not entirely correct. Firstly, as discussed earlier, the primary reason cited by most of the members who were against the bill was fear of political misuse and increase in space for executive action. Secondly, the proceedings of Assembly also reflected sharp divisions on religious lines. It would not be entirely correct to claim, as Neeti Nair does, that the leaders rose above their loyalties and affiliations (2013: 317). In contrast, they seem to hold strongly religious lines of arguments.[38] Most of the Muslim legislators were in favour of the bill, and among those who voted against the bill, most were Hindus.[39] The charges levelled by several Hindu members that the bill was an extension of a Muslim appeasement policy of government has already been discussed. In fact, many of those Hindu members who supported the bill did so only because they believed that prohibition and check on scurrilous writings would be equally beneficial for all religious denominations. Thirdly, though the concern for freedom of expression was raised, it was not centrally addressed. Doubts about the bill's impact on freedom of expression largely remained confined in the arguments of professional pressmen, who feared that such law would directly impact their lives. At all other times when the concern was raised about its impact on historical research or religious reforms, it was never seriously dealt with, and no remedy was therefore suggested. It was not surprising that the claim about the bill's impact on freedom of speech and expression was easily overshadowed by the concern for the emergent communal situation and thereby the need to empower the state to maintain public order and tranquility. It is for this reason that a 'consensus', as claimed by Nair, could be reached. But the fact remains that the debates in the Assembly lacked any serious discussions about the fate of freedom of speech and expression, and at the same time the participants overwhelmingly used overtly religious arguments in order to underline the need for such laws. Law was seen as an instant means to protect emotional subjects from hurt in a context where vilification of religion and religious figures had become a regular phenomenon. I doubt that this approach can be called 'legislative pragmatism', as Nair has claimed. If anything, the role of the Indian representatives in the Assembly reflects a sense of urgency and short-sightedness. In an attempt to provide instant protection to religious sensibilities from hurt, they failed to contemplate the long-term repercussions that such a law could have on the basic rights of people.[40] The most significant aspect of the debates in the Assembly was that native leaders engaged in a process of deliberation on a law that was going to govern their lives and impact their basic liberties in a fundamental way. However, a consensus was implicit in the process of deliberation that some rational limits had to be drawn in order to check religiously offensive speech acts. This aspect dominated the proceedings of the legislature, and the importance rendered to such a law in overcoming topical issues marred the possibility of an assessment of its probable implications.

The Nationalist Discourse and the Dichotomy over Freedom of Expression

Running parallel to the attempts at censorship by British authorities was also the story of nationalists' struggle for 'fundamental rights'. The first explicit demand for fundamental rights appeared in the Constitution of India Bill, 1895. Article 16 of this bill included a variety of rights like free speech, free education and others (Rao 1967). A series of congressional resolutions adopted in the period 1917–1919 also reiterated the concern for civil liberties. During this time, the central concern was to gain equal rights as the British in India and as the Britons had among themselves in England. However, by the mid-twenties the aim was changed, and with the demand of *swaraj* taking centre-stage, the comparisons were replaced by a thesis about complete freedom (Austin 1997: 50). Mrs Besant's Commonwealth of India Bill (1925) was reflective of this spirit. It laid down that individual liberty, freedom of conscience, free expression of opinion, free assembly and equality before the law were to be ensured. The *Nehru Report*, prepared by a committee headed by Motilal Nehru and formed by a resolution by the Madras Congress, reiterated this position. It declared that the first concern of Indians was to 'secure the fundamental rights that have been denied to them'. In this report, the desire to afford protection to minorities was especially prominent. For example, the right to freedom of conscience and to the free profession and practice of religion was included explicitly to prevent 'one community dominating over another'. It declared,

> Another reason why great importance attaches to a declaration of rights is the unfortunate existence of communal differences in the country. Certain safeguards are necessary to create and establish a sense of security among those who look upon each other with distrust and suspicion. We could not better secure the full enjoyment of religious and communal rights to all communities than by including them among the basic principles of the constitution.[41]

It is explicit that in nationalists' understanding, religious and communal rights were not seen as antithetical to individual rights; rather, it was held that they could co-exist harmoniously. The Karachi Resolution of Congress (1931) on Fundamental Rights and Economic and Social Change, which was both a declaration of rights and a humanitarian socialist manifesto, took the demand forward (Austin 1997: 56). Continuing this spirit was the *Sapru Report* of 1945 that declared:

> What the constitution demands and expects is perfect equality between one section of the community and another in the matter of political and civic rights, equality of liberty and security in the enjoyment of the freedom of religion, worship, and the pursuit of the ordinary application of life.
>
> (Sapru 1945: 260)

All these were important reference points when the fundamental rights were debated in the Constituent Assembly, and freedom of speech and expression featured in all these documents, reflecting a kind of unanimity on the issue.

Situations like the *Rangila Rasul* controversy exposed the lack of clarity among the nationalists on the question of freedom of speech and expression. On the one hand, they were demanding greater freedom to criticize the colonial government,[42] and on the other hand, they were not very sure how to respond when such freedom was used for vilification of religious symbols and personalities. This was further evident when *Satyarth Prakash* (The Light of Truth), the most important book of Arya Samaj, was banned in Sind in 1944. The demand for the ban had been made time and again by several Muslim groups since its publication in 1875, as they insisted that it contained severe insulting references to the Prophet Mohammad and to Islam, which according to them was offensive to Muslims all over the country. But the British did not endorse their position. In December 1943, during a public meeting in Karachi, the Muslim League reiterated this demand and appealed for action. In 1944, due to immense pressure from Muslim public opinion, the Sind government, led by the Muslim League, announced the ban. Gandhi was distressed with the ban. He maintained, 'Satyarth Prakash enjoys the same status for 40 lakhs of Arya Samajists as the Koran for the Muslims and the Bible for the Christians' (*Harijan*, 3 November 1946). He argued in his article entitled *Sind bans Satyarth Prakash*:

> The virtue of toleration is never strained, especially in matters of religion. Differences of religious opinion will persist to the end of time. Toleration is the only thing that will enable persons belonging to different religions to live as good neighbours and friends. Religion never suffers by reason of the criticism – fair or foul of critics, it always suffers from the laxity or indifference of its followers.
>
> (*Harijan*, 3 November 1946)

Ironically, about the same book, writing in *Young India* in 1924 in an article entitled 'Hindu-Muslim Tension: Its Cause and Cure', Gandhi had said:

> I have read Satyarth Prakash, the Arya Samaj Bible.... I have not read a more disappointing book from a reformer so great.... He has unconsciously misrepresented Jainism, Islam, Christianity and Hinduism itself.... One having even cursory acquaintance with these faiths could easily discover the errors into which the great reformer was betrayed.

Although he was extremely critical about *Satyarth Prakash*, he believed the banning of the book was uncalled for. Gandhi's position with regard to *Satyarth Prakash* indicated his approach to the question of tolerance and his discomfort with the idea of banning any form of publication. Rather, the remedy he suggested to counter writings containing vilification or denigration of other religions was different. In his article 'Hindu-Muslim Tension:

Its Cause and Cure', Gandhi was particularly critical of writings – tracts and pamphlets – which according to him had played a significant role in heightening Hindu-Muslim tensions. But he believed that the best mechanism to counter this competitive vilification of each other's religion was the role that local community leaders should play, for instance, by taking measures to find ways of 'stopping these publications or, at least, discrediting them and distributing clean literature instead, showing tolerance for each other's faith' (Gandhi 1967: 261). He also insisted on creating a public opinion that could reject such incitements. He believed that the regulatory and legal mechanisms failed 'to serve the purpose intended, except temporarily, and in no case do they convert the writers.... The real remedy is healthy public opinion that will refuse to patronize poisonous journals' (*Harijan*, 28 May 1931).

Gandhi's was a moral position on the subject and also reflective of his general aversion to the role that law and government should play in an ideal society. Rather, he insisted on building local networks to counter the threat posed by offensive publications. However, many other nationalists would not uphold this position. Though they were critical of the ban on *Satyarth Prakash*, they had their own reasons. For example, Nehru claimed it to be a larger issue of religious freedom. He was worried that 'this may become a precedent for future invasions on all civil rights and liberties' (*Harijan*, 5 October 1945). Nehru asserted that 'I shall always endeavour to have civil liberties in all forms maintained and practised in India and to resist any encroachment on them'. For Nehru, to take a principled position when the ban was called by the Muslim League's government in Sind was easy, but one can contrast this view from his position in 1937 after the Indian National Congress had emerged in power in most of the provinces. When communal tensions increased in some regions and was further frenzied by vernacular press, he wrote in *Harijan* on 23 October:

> Inspite of every desire to avoid it, coercive action may become necessary and in such cases ministries will inevitably have to undertake it. Such coercive action should only be undertaken where there has been violence or incitement to violence or communal strife.

Nehru's approach was more realistic than Gandhi's, as he saw the inevitability of the state's role in regulating free speech in certain circumstances, especially when it increased communal tensions. He insisted that in such cases, governmental interferences were necessary, a position that he maintained even after India became independent. The opposition to the ban seemed to situate Nehru on the same side as S. P. Mookherjee,[43] who also criticized the ban, however, for completely different reasons. Mookherjee condemned the ban as an attack on Hinduism. He took the opportunity to appeal to the Arya Samajists to work in cooperation with other parties for the consolidation of the Hindu forces and freedom of Hindustan (Madok

2001: 53). The Arya Samajists organized a massive *satyagraha* (non-violent protest) in Sind but in vain.[44] The book remained banned even after all such agitations.

It was evident that though the ban was opposed by the nationalists, different sections had different reasons for their oppositions. It was particularly true in cases where the freedom of speech and expression was seen as being in collision with religious values and identities. So, whereas Gandhi was in principle against the use of government machinery for such a cause, Nehru's opposition was based on his arguments for religious liberties, and Mookherjee saw it as a conscious ploy by Muslim fundamentalists. The divergent arguments reveal no unanimity over the criticism of the ban, but rather ambiguities in nationalist positions regarding censorship. These issues once again came out in the open when these personalities sat down to write the Constitution for Independent India.

Conclusion

What ramifications did the debates over censorship during colonial times have on the understanding about freedom of speech and expression? On the one hand, the legal provisions and limitations introduced by the British formed the guiding principles for the free speech discourse in India, and on the other hand, in the absence of any comprehensive civil liberties movement, the mediums of nationalist responses like the vernacular press, tracts, books and iconographies became the rallying point around which the freedom of expression debate centred.[45] Freedom of expression remained largely dependent on the interpretations of law offered by the colonial authorities. Neither the British nor the Indians treated freedom of expression as a fundamental individual right. It was invoked based on the utility it served for the community at large. The British attitude to freedom of expression in relation to offence or insult to religious identities reflected a subtle dichotomy. On the one hand, in legal and legislative language, the limits to free expression were pronounced and kept on growing (in the form of section 153[A], or section 295[A] of the IPC and other similar regulations); on the other hand, post-1857 they claimed to maintain a policy of non-interference in the religious activities of the natives. The use of colonial laws, however, was subject to the interests of the imperial design, which was believed to be best served by the colonial state maintaining an image of a neutral arbitrator of religious conflicts. So, at times due to the fear of being branded as biased towards a particular community, and at other times, in order to extract maximum benefit from such antagonisms, they exercised 'selective censorship'.

On the part of the colonized Indians, the response was equally diverse. The early liberals like Rammohan Roy argued for some limits to freedom of speech and expression especially in conditions of libel and sedition but thought it to be a potent weapon to respond to the challenges of Christian missionaries. But gradually the same freedom was used by Hindus and Muslims against each other. As these antagonisms escalated and began to take violent shape, there were demands from within the Indian communities to restrict freedom of expression. There was no clarity in the position of Indian nationalists on the subject. The nationalists questioned the British claim that they had conferred religious liberty and toleration on Indian society through their policy of impartiality in the domain of religion and argued that it only allowed men of various creeds to play fast and loose with religion (Jalal 2000: 80). Though they were struggling for greater freedom of expression to criticize the authorities, they were not sure if similar freedom should be allowed in religious matters. Legislative debates of the time reveal that they were not just mute observers in the lawmaking process; rather, they participated actively in critically analysing the scope and limits of such laws. During the making of sections 153(A) and 295(A), Indian legislatures made a significant impact both in criticizing the colonial government and, at the same time, pitching a rational law that could prevent vilification of religious personalities and incitement to religious hatred.[46] Several leaders also cautioned against granting too much power to the executive, as it could impact the freedom of speech and expression in significant ways.[47] However, an overwhelming support for the proposed amendments and additions in the IPC reflected a general consensus among Indians leaders that freedom of speech and expression should be limited in cases where it could cause religious harm or incite hatred in the name of religion or other forms of community-based identity.

This analysis presents a picture of free speech debate in colonial period in a different way than the one forwarded by legal scholar Arun K. Thiruvengadam, who characterizes different historical periods in India's free speech experience and argues that during the anti-colonial struggle it presented a 'universalist' nature that subsequently got replaced by 'particularistic' concerns during the constitution-making process and led to the inclusion of several grounds of restrictions.[48] As the discussions in this chapter highlight, such a 'universalist' approach never existed. Indian leaders, in the name of harm that publications vilifying different religions had caused, aggressively advocated curtailment of freedom of expression through legal means. It can be concluded that when India became independent, it carried with itself an ambiguity, vis- à-vis the position over freedom of expression, particularly in relation to religious offence. There was, however, a looming consensus that such freedom needed to be controlled and regulated through law. This history of contradictions and the role of the vernacular press in communal violence had a significant impact on the future of freedom of speech and expression when it was being debated in the Constituent Assembly.

Notes

1 Buckingham was the editor of the *Calcutta Journal* until 1823, when he was deported.

2 Fair was the editor of the *Bombay Gazette* and was deported in 1824.

3 Henry Maine also believed that India was 'empty of laws' before the British started to legislate. He wrote, 'Nobody who has inquired into the matter can doubt that, before the British government began to legislate, India was, regard being to its moral and material needs, a country singularly empty of law'. See 'Minute on Codification in India', dated 17 July 1879, NAI, Home (Legislative) August 1879: 217–220.

4 His provision simply states: 'Whoever, by words either spoken or intended to be read, or by signs, or by visible representations, attempts to cause any imputation concerning any person to be believed in any quarter, knowing that the belief thereof would harm the reputation of that person in that quarter, is said except in the cases (hereinafter mentioned), to defame that person'. See 'Of Defamation' in *A Penal Code Prepared by the Indian Law Commissioners* (Kolkata: Bengal Military Orphan Press, 1837), p. 124.

5 See 'Notes J', in *A Penal Code Prepared by the Indian Law Commissioners*, p. 49.

6 Section 298 in the original IPC is present as section 282 in the Report in *Penal Code Prepared*, 71. It rendered everyone liable to a year's imprisonment who, 'with the deliberate intention of wounding the religious feelings of any person, utters any word or makes any sound in the hearing of that person, or makes any gesture in the sight of that person, or places any object in the sight of that person'.

7 'Indirect rule' was basically the rule through native institutions. Scholars like Maine argued that there was fundamental difference between native societies and the British. Based on this argument, he urged that the aim of British rule should be to use the internal coherence of native institutions rather than its dissolution. Indirect rule became the foundational principle of late-imperial philosophy in Asia and Africa. For a detailed analysis see Karuna Mantena (2009).

8 There are commentators like Chatterjee who don't agree with the idea of shift in the policy. He argues that the essentialized difference between colonizers and colonized justified colonial authoritarianism, and so although British administrators promised that colonialism would eventually eradicate differences, once the colonized 'other' became modern subjects, colonial control would have lost its ideological foothold. So, in *The Nation and Its Fragments* (1993) he maintains that 'colonial difference' was always at the centre of imperial policy, and the case of legal reform was no different. But even he agrees that the British maintained an essential difference between criminal and personal laws.

9 In the English law the provision for enmity between classes was included in the section dealing with offences against the state.

10 Lord Lansdowne et al., memo, 27 December 1893, *India Office Library/Records*, London (Henceforth IOL/R), L/P & J/6/365, File no. 84, p. 4.

11 'Note on the Cow Protection Agitation in Gorakhpur District', 1894, IOL/R, File no. 84, pp. 1–2 (emphasis added).

12 See Wheeler note (27 November 1913), Government of India Home Political Proceeding (GIPOL) December 1913, 9D, as quoted in Barrier (1974: 61).

13 *Lauh-i-Mahfuz*, Moradabad, 29 August 1879, Selections, L/R/5/56, IOL/R, p. 698.

14 *Samaya Vinod*, 1 November 1876, L/R/5/53, IOL/R, p. 627.

15 Barbara Daly Metcalf (1992) has argued that these were the new leaders who became experts in religious tradition, though they did not receive traditional teachings and training like the pundits or *ulemas*. They became more popular due to their use of modern techniques like print in professing and popularizing religion. An example of such leaders, according to Metcalf, was Arya Samaj founder Swami Dayanand Saraswati.
16 It was based on this recognition that Gandhi, in his attempt to bring different communities together, rejected the idea of historicization of the past as it could lead to a divisive and self-defeating project for Indian nationalism. He prioritized 'civilizational consciousness' over 'historical consciousness'. 'I believe in the saying that, a nation is happy that has no history', he maintained. As quoted in R. Iyer (1986: 187).
17 *Lauh-i-Mehfuz*, an Urdu journal, exposed that instead of using the mission funds for supporting the poor, the money was being wasted on the 'publication of books written with no other object than to expose, to ridicule and hold in contempt the Hindus and Mussalman religion'. *Lauh-i-Mahfuz*, Moradabad, 14 September 1874, Selections, L/R/5/52, IOL/R, p. 484.
18 The common enemy appeared in the form of Muslims because beef formed an important part of their diet, and the same was prohibited in both Hindu as well as Sikh religious traditions, which considered the cow to be sacred (Barrier 1992; Metcalf 1992).
19 Nizam-l-Akhbar, 27 August 1876, Selections, L/R/5/53, IOL/R, p. 471.
20 Christopher Pinney (2009) considers this phenomenon in Indian politics as 'Iatrogenesis' i.e., an illness that comes about as a direct result of the physician's intervention.
21 The real author of the tract remains unknown. However, some scholars have claimed that it was Pandit Chamupati, a popular Arya Samajist (Kumar 1997: 50; Thursby 1975: 40).
22 The main source of the case and judgments is POLITICAL/1927/File 132/I, NAI (National Archives of India). Judgement of the final appeal also was published as *Raj Pal v. King Emperor* (1927) 14 AIR 590 (Lahore).
23 This incident was widely publicized in the press. See, 'Deputation to the Governor', *Tribune*, 14 June 1927. Also see Hailey's letter to the Home Department on 23 June 1927, in POLITICAL, 1927, File No. 132.
24 Mohammad Iqbal was shouted down by an agitated crowd at Lahore on 9 June 1927. 'Muslims Climb Down', *Tribune*, 10 June 1927.
25 The article 'Resign' published in *Muslim Outlook* also tried to make sense of the judgement in the light of the religious identity of Dalip Singh, who was a Christian. See, 'Alleged Contempt of Court', *Times of India*, 17 June 1927.
26 'Clear Contempt of Court: Lahore Editor to Jail', *The Times of India*, 22 June 1927; 'Lahore Editor Jailed: "In Perfect Good Faith"', *Times of India*, 23 June 1927.
27 Telegram, Hailey to Broadway, 6 July 1927, *Hailey MSS* Eur. E 200, IOL/R, London.
28 'Hartals in UP Towns: Hindus Agitated: Aftermath of Vartman Judgment', *The Times of India*, 10 August 1927.
29 'Hailey's letter to the Home Department', 12 August 1927, in POLITICAL, 1927, File No. 132.
30 B. P. Naidu, *The Legislative Assembly Debates*, vol. 14, 16 September 1927, 4478. All volumes of *The Legislative Assembly Debates* are available at the NAI. All the citations regarding the debate follow from same source, so until mentioned, the reference remains same and only the column number will be mentioned with the names of the speakers.

31 K. C. Roy, 4468. Roy held that the demand had only come from 'a handful of men in the Punjab, thoughtful perhaps, patriotic perhaps, but really, the inner working came from a set of men who are responsible for the communal disturbances in north India'.
32 Amar Nath Dutt, 4484–4486.
33 M. K. Acharya, 3433–3436; Thakur Das Bhargava, 3951–3952; Roy, 4467–4468.
34 Lajpat Rai, 3930–3931; M. A. Jinnah, 3932–3933; Kunzru, 3941; M. M. Malviya, 3948.
35 The details of amendments that were tabled are available in The Legislative Assembly Debates, vol. 14, 16 September 1927, 4502–4584.
36 Dr. Belvi, 4469–4470. He had raised this issue in the Assembly.
37 Julia Stephens (2014) has also developed this point, arguing that the case reflects an inextricable relationship between 'religious sentiments, colonial politics and secular laws'.
38 There were attempts to derive the idea of tolerance from religious scriptures like the Koran, the Gita and others. There were also attempts to pass the buck on the other community and blame them for starting the problems. See Abdul Haye, 3928; Acharya, 3433–3436; Mohammad Shah Nawaz, 3443–3444; Malviya, 3448; Bhargava, 3451–3452.
39 None of the Muslim members voted against the bill. List of who voted 'for' and 'against' the bill is available in POLITICAL, File No. 132/27, 1927, 26.
40 Nair (2013: 331) also agrees that most of the votes in favour of the bill were 'reluctant' and only responding to the 'emergency situation'.
41 All Parties Conference, 'Report of a Committee to Determine Principles of the Constitution for India', *The Nehru Report*, pp. 89–90.
42 All the major documents brought out by the nationalists reiterated this demand like the Constitution of India Bill (1895), Commonwealth of India Bill (1925), Nehru Report (1928), The Karachi Resolution of Congress (1931) on *Fundamental Rights and Economic and Social Change*, and The Sapru Report (1945).
43 Member of the Congress Party considered very close to religious nationalists of the time, and who later founded the right-wing nationalist party Bharatiya Jana Sangh.
44 'Satyagraha in Sindh launched', *The Times of India*, 17 January 1947.
45 This, however, changed after the 1870s, when tracts, books and iconography also became sites of contestations and debates. See Pinney (1997: 834–867).
46 For example, during the discussions over the introduction of section 153(A) in the penal codes, Select Committee member P Ananda Charlu described the enactment of section 153(A) as 'a dangerous piece of legislation and has been impolitic (among other reasons) by necessitating Government to side with or to appear to side with one party as against another'. He said, 'In my humble judgment it will only accentuate the evil which it is meant to remove. Far from healing the differences which still linger, or which now and then come to the surface, it would widen the gap by encouraging insidious men to do mischief in stealth'. See, Select Committee Report, *Gazette of India*, Part V (5 February 1898), 15. Although as a member of the Select Committee he registered his dissent, he voted for the bill in the Council, and section 153(A) was passed there with 18 members in favour and 4 against the amendment to the criminal laws.
47 These concerns were raised by Indian representatives like Ananda Charlu and the Maharaja of Darbhanga during the debates over section 153(A) in 1898 and members like Lala Lajpat Rai and Mohammad Ali Jinnah among others, during the debates over section 295(A) in 1928.

48 Arun K. Thiruvengadam, 'The Evolution of the Constitutional Right to Free Speech in India (1800–1950): The Interplay of Universal and Particular Rationales', University of Washington Trans-Pacific Comparative Constitutional Roundtable on 6 December 2013; Centre for Asian Legal Studies, National University of Singapore, Working Paper Series, Available at http://papers.ssrn.com/sol3/papers.cfm? abstract_id= 2470905 (last accessed on 17 July 2017).

2

FREEDOM OF EXPRESSION AND RELIGIOUS VILIFICATIONS

Decoding the Constitutional and Legal Definition of 'Limits'

When India became independent, celebrations of the birth of a new nation were accompanied by the general feeling of hope that everything associated with colonial rule would be undone, and independence along with formation of a new state under the leadership of the nationalists would usher a fresh sense of freedom with an uncompromising respect for civil liberties (U. Mehta 2011: 17). However, the challenge of nation-making and the pressure of the context did not allow space for such ambitious intervention. This dichotomy was clearly evident in the Constituent Assembly Debates (henceforth to be called CAD) and the constitution that took shape thereafter. Sudipta Kaviraj has significantly argued that 'before independence as power was not in the hands of the nationalists, political and ideological positions could be articulated only as ideas, which allowed the liberty to think beyond barriers, almost a utopian imagery of independent India' (2011: 76). The real challenge, therefore, was visible when the same nationalists occupied positions of power and responsibility to shape the future of the nation.

The Constituent Assembly and the Idea of Freedom of Speech and Expression in the Constitution

The Constituent Assembly became the site where divergent visions about India's future interacted to produce a document which could become the 'statement of Indian identity' (Parekh 2008). The discussions in the Assembly over freedom of speech and expression lacked any political or philosophical argumentation about the importance or need for such a right in a democracy. Its inclusion in the constitution was considered sine qua non, partly because of the historical background of the struggle for Independence and more because of the fact that the most part of India's constitution was borrowed from the declarations or constitutions of the then-successful democracies. The Bill of Rights, the debates over the First Amendment in the US and others were clear in the minds of the constitution makers. But it was not an exclusive case with freedom of speech

DOI: 10.4324/9781003369257-3

and expression. Many political concepts that were used and included in the constitution were little debated or reflected upon by the constitution makers. Though Nehru claimed in the Assembly on 13 January 1946 that 'we have laid down no theoretical words', the constitution was full of political concepts and ideas that required far more clarity than was rendered (Gopal 1991: 247). Sunil Khilnani has rightly argued that such evasion 'retracted attention from how these elements might interact with one another over time, producing mutations in the forms of democracy, while also changing the internal character of the nature of representation, rights and equality' (2005: 70). However, it did not mean that the ideas were not discussed at all. For example, in relation to freedom of speech and expression, the members debated extensively about the appropriate limits to such freedom.

The issue about the restrictions and its rationale came up at an early stage when the *Draft Report* submitted by the sub-committee to the Advisory Committee for consideration subjected freedom of speech and expression to 'public order' and 'morality'. It also included provisions for action against 'publication or utterance of seditious, obscene, slanderous, libellous or defamatory matter' (Rao 1966–1968: 138). Pointing out the lacunae, members like K. T. Shah[1] argued that the limitations should be minimal and terms like 'morality' should be avoided, as they were vague and could be misused (ibid.: 157). On the opposite of the spectrum were members like A. K. Ayyar,[2] who argued that exceptions were too narrow and should be broadened in order to be used by the state for security and other emergencies. These discussions forced early amendments and the *Interim Report on Fundamental Rights* that was presented to the Constituent Assembly by the Advisory Committee read:

> 8. There shall be liberty for the exercise of the following rights subject to public order and morality or to the existence of grave emergency declared to be such by the government of the union or the unit concerned whereby the security of the union or the unit, as the case may be, is threatened:
>
> a) The right of every citizen to freedom of speech and expression: provision may be made by law to make the publication or utterance of seditious, obscene, blasphemous, slanderous, libellous or defamatory matter actionable and punishable.
>
> (CAD, Vol. III: 2)

This draft attracted severe criticism from different ends. For example, Somnath Lahiri[3] argued that the provisions seemed to have been framed 'from the point of view of a police constable'. He also warned that the phrase 'grave emergency' was one open to interpretation, and hence its misuse by the executive was possible (CAD, Vol. III: 384–385). Looking at the kind of hostility it had generated, Patel moved clause 8 the next day, omitting the provisos contained in clause 8(a). Based on the committee reports and their discussion in the Constituent Assembly, B. N. Rau[4] prepared the Draft Constitution, which was cleared by the Drafting Committee before being placed in the Assembly. Interestingly, the Draft Constitution included a set of new provisos and read as follows:

> 13. (1) Subject to other provisions of this article, all citizens shall have the right- (a) To freedom of speech and expression;
>
> (2) Nothing in sub-clause (a) of clause (1) of this article shall affect the operation of any existing law, or prevent the state from making any law, related to libel, slander, defamation, sedition or any other matter which offends against decency or morality or undermines the authority or foundation of the state.

These new inclusions received polarized reactions, some opposing the provisos and others in support. Those opposing included K. T. Shah, Damodar Swaroop Seth,[5] Mahboob Ali Baig,[6] Sardar Hukam Singh[7] and Pandit Thakur Das Bhargava,[8] among others. They invoked the Bill of Rights of the US Constitution and argued that the fundamental rights should be absolute and not subject to exceptions. It was feared that the presence of provisos made the liberty insignificant. Damodar Swaroop Seth said: 'Rights guaranteed in article 13 are cancelled by that very section and placed at the mercy of the high handedness of the legislature' (CAD, Vol. VII: 712). There was a general feeling that the presence of provisos in the article seemed as if the right was 'given by the right hand and taken away by the left'. They were concerned about the executives in the future acting like the British in the past and using laws to curb political dissent. Most of the advocates of such unconditional institutional protection for civil rights belonged to political minorities: Muslims, Communists and the Hindu Right. Based on their distrust of government's role, they argued that the decisions about regulation of freedom of speech and expression should be left exclusively for the judiciary, which could decide on a case-by-case basis.

Contrary to this view were those who believed that some form of censorship was important for government to enable it to handle the turbulent times that the country was undergoing. For example, Shri K. Hanumanthaiya[9] said:

> We went through a course of suffering and sacrifice which were imposed upon us by the repressive laws of British imperialism; this naturally made us votaries of unadulterated fundamental rights and that was our hope. But, ultimately when we emerged out of those innumerable difficulties, we are faced, within our own society, with elements who want to take advantage of those rights in order to do violence to men, society and laws.... No man who believes in

> violence and who wants to upset the State and society by violent methods should be allowed to have his way under the colour of these rights. It is for that purpose that the Drafting Committee has thought it fit to limit the operation of these fundamental rights.
>
> (CAD, Vol. VII: 754–755)

Those in favour of restrictions insisted on the need to show faith in the executive's commitment not to misuse power since it was under democratic oversight.[10] Defending the presence of provisos, T. T. Krishnamachari[11] argued that it just reflected the middle path adopted by the government to balance freedom with responsibility (CAD, Vol. VII: 770–773). There were others, like Amiyo Kumar Ghosh, who were not against the idea of including provisos, but believed that the vagueness of the terms used to limit such freedom should be avoided, as it could lead to ambiguity and misinterpretations (CAD, Vol. VII: 769–770).[12] However, there seems to have been no serious response to such arguments.

At the end only K. M. Munshi's[13] amendment to delete the word 'sedition' from article 13(2) was accepted and the re-numbered provision, finally adopted, read as follows:

> 19. (1) all citizens shall have the right- (a) to freedom of speech and expression;
>
> (2) nothing in sub-clause (a) of clause (1) shall affect the operation of any existing law in so far as it relates to, or prevent the state from making any law relating to, libel, slander, defamation, contempt of court or any matter which offends against decency or morality or which undermines the security of, or tends to overthrow, the state.

CAD and the Central Concerns regarding Freedom of Expression

The debates in the Constituent Assembly reflected three broad concerns related to freedom of speech and expression in particular: (1) there was concern about any continuity to the British form of rule and colonial laws, and at least symbolically there was a unanimous negation of it; (2) there was concern about whether the government could always be trusted on questions relating to freedom of speech and expression, and there was agreement on the need for a 'two-tiered' response system, as it was agreed that the judiciary should play an important role as the protector of fundamental rights; and (3) set against the backdrop of Partition, the constitution-makers were also taking into account and reacting to the new set of challenges connected with communal antagonisms.

The Fear of Continuing Aspects of British Rule

The concern that the restrictions on freedom of speech and expression by the government represented a continuing aspect of colonial policies of control was reflected in the way the reference to British rule was invoked to either criticize the government or question its intentionality. For example, Mr. Mohammed Ismail Sahib[14] raised his concern about the scope of the provisos and said:

> It was different when the Britisher, the foreigner was in the country and that now it's our own rule. True, but that does not mean that we can deal with liberty of the citizens as we please.... Therefore, Sir, the citizen must be protected against the vagaries of the executive in a very careful manner as other self-governing countries have done.
>
> (CAD, Vol. VII: 725)

A similar attitude was reflected when other members compared the expectations from the constitution of a new state with the history of denial of such rights by an autocratic government. For example, Somnath Lahiri in the course of debate accused Sardar Patel (then Home Minister and the Chairman of the Advisory committee on fundamental rights) of trying to arm the future legislature and executives with more powers than the British government itself, which according to him, was 'not the basis of democracy' (CAD Vol. III: 2, 384–385). It is ironic, however, that though there was a firm determination to be different from the British in forms of administration and rule in general – or to say so at least in the visible forms of governmental manifestations – the fact that more than one-third of the constitution was taken from the 1935 act and further, article 372 allowed all the then-existing laws to continue (subject to the review power of the judiciary) did not seem to be in consonance. The fear of existing laws affecting the sanctity of these rights was raised at several instances. Mahboob Ali Baig pointed out that the laws like the Press Acts, Criminal Law Amendment Acts and Security Acts were promulgated by British for repressive purposes, and the continuation of such laws was both unwarranted and useless in a democracy (CAD, Vol. VII: 728). A similar fear is reflected in Sardar Bhupinder Singh Mann's[15] claim that 'to apply the existing law in spite of changed conditions really amounts to trifling the freedom of speech and expression' (CAD, Vol. VII: 750). One could also see a fierce opposition launched to include the word 'sedition' within the provisions restricting freedom of speech and expression. The history of bitter experiences faced by the leaders of nationalist movement at the hands of the British, and the scope for its misuse in the future, were cited as primary reasons for such opposition.[16] Eventually the word 'sedition' was dropped.

A special clarification had to be offered by Nehru and Ambedkar, claiming that no such intrusion was intended. It was forcefully argued that article 8 (article 19 in the present constitution) would be a safeguard against any such attempt by future authorities in power. It was further assured that any law which was in force in any part of the land should be held as void if the judiciary found it to be inconsistent with the provisions guaranteed under fundamental rights.

Uncompromising Faith in the Judiciary

It was almost unanimously held that the judiciary should be the sentinel of the rights promised by the constitution. This confidence in the judiciary was encouraged by the concern that the executives in the future could misuse their capacities if these rights were not granted such protections. Sardar Hukam Singh and Pandit Thakur Das Bhargava argued that if the fate was left in the hands of the authorities in power, the fundamental rights would become 'illusory' and hence the Supreme Court should have the 'final say with regard to the destinies of our nationals' (CAD, Vol. VII: 733–745). There was a strong set of voices in the Assembly arguing that 'unconditional' rights be granted by the constitution, and in cases of disputes, the judiciary could judge its validity, as in the US case.

The faith in the judiciary was also shaped by two other factors: first, the positive role that the judiciary had played in preservation of civil liberties against executive excesses in other successful democracies. The US case was an instant reference point. Mahboob Ali Baig cited the Fourteenth Amendment of the US constitution and the British experience to highlight the primacy of the judiciary contrary to the German experience, where power was misused by the legislature and the executive under Hitler's rule (CAD, Vol. VII: 728). Second, the enthusiasm also flowed from the experiences of the workings of the Supreme Court at home, especially in its last phase before Independence. As legal historians like Rohit De have demonstrated, there were instances of severe confrontation between the colonial state and the federal judiciary when the latter struck down a number of emergency wartime legislations. This not only took both the colonial officials and Indian public by surprise, but also encouraged a degree of faith in the judiciary among Indians themselves (De 2012: 59–90).

All these factors invoked a deep reverence for the judiciary as the protector of such rights. However, there was a small section, mostly amongst Congress loyalists, who were not enthusiastic about giving extensive powers to the courts. For example, K. Hanumanthiya doubted the court's capacity to come to grips with rapid changes within the country. He also argued that the function of courts was only to interpret, and the legislature should therefore frame laws that could adjust according to the demands of changing times and not depend on the judiciary for its innovations (CAD, Vol. VII: 754–755). Similarly, G. B. Pant[17] was afraid that the future of the country would be determined 'not by the collective wisdom of the representatives of the people but by the fiats of those elevated to the judiciary'. 'We cannot be subject to varying court judgements, to the whims and vagaries of judges.... If we can't put mischief makers in jail, there is no end to communal disorders', he said (as quoted in Austin 2003: 85). It seems that in order to maintain a balance, although the judiciary was assigned a central role via article 13 and article 32 of the constitution, the space for such judicial intervention was in some ways limited by pronouncing provisos to freedom of speech and expression under article 19(2).

Responding to the Complicated Context

The making of the constitution took two years, eleven months and eighteen days. This period was full of turmoil and disturbances in the country. Though the period was marked by the transition from a subjugated colony to a free nation, it was accompanied by partition and widespread communal violence. Such transformation posed serious challenges to the project of nation-building facing the framers of the constitution. A central question they had to confront concerned the fate of the religious minorities who had chosen to stay back. There was, on the one hand, the fear among minorities of being suppressed by the Hindu majority, something about which the Muslim League had long been warning. On the other hand, there were expectations of some 'reward' in return for their decision to stay back – rewards in the form of institutional protection of their political and cultural rights as promised by the nationalists during the course of the freedom struggle and as they had enjoyed during the last phase of British rule (Jaffrelot 2010: 8). It was also a test for the new Indian leadership, since they were required to refute the historical claim made by the British that the British had special obligations to protect the minorities as they could not find justice if left in the hands of other Indians (Austin 2003: 59). So, Patel made it explicit in the first meeting of the Advisory committee on 27 February 1947 on minority rights that:

> It is for us to prove that it is a bogus claim, a false claim, and that nobody can be more interested than us in India, in the protection of our minorities. Our mission is to satisfy everyone of them ... at least let us prove we can rule ourselves and we have no ambition to rule others.
>
> (As quoted in Rao 1966–1968, Vol. II)

There was mounting pressure on the Assembly to handle in tandem the issues of rights and liberties and the concerns of minority protection and national integration. Though these were not mutually exclusive goals, the real challenge was to derive an acceptable and workable balance among them all. In the process, the Assembly arrived at remedies that had lasting impact on and consequences for the future of Indian democracy. At least three of these deeply affected the discourse on free speech: (1) the location of the value of liberty in relation to equality and fraternity in the democratic discourse; (2) individual versus group in the constitutional vocabulary; and (3) freedom of speech and expression vis-à-vis 'communal hatred'.

The Location of the Value of Liberty in Relation to Equality and Fraternity

In the Indian context, it seems that the values of equality and fraternity were placed at a higher pedestal than that of liberty. The constitution makers of a nation which had experienced police repression, arbitrary governmental action and brutality under the colonial regime showed little respect for civil liberties and individual freedom. The enunciation of fundamental individual rights was conjoined with a set of conditions under which the state could exercise its power and limit such liberties to realize a broader national and political vision. So, a broad understanding was achieved that individual liberties would attain a subsidiary position within the constitution, and more emphasis was rendered on the values of equality and fraternity. Ambedkar's statement in the Assembly on 4 November 1948 is significant in this regard. While distinguishing between non-fundamental rights and fundamental rights, he argued that while the non-fundamental rights are created by agreement between parties: 'Fundamental rights are gifts of the law. Because fundamental rights are the gift of the state it does not follow that the state cannot qualify them' (CAD, Vol. VIII: 40). So, if the need be, the state had every legitimate right to compromise such individual rights and liberties for larger goals. In a context marred by riots and political violence, it was considered imperative that the state should assert its prerogatives and, with extensive powers under its command, should guide the process of nation-building by inculcating a sense of trust and faith among communities which in turn required projecting the values of fraternity and promises of equality where necessary (CAD, Vol. VII: 754–755).

Broadly speaking there were two positions amongst those who supported such limitations of individual liberties: (1) The first was expressed by CAD members who argued that extensive powers in the hands of the state was required in order to control the conflictual situation that had arisen post-Independence. The state was expected to maintain peace and order in society not only by enforcing law and order but also enabling solidarities and trust to emerge among various communities, especially between Hindus and Muslims. This idea was articulated by members like Hanumanthaiya and T. T. Krishnamachari. (2) The other position was held by those CAD members who believed that by its very nature liberty was different from licence, and the role of the state was important also to ensure that clashes of different perceptions of liberty did not occur. No rights therefore could be absolute. This position was held by members like Ambedkar, Patel and others. As the proceedings of the CAD turned out, these voices were dominant in the house and led to the fact that the provisions in the constitution favouring individual rights were made conditional to the authority of the state to manage liberties to ensure equality and fraternity in society.

Individual Rights versus Group Rights in the Constitutional Vocabulary

The prevailing context and the history of national movement also had a deep impact on the way individual rights were perceived in relation to group rights in the constitution. Within the Constituent Assembly, there was a significant section who wanted individuals and not groups to be the bearers of rights. For example, G. B. Pant condemned the practice of invoking the category of 'community', thereby undermining the value of the 'individual', who was the citizen and therefore should be the centre of concern (CAD, Vol. I: 332). This attitude, as Christophe Jaffrelot argues, represented a classical 'Jacobin rejection of communities' (2010: 7). It was also reflected in the ideas of Nehru, Patel and Radhakrishnan, among others. This rejection of communities was based on two central arguments: (1) the project of nation-building required a strong unity of the nation, which could be hampered by due allegiance to intermediary forms of identity such as religion or caste; and (2) the fear that recognition of minority identities would inevitably lead to the isolation and neglect of these communities by the majorities in the future. It was reflected in Nehru's concern that '[in] a full-blooded democracy, if you seek to give safeguards to a minority, and a relatively small minority, you isolate it' (CAD, Vol. III: 330).

There was yet another section among the Constituent Assembly members who invoked individual rights and national unity considerations virtually interchangeably. This position was represented by Rajkumari Amrit Kaur,[18] Hansa Mehta[19] and Minoo Masani.[20] Their opposition to community recognition was based not only on the importance of equal rights for all citizens in nation-building, but also on a fear that if the cultural communities were thus recognized without drastic internal reform among these communities, it would mean the continuation of the subjugatory illiberal practices within each such community, which would be contrary to the interests of large sections within these communities that were vulnerable, like women.[21] So, they preferred the individual-based concept of rights, equal for all. This was reflected in their consistent support for the Uniform Civil Code and opposition to the addition of 'practice' and 'propagate' religion as a fundamental right.

Contrary to all these positions were the views of other members like K. T. Shah, K. M. Munshi and representatives of different minority communities who argued for recognition of the rights of communities based on the significance of religious identity to the self (Mahajan 2008: 300). Eventually, as it happened, this latter position was in part accepted, and space was made for recognition of groups and the claims of community rights. However, with Independence, the context had changed, and partition in the name of religion had convinced the members that though minorities' right to culture should be protected, they should have no claim to benefits in political rights either in the form of reservations or separate electorates (Bajpai 2011; Chandoke 2005). Many of the minority leaders, including several Muslim leaders, welcomed the decision.[22]

In the case of religious and cultural rights, on the one hand the leaders of religious minorities wanted no interference of the state on issues of institutional and cultural practices internal to religion, but at the same time they expected protection and support in the form of social welfare programmes that included education and propagation of cultural values. About the abrogation of political benefits and protection of socio-cultural rights, Gurpreet Mahajan (2008) is of the opinion that in the post-partition phase, minority leaders were more interested in preserving their cultural rights of their communities than in upholding the political rights that they previously enjoyed during the British rule. Rochana Bajpai (2010, 2011) adds to this understanding by demonstrating that unlike political safeguards, the language of cultural rights of minorities found support in key nationalist ideals. Preservation of such rights was seen as a part of the secularism that the new state was expected to follow, whereas political safeguards in the form of either separate electorates or reservations were considered a threat to national unity. It is not surprising therefore that unlike the standard liberal position, groups as well as individuals were recognized in nationalist opinion as the subjects of rights and entitlements (Bajpai 2010: 291). The Constituent Assembly took a balanced position on this issue: on the one hand, the right to religion – to profess, practice and propagate – was conferred to all persons; on the other hand, the freedom was not left unfettered – state intervention was authorized in the interest of protecting 'public order, morality and health' (Bajpai 2010: 293). It is equally true that cultural pluralism, rather than liberal individualism, became the operative principle of democracy, and though the constitution had guaranteed a set of individual political rights like freedom of speech and expression, almost all of these were severely circumscribed. Cultural community, on the one hand, and national interest, on the other, curtailed the free expression of these rights (Mahajan, 2008: 38). This position was indicative of the approach of the government in cases where individual rights came in collision with group rights. For example, when the claim of religious 'offence' is presented as a claim for protection promised under the right to freedom of conscience and free profession, practice and propagation of religion under article 25, and is shown to be threatened by someone's freedom of speech and expression guaranteed under article 19 (1) (a), it presents a complicated situation because though each of these rights is legally treated as an individual right, the practical implications of the former is for a wider public.

Freedom of Speech and Expression and the Issue of 'Communal Hatred'

The context in which the constitution was being drawn also brought in question the relation of freedom of speech and expression to communal harmony. The role of the press and publications as a means for propaganda to incite communal hatred had been significant. Several members were convinced that such incitement to religious and communal hatred should be prevented by the state. So, during the meeting of the Advisory Committee on Fundamental Rights, A. K. Ayyar insisted on the inclusion of the words 'calculated to promote class hatred' as a condition to limit freedom of speech and expression.[23] This idea was supported by K. M. Pannikar, who wanted the addition of 'class or religious hatred' as one of the provisos under article 19(2).[24] On this, Rajagopalachari noted that some of the provisions for such action were already present in existing laws within the IPC, especially under section 153(A); therefore, he argued that the best way to deal with it was by re-drafting the whole clause and saying – 'The right of every citizen to freedom of speech and expression, subject to criminal law'. Rajagopalachari opined that 'the fundamental peace and orderly progress' of the country depended upon 'communal peace and harmony', and if the 'speeches and utterances likely to foster communal hatred' were not prevented, 'we cannot have progress.'[25] What Rajagopalachari was suggesting was extremely dangerous, as it would have meant that the fundamental rights would become subordinate to criminal laws of the land, which incidentally were devised by the British, and were not at all amended as of then. It would have definitely made the limits placed upon such rights more central and seminal than the idea of liberty itself. It was to be expected that such attempts to curtail liberties faced severe criticism from among the members. S. P. Mookherjee thought that such expression could cut both ways. It was possible that simply expressing opinions against the party in power might be construed as class or communal hatred and punished (Rao 1966–1968: 157). Bakshi Tek Chand[26] and H. C. Mookherjee[27] pointed out that their worries about abuse were rooted in their experience under the British rule and feared that such powers in the hands of future executives could be extremely dangerous (Rao 1966–1968: 231–232). K. M. Munshi took the debate forward and argued that 'class or communal hatred' was omitted as it was feared that the state units would make drastic laws under such provisions in order to curtail even the basic forms of free expressions. For him 'breach of peace or public order' should be important for restrictions. He said:

> The right of free expression is now recognized all over the world, and it has been felt that speeches or writings tending towards

> communal or class hatred, if they do not go to the extent of causing violence or crime, may be permitted.
>
> (As quoted in Rao 1966–1968: 231)

As none of the sides was ready to relent, the amendment was put to a vote whereby the amendment proposed by Rajagopalachari was defeated. Even though the amendment failed, it seems that the framers saw some merit in the argument related to communal hatred and in the *Interim Report of the Advisory Committee on Fundamental Rights*, one could find the mention of 'blasphemy' as one of the provisos. However, in the drafting stage, when the provisos reappeared (after it was dropped by Sardar Patel during debates in the Assembly), the word 'blasphemy' was found missing. Interestingly, there is no evidence of any opposition or protest against such move, neither within the drafting committee, nor during the debates of the assembly.[28]

A similar issue appeared when, during the course of debate on the Draft Constitution, Mohd. Tahir[29] argued that invoking 'communal passion' should be made an offence against which the state should have the right to make laws to limit freedom of speech and expression. 'Communal passion', according to him, included 'agitating or exciting the minds of one community against the other'. He pointed to the great 'loss and disservice' that such offences had done to the country and to the neglect of such laws by the British as it served their interest. But after independence, he believed, such stringent laws were important (CAD, Vol. VII: 742). This initiative also found support among others like Syed Karimuddin,[30] who argued that 'whether Muslims are responsible or the Hindus are responsible for communal passions it has eaten away everything that is good in society' (CAD, Vol. VII: 757). Hence, he maintained that inciting communal passion in any form should be made an offence. This concern was reflected in the amendment suggesting the inclusion of 'inciting communal passion' as a proviso to restrict freedom of expression.[31] This amendment was vociferously opposed by members like M. A. Ayyangar,[32] who argued that there were already laws under the IPC to deal with such issues and hence such inclusions were not required. The amendment was put to a vote and was eventually defeated.

The demand for making 'promotion of communal hatred' or incitement of 'communal passion' as a proviso to limit freedom of expression was based on the premise that Indian citizens could easily be misguided by communal elements, and therefore the state needed to step in more prominently to protect them from such propaganda. Though incitement of communal passion or promotion of communal hatred did not form a part of the caveats introduced under article 19(2), it was primarily because the lawmakers showered extensive faith on statutory laws like section 153(A) and 295(A), as credible tools in the hands of the officials to deal with situations where communal hatred was being promoted. It not only hinted at their support to the statutory laws (which had colonial origins), but also gave a sense that they wanted the officials to use it extensively, in order to suppress fissiparous tendencies among some Indians to incite communal hatred.

Looking at the final draft, one can say that the opponents of the provisos failed in their efforts because not only were the provisos entered, the final clause wasvague in its content and intent, which made it open to misuse and misinterpretations by different parties. It was also clear that the lawmakers thought that though freedom of speech and expression was important, its misuse for communal polarization that led to violence was detrimental to social harmony, and hence it was necessary to curb it. A broad consensus was reached that in the interest of national integration, freedom of speech and expression should carry important provisos, which significantly limited its scope in practice. It now remained upon the courts to protect the fundamental rights of citizens from any form of intrusions by either the state or society.

Constitutional Amendments and Other Legal Apparatuses

Within a few months of its introduction, the judiciary and the parliament were at loggerheads over the interpretation of the constitution. Both these institutions seemed to have diverse views regarding some key constitutional aspects. It was felt that political stability and national integrity was in conflict with the democratic rights to freedom of expression and personal liberty. Responding to the situation, Nehru's government introduced the First Amendment Bill in 1951. The situation arose primarily because of decisions of courts in the *Crossroads* case (*Romesh Thapar v. State of Madras, [1950] AIR 37*), the *Shailabala Devi* case (*State of Bihar vs Shailabal Devi [1952] AIR 329*) and the *Brij Bhushan* case (*Brij Bhushan v. State of Delhi [1950] AIR 37*). In each of these cases, the state governments took action under some version of the 'Public Safety Act', and each defendant turned for protection to the first clause of article 19. In the *Crossroads* case, dangers of the 'communist threat' were used by the government to justify press censorship and laws of Preventive Detention against Romesh Thapar, the editor of the communist mouthpiece. The Patna High Court in the *Shailabala Devi* case rejected the contention that the pamphlet incited violence, and the Supreme Court unanimously upheld this judgement. In East Punjab, the Public Safety Act, 1950, was struck down by the Supreme Court on the grounds that pre-censorship restricted the liberty of the press. The laws were all struck down on grounds of 'over-breadth' – the courts claimed that their ambit was much greater than the exceptions provided within article 19(2).

This led to wide-ranging political reactions, some of which were particularly significant. Sardar Patel thought that the *Crossroads* decision knocked 'the bottom out of most of our penal laws for the control and regulation of the press'.[33] Ambedkar, the erstwhile Chairman of the Drafting Committee, and Law Minister at the time of the First Amendment Bill, opined that the Supreme

Court had decided the issue incorrectly.[34] Central to Nehru's arguments regarding amendment to article 19 was his unease with some of the press, which according to him seemed irresponsible: 'some two page news-sheet... full of vulgarity, indecency and falsehood'. New provisos in the form of 'public order' and 'incitement to an offence' were added as Nehru maintained that a constitution should not limit the 'power of the Parliament to face a situation'. The 'concept of individual freedom has to be balanced with social freedom and the relations of the individual with the social groups', Nehru argued.[35]

The opposition to the amendments came from different directions. There were criticisms about the high-handedness of the government thereby undermining the importance of freedom of speech and expression (S. P. Mookherjee, PD, 8838). Questions were also raised about the timing of such introduction (just before general elections) and the technical subject about whether a Constituent Assembly (largely unelected) had such rights to introduce so significant an amendment (Austin 2003: 47).

However, it was H. V. Kamath's[36] suggestion about the need to include 'reasonable' as qualifying any restrictions on speech that attracted the most attention (PD, 8913–8924). Amidst a lot of pressure, both from the opposition and from within the cabinet (especially from the Law Ministry), Nehru agreed to include this proposal, but he was not very happy as he feared that such inclusion could invite each such case to go to the courts and hence more intervention of the courts in executive decisions (Gopal 1991: 189). Finally, the Assembly passed the bill by a vote of 228 to 20. It retroactively and prospectively empowered government to impose 'reasonable restrictions' on freedom of expression 'in the interests of the security of the State (replacing the words 'tends to overthrow the state'), friendly relations with foreign states, public order, decency or morality, or in relation to contempt of court, defamation, or incitement to an offence' (Austin 2003: 49).

Other than broadening the scope for government intervention, there were three important aspects in the debates: (1) The First Amendment received, as expected, comparisons with the First Amendment in the US. It was pointed out that while the First Amendment had extended individual rights, 'our First Amendment did the opposite by curtailing individual freedom' (S. P. Mookherjee, PD: 8912–8913); (2) There was pointed discussion and criticisms about the courts. Nehru charged the courts of practicing conservatism (PD: 8818), and Congress leader N. G. Ranga extended the charge to the judges of the courts (PD: 8681). All the top leaders including Ambedkar, Patel and Rajagopalachari questioned the wisdom of the courts in interpreting the constitution and argued that the amendment was necessary as such interpretations had been made possible because of the error in the founding of the constitution itself; and (3) The addition of 'reasonable' to qualify the restrictions on freedom of expression was a significant move. It provided the judiciary with the test of 'reasonableness' in order to assess whether the action of the executive in cases dealing with freedom of speech and expression were justifiable.

Significant transformation again occurred in 1963, when both external and internal situations forced another amendment of the constitution. The threats emanating from the Chinese invasion in the northeast and concerns over the demands of regional autonomy reflected in Tara Singh's fast for the Sikh state and Dravida Munnetra Kazhagam's (DMK) call for 'Dravidanad' led to the Sixteenth Amendment to the constitution, which added that the government might place restrictions on expression in the interest of 'the sovereignty and integrity of India', the qualifier 'reasonable' remaining in place (Austin 2003: 50). After all these changes, the constitutional provision for freedom of expression as it stands today reads as follows:

> 19(1) The citizens shall have the right-
> (a) to freedom of speech and expression; and the proviso under 19 (2) reads:
>
> Nothing in sub-clause (a) of clause (1) shall affect the operation of any existing law, or prevent the State from making any law, in so far as such law imposes reasonable restrictions on the exercise of the right conferred by the said sub-clause in the interests of the sovereignty and integrity of India, the security of the State, friendly relations with foreign States, public order, decency or morality, or in relation to contempt of court, defamation or incitement to an offence.

Amendment of Statutory Laws and Its Implication for Freedom of Speech and Expression

The challenges facing Indian society in its post-Independence phase forced the government to relook into the existing statutory laws. Incidents of communal violence and the role of print media in it, especially the vernacular press, allowed interventions which ensured that the scope of sections 153(A) and 295(A) of the IPC was significantly altered. The government wanted to curb the misuse of the press to spread communal hatred, but changes initiated were also going to affect pamphlets, tracts and books, as the laws governing all these forms of publications remained the same. A strong will to introduce new changes to these laws was reflected as early as 1956, when the controversy surrounding the publication of the book *Living Biographies of Religious Leaders* and the subsequent role of some sections of Urdu press in Uttar Pradesh led to communal riots in Aligarh and surrounding areas (Brass 2003).

The book *Living Biographies of Religious Leaders* was written by Henry Thomas and Dana Lee Thomas and was originally published in the US. It was already in circulation when Bharatiya Vidya Bhawan, Delhi, decided to reprint it.[37] The protests against the book began in Aligarh with students of Aligarh Muslim University playing a pivotal role in organizing strikes and demonstrations (*The Times of India*, 14 September 1956). It was argued that the book contained a chapter on Prophet Mohammed, and it presented the Prophet in the wrong light. The protests also targeted K. M. Munshi, who was then the Governor of UP and closely associated with Bharatiya Vidya Bhawan as a founding member and one of the editors. Because of the fear that the controversy would scale up, the book was quickly withdrawn, and Munshi also published an unconditional apology along with requests to the protestors to allow the matter to rest (*The Times of India*, 7 October 1956). However, the controversy did not die down.[38] The offending passages from the book were reproduced in Urdu newspapers, and these were distributed to mobilize Muslims against the attitude of the Indian government in general and Munshi in particular. There were significant communal clashes in different parts of Uttar Pradesh (Brass 2003).

The controversy further took an international dimension. The Hindu groups argued that protesting Muslims were getting support from Pakistan as the Muslim organizations in Pakistan had voiced their concerns against the book, and thereby the protestors were also referred as 'anti-national elements'.[39] The crisis was later resolved by the involvement and interventions by Zakir Hussain, the retiring Vice Chancellor of the Aligarh Muslim University; Maulana Azad, Education Minister; and Nehru, the Prime Minister.[40]

This episode highlighted some deep concerns regarding freedom of speech and expression and the question of religious offence. Most leaders criticized the manner in which Muslim demonstrations turned violent, and a counter-movement was launched by Hindus in north India. Another important issue of concern was the role of print media in promoting communalism; objectionable portions of the book were reprinted by the vernacular press, which further escalated the feeling of offence among the Muslims in those areas. Nehru in particular saw it as a major challenge to be strongly dealt with in the future and was eager to come up with a legislation to prohibit such acts. He wrote to the Chief Ministers that if they were 'convinced that a newspaper editor or any other individual has spread communal hatred or incited people to communal violence, we should arrest him and either proceed against him in a court of law or keep him under preventive detention'.[41] In an attempt to devise a zero tolerance attitude for incitement of communal violence, Nehru also encouraged the executive to take direct action against such violators, which could be seen as a dangerous step as there was every possibility that some official could misuse this power for political ends. In another letter addressed to the Chief Ministers Nehru wrote:

> I have personally come to the conclusion that we must have fresh legislation to deal with the spread of communal hatred by newspapers, etc. I would confine this to offensive communal writings, and not extend it at all in the political or other fields.

The urgency expressed by Nehru reflects the impact the protests and the violence that followed had on national politics. Further, this attitude was also reflective of the understanding that amendment to the existing laws was warranted, and if need be, the political class was prepared to intervene in order to counter the threat of communal violence. Stronger and wider laws were seen as an important tool in the hands of the state to maintain public tranquillity. The incidents that occurred also had connotations for publications that were considered to be religiously offensive. It was clear that the book was already available in India much before the publishers decided to reprint it, and the timing of the furor could therefore be questioned. But contrary to this, the government seemed to consider removal of the book from the public sphere as an easy and instant remedy to the hurt sentiments of the protesting Muslims. This approach of the state laid the foundation of a trend in the future where claims of religious offence obtained a sense of legitimacy, and the tendency to take to the streets against publications considered offensive became a legitimate democratic means to pulp such publications.

Though Nehru wanted to strengthen statutory laws in order to counter the tendency of spreading communal tension by means of the vernacular press, government did not initiate any legislation in this regard. Things, however, changed in 1961. Recurrence of communal violence in different parts of the country, and particularly in Assam and Jabalpur, forced the Nehru government to form a special committee under Indira Gandhi to study the causes of such incidents and strategies to counter them. The Committee recommended important changes in statutory laws, including section 153(A) and section 295(A) of the IPC. These recommendations were further approved by the Conference of Chief Ministers, a forum that took the shape of the National Integration Council in 1962. Based on the suggestions from both these groups, the government introduced a bill in the Parliament which later became Act XLI of 1961.

The bill was introduced in the Lok Sabha on 11 August 1961 by Home Minister Lal Bahadur Shastri as the Indian Penal Code Amendment Bill, 1961, and a detailed discussion took place in the house on 30 August after the bill returned from the Select Committee stage. Debates in both the houses of Parliament reflected similar concerns about the scope of the amendment, the fear of misuse of extended power by the executive and the attack on freedom of speech and expression. While initiating the debate, Minister of State at the Ministry of Home Affairs, Mr. Dattar, stressed that the amendment was being introduced as a constructive step in order to assure 'the integration of the nation in the fullest sense of the term' (Dattar, LSD: 5884) by preventing 'fissiparous tendencies within different religious and other groups that impact the peace in which all religions stay together' (Dattar, RSD: 2030).

The amendment proposed some significant changes in the statutory laws, especially section 153(A) of the IPC. Firstly, it made the grounds of conviction explicit in sections 153(A) by allowing punishment for the acts that 'promote or attempt to promote feelings of enmity or hatred' on grounds of 'religion, race, place of birth, residence, language'. Further, it proposed to increase the quantum of punishment under section 153(A) and section 295(A) of the IPC from two to three years. It also proposed to insert an additional clause (c) to section 153(A), which made punishable any act that was 'prejudicial to the maintenance of harmony between different religion, racial or language groups or castes or communities and which disturbs or is likely to disturb the public tranquillity' (LSD: 5884). But the most fundamental change was the removal of the explanation that was associated with section 153(A) since its inception as a colonial law in 1898. The explanation said:

> It does not amount to an offence within the meaning of this section to point out *without malicious intentions* and with an honest view to their removal, matters which are producing or have a tendency to produce, feelings of enmity or hatred between different classes of citizens.

This explanation put the onus of proving malicious intentions on the prosecutor. However, its removal meant that the responsibility to prove innocence would completely fall on the person charged with the crime.[42]

Debates over the bill in both houses of Parliament centred around a set of issues which were very similar to the ones raised during the colonial period, when these laws were inserted to the penal codes. Opposition to the respective bills were also based on similar grounds. The opposition charge was led by Jan Sangh, leader and future Prime Minister of India Atal Bihari Vajpayee in Lok Sabha, and Communist leader Bhupesh Gupta in Rajya Sabha, who demanded that the bill should be sent for wider consultation, and public opinion should be sought before inserting amendments. Vajpayee claimed that the exercise would not only be representative of the true democratic process but also 'help in educate and train people to national integration' (LSD: 5900). But the demand to send the bill for wider consultation was defeated in the house by an overwhelming majority of 116 votes against 22 as it was seen as a delaying tactic on the part of the opposition.

One of the foremost arguments against the bill was that already-existing laws were potent enough, and there was no need for fresh amendments. A. Krishnaswamy, an independent MP from Tamil Nadu, and M. S. Aney, independent MP from Nagpur, argued in Lok Sabha that the step showed the failure of government to use the available laws properly. Krishnaswamy also pointed out that a new law would be counter-effective as it would only ensure that the oppositional and disintegrative forces go underground, and thereby it did not provide a good solution to the problem of communalism (LSD: 5924). There were other opposition leaders who strictly rejected the need for any legislation of that sort. H. Hynniewta, an independent MP in

Lok Sabha representing hill regions of Assam, along with others like Socialist leader Ramsevak Yadav considered the bill a threat to freedom of speech and expression as it widened the space for state interventions (LSD: 5998). Similar views were put forward by Communist leader Bhupesh Gupta and Republican Party of India MP B. D. Khobragade in the Rajya Sabha (LSD: 6217). There was also opposition to the removal of the explanation from section 153(A), as it was believed that the change would make the law amenable to misuse and make it difficult to prove innocence in cases where the charges were falsely implicated. Congress leaders like Mahavir Tyagi (LSD: 5937–5940) and Thakur Das Bhargava (LSD: 5945) were vehemently opposed to this move. They argued that the removal of 'malicious intentions' from the necessary requirement to convict individuals under the law as contained in the explanation to section 153(A) would be a direct attack on freedom of expression. Hridaynath Kunzru remarked in the Rajya Sabha: 'We are now trying in the name of national integration to adopt a more stringent measure than Government considered it necessary to adopt during the war' (RSD: 3166). A similar attitude was reflected by All India Mahasabha Vice President V. G. Deshpande, who in a press conference on 12 August 1961 charged that the 'section has become too wide in scope and will make innocent activities for social reform also a criminal offence' (*The Times of India*, 13 August 1961).

The Congress Party was well armed to counter these opinions and justify its decision to introduce the amendments. The foremost justification extended in support of amendments was that they were required to protect the secular character of Indian polity. Congress members like Raghubir Sahai (LSD: 5968) and Sriram Sahay (RSD: 3168) argued that it was necessitated by the activities of communal parties which tried to polarize votes by invoking religious contentions. Santosh Kumar Basu, Congress MP from West Bengal (RSD: 3194), along with other members like Kasliwal (LSD: 5922) and Akbar Ali Khan (RSD: 3174), argued that government needed such laws in order arm itself to curb the intentions of communal parties of all hues. Khan even recommended that the guilty should not just be jailed but be hanged (RSD: 3174). Reply to the opposition was led by the Minister of Home Affairs Lal Bhadur Shastri, who defended his government's position aggressively. He not only rejected the need for circulation but also argued that unlike the opposition's claims, section 153(A) was being made more pointed and grounded according to the needs of the time (LSD: 6218). On the subject of removal of explanations, he argued that the onus to prove that the intention of the accused was neither mala fide nor malicious should be the responsibility of the accused and not the prosecutor, else it was very difficult for the executive to act even in most disastrous situations. The explanations, he remarked, gave an undue advantage to the accused (LSD: 6220). The overwhelming presence of congressmembers in both houses of Parliament ensured that the bill was passed without any difficulty.

As is visible, overall debate in both houses of the Parliament concentrated on issues of communal violence and the role of the press. The question of freedom of expression remained important but was overshadowed by harms that an excess of it had caused to society. The need of the hour, it was widely acknowledged, was to curb such liberty to promote values of 'national integration' and 'toleration' (Dattar, LSD: 5884). Though the question of religious offence did not figure at all in the debates, there were clear signs that the legislation was going to have serious ramifications on the subject. So, any form of publication which could incite religious passions could face punitive action. Further the amendment to section 153(A) also meant that the scope of preventive laws under section 99 of CrPC was also widened, and hence any such publication could also be proscribed without any consideration about the intentions of the author. Furthermore, the way in which government introduced the amendments in response to communal violence in different areas meant that strengthening the laws was seen as an important and easily available remedy to counter such attempts. It was overlooked, however, that these changes would have long-term repercussions on the freedom of speech and expression, and its impact would not be limited to the communal press but could also affect other mediums of expression. The congressmembers like S. S. N. Tankha (RSD: 3174–3179) insisted that Parliament should have faith in the elected government that the laws would not be misused, but in practice it was no guarantee to the way in which the executive would translate and use such powers in its dealing with contentious subjects like publications that were claimed to be religiously offensive. At the least, an increase in the scope of sections 153(A) and 295(A) meant a direct attack on the scope of freedom of speech and expression, a relation that most lawmakers overlooked, considering it a necessary step to curb tendencies of communal disturbances.

Similarly, in 1968, after a series of communal riots, most significantly in Srinagar, Ranchi and Aurangabad, the National Integration Council recommended further amendments to these laws and recommendations the government readily accepted.[43] Following this, the government introduced the Criminal and Election Laws Amendment Act, 1969, in the Parliament, which became Act XXXV of 1969. While introducing the bill in the Rajya Sabha, Vidya Charan Shukla, Minister of Home Affairs, pronounced that the aim of the legislation was to counter 'growing trends of communalism, factionalism and regionalism' in the country (RSD: 5482). He specified the role of the communal press in disturbing the peace and harmony of the country and inciting religious hatred among common people who are easily swayed by such propaganda material (RSD: 5483). He specifically accused the RSS mouthpiece, *Organizer*, and journals like *Mother India*, of misguiding citizens on communal lines. The most significant amendments that the bill proposed to undertake in relation to freedom of speech and expression included: (1) The scope for intervention of the executive under section 153(A) was enlarged. So, unlike earlier, when promoting feelings of enmity or hatred were punishable, promotion of 'disharmony' and 'ill-will' was also added as eligible for conviction. However, the terms like 'disharmony' and 'ill-will' remained undefined, and also there was no discussion about what parameters would be used to judge a particular publication's capacity to promote 'disharmony' or 'ill-will' among different communities. (2) Along with the change in the scope of 153(A), section 196 of CrPC was also amended whereby the offence under section 153(A) was made cognizable and unlike earlier, the District Magistrate could act *suo motu* in such cases without permission of the state government or any court. As Shukla claimed on the floor of the house, the District Magistrate could now directly take cognizance of such inflammable matters to 'not only stop that sort of writing, but also seize the printing press' (RSD: 5484). It is explicit that both these measures were detrimental to the scope of freedom of speech and expression as they increased the space for subjectivity in executive action. These amendments only made the laws more prone to subjective intervention and hence available for misuse by the executive.

As in the case of the amendments in 1961, debates in both houses of the Parliament revolved around the issue of communal violence. The opposition concentrated on highlighting the failures of the Congress government to stop communal riots. It was claimed that statutory laws, if used properly, had enough scope to deal with the situation, and there was no need to increase them further. It was maintained that the continuing spree of communal violence was representative of the inability of government and not the inefficacy of laws.[44] The Jan Sangh leaders like Niranjan Verma accused government of practicing pseudo-secularism and argued that it had failed to inculcate the values of 'toleration' and 'national integration' among citizens (RSD: 5505–5507). The Communist and Socialist members doubted the intentions of government in widening the powers of local authorities.[45] On the contrary, congressmembers and other supporters of the bill defended the step of government by citing the NIC recommendations.[46] They criticized the politics of political parties like Jana Sangh and the Muslim League in religious polarization and pointed to the role of the press in corrupting the minds of vulnerable masses that fall prey to their political propaganda.[47]

The subject of freedom of speech and expression remained largely absent in these debates. Among all participants in the debates in both houses of Parliament, the only member who raised the issue of freedom of speech and expression extensively was Pranab Kumar Mukherjee, a Congress Party member and first time MP of Rajya Sabha representing West Bengal. Though Mukherjee supported the bill, he raised serious issues about the attitude of politicians regarding freedom of expression. He remarked:

> Whatever be our feelings about any particular journal, whatever be our feelings about any particular press, whatever be our sentiments about the opinions expressed in a publication, we cannot advocate on the floor of the house that the freedom of the press be curtailed. (RSD: 5548)

He was critical about any attempt by government to curtail the freedom of press, and though he belonged to the ruling party, he raised doubts about the future of freedom of expression if the power of the executive was increased. He said:

> If we want to curtail the freedom of the press only from the view of stopping communalism, it will not stop there. If we give this power to the government of India, give this into the hands of the bureaucrats, they will control them and will say what should appear. It will not stop there, will go further. So, I think there should not be that power which can control the press.
>
> (RSD: 5548)

He raised objections with clause 6 of the bill, which maintained that freedom of expression could be restricted for maintaining communal harmony. According to him, eight exceptions were mentioned in article 19(2) of the constitution, and maintenance of communal harmony did not figure there, and therefore he was not sure if the bill itself was in accordance with the spirit of the constitution (RSD: 5549). Mukherjee asked pointed and pertinent questions regarding the constitutionality of the bill as well as on the subject of freedom of expression. Unfortunately, when the concerned Minister Vidya Charan Shukla delivered his final comments on the bill, he continued his attack on leaders belonging to the Jana Sangh as well as the Communist and Socialist parties but evaded throughout his speech any discussion about the probable impact of the bill on the scope of freedom of speech and expression. Mukherjee's name or concerns raised by him did not even appear in the speech of Shukla. The context of communal violence trumped any concern for freedom of speech and expression, and as in 1961, the amendments to statutory laws in 1968 were dominated by the aim of the government to control the communal press from inciting and spreading communal hatred. It resulted in further strengthening the hands of the executive by widening the scope of statutory laws.

Attitude of the Lawmakers towards Freedom of Speech and Expression in Independent India

Two aspects dominated the attitude of lawmakers in the debates of Parliament, during the amendments of constitution and the statutory laws. The first was the sense of urgency, and the second was the sense of paternalism reflected by the lawmakers. The urgency of the context – communal violence and the role of the press in it – guided these debates. In order to respond to the threats of communal violence, the lawmakers concentrated on enlarging the space for executive action. Though a constitutional right, freedom of speech and expression was considered a threat for maintenance of communal and social harmony. The sense of urgency is reflected throughout the debates, where leaders consistently argued for the need of making laws more stringent in order to strengthen the process of 'national integration' by curtailing 'fissiparous tendencies' and enforcing 'toleration' and 'communal harmony' among the citizens through fear of punishment for deviants. In order to curb the capacity of the communal press in the context of a disturbed communal context, it was overlooked that an amendment to the law would not only affect newsprint but would be detrimental to all forms of expression, and the increased scope for applicability of such laws ensured that the right to freedom of speech and expression would remain conditional on what the executive thought was permissible within the law.

The debates also reflected another important aspect in the attitude of the lawmakers, that is, the sense of paternalism. Repeated concern was raised about the vulnerability of Indian citizens and how they were being easily misguided by the communal press. For example, during the debates over the First Amendment, it was argued that most Indians were 'ignorant and illiterate' and, therefore, 'easy to mislead' (Bhargava, PD: 9717). When the opposition criticized the government by citing examples from other democracies, it was held that other countries had a long tradition in freedom, and that had 'instilled discipline and restraint' in them. It was also argued that Indians 'respond to incitement easily', unlike citizens of other countries, and therefore the comparison was faulty (Rev. D'Souza, PD: 9692). Similarly, while introducing the amendment to the statutory laws, B. N. Dattar, the then–Minister of Home Affairs, claimed that the bill was aimed to contain 'fissiparous tendencies' and was required because 'each man often times here and there thinks more of his religion … than common binding links of the Indian society' (RSD: 3019–3020). It was therefore considered the duty of the government to protect citizens from the impact of a communal press that was misguiding them. The above discussions reflect that in the context of urgency, the attitude of the lawmakers was paternalistic and reactionary, and a debate about the ramifications of the proposed changes to the law on the fundamental right to freedom of speech and expression was avoided.

Conclusion

In the Indian case, the right to freedom of speech and expression was considered a natural ally to independence, and therefore its inclusion in the constitution as a fundamental right was neither doubted nor debated. In the process, an opportunity was lost to seriously reflect about its importance and the role it could play in making Indian democracy more vibrant. Rather, the need for national unity and public order motivated the constitution makers to severely limit its scope. Uday Singh Mehta has very well presented the situation as an irony 'that the successful culmination to free oneself from imperial subjection led almost immediately to freedom itself becoming a subsidiary concern; that is subsidiary to national unity, social uplift, and a concern with recognition' (2011: 17). But for the constitution makers, it was not an irony, but rather an 'ideal' produced under compulsion of the complex context in which they were operating.

The Constituent Assembly faced the classic dilemma of how to preserve individual freedom while promoting the public good (Austin 1997: 50). It attempted to create a happy marriage between different ideal values, overlooking the possibilities of clashes among them. The debates that followed reflected three important strands: (1) The idea of liberty, though important, was seen as subsidiary to the promises of social equality and the need for fraternity. So although important freedoms were included as fundamental rights, they were accompanied with caveats that made space for state intervention; (2) There was an attempt to balance individual rights with community/group rights, but as was visible, in relation to freedom of speech and expression, it further increased the ambiguity of state intervention, as it did not say anything about the situation when both these aspects could clash; and (3) Though the assembly did not approve the inclusion of 'communal hatred' as a proviso for state intervention, it was not because they did not recognize it as a threat, but because they believed that other laws especially under the IPC were enough to deal with such issues. These strands made space for state intervention from three directions: firstly, through the constitutional provisions whereby laws could be made to limit freedom of speech and expression; secondly, through the ambivalence created by not considering the situation where individual and group rights might clash in the form of potential contradictions that were yet undeveloped; and thirdly, the recognition of criminal laws as a deterrent to excesses of free speech, which incidentally, were to be imported as formulated during British rule.

Soon after its formulation, the constitution faced newer contradictions, resulting in its amendment. However, again, rather than engaging in a debate about the prospects of free speech, it was posed as a threat to state capacity and hence resulted in increased powers to the state against such freedom. It can be said that different contexts call for different ways of treating the issues of rights and liberties, and it often depended on the socio-cultural and political contexts. Some scholars have pointed at the 'paradox of constitutional democracy', which assumes a strange merger of 'constitution' and 'democracy', which often stand for contradictory values and ideals (Habermas 1996; Michelman 1998). Habermas has argued that such paradox can only be settled if we try to understand the principle of 'co-originality' – that private and public autonomy require each other. The argument is not therefore that there should or should not be limitations; rather, it is about the kind of limitations forwarded and whether they improve the space for liberty or restrict it (Habermas 2001: 767). The laws in such cases should consider freedom at its core, which apparently did not happen during the CAD. The terms used to delimit the scope of freedom of speech and expression – libel, slander, defamation, contempt of court, decency, morality – are vague and uncertain; there is every possibility for multiple interpretations. This not only invited state intervention but increased the possibilities of its misuse. Adding to these were the already existing and newly developed legal instruments, be it either in the form of the IPC, CrPC or the state-based laws which did not only severely limit but also introduced similar ambiguities about the scope of free speech as experienced during colonial times.

The attitude of lawmakers and executives towards freedom of expression is equally a matter of concern. The way in which this freedom was juxtaposed to the maintenance of social harmony reduced its scope – both legal as well as substantive. As the debates in both houses of Parliament during the amendment to penal codes in 1961 and 1969 show, lawmakers were not interested in discussing the issues of freedom of expression, and even in cases where the concerns were raised; it attracted little attention due to the context in which the legislations were introduced. A series of communal violent incidents and the role of the press in escalating polarization convinced the legislators that freedom of speech and expression needed to be curbed. However, the repercussions of amendments were largely overlooked. It affected not only the communal press, but also other forms of expressions like books and others. Also, an increase in powers of the executive to act upon such laws meant that the space for freedom of speech and expression was further left conditional to the prerogative of the administrators. Two conclusions can be drawn from such exercise: (1) Freedom of speech and expression as a fundamental right did not enjoy any significant status in India. It was allowed with several caveats that defined its scope; (2) The political class was insistent in allowing greater space for government intervention in the free exercise of freedom of speech and expression. It was believed that on the one hand, it was the responsibility of the government to maintain communal harmony and social cohesion, and therefore there was the need to balance freedom of expression with such challenges; on the other hand, it was considered the duty of government to adopt a paternalistic role to inculcate values of national integration and toleration among its citizens, and therefore there was the need to allow excessive powers under its command on contentious subjects like freedom of speech and expression.

Notes

1 K. T. Shah was an alumnus of London School of Economics and a left-oriented member representative from Bombay.
2 Ayyar was a well-known lawyer from the Madras constituency and represented the liberal school within the Congress Party.
3 Lahiri was a Communist leader from West Bengal.
4 He was a civil servant and appointed as the Chief Advisor to the Constituent Assembly. He played a key role in this capacity in formulating the Indian Constitution.
5 Seth was a Socialist leader representing United Provinces.

6 Baig was a prominent Muslim representative from Madras.
7 Sardar Hukam Singh was one of the two members included as a Sikh representative. He belonged to Shiromani Akali Dal and was Secretary of the National Democratic Front formed by S. P. Mookherjee. Later he joined the Congress Party and became the Speaker of the Lok Sabha in 1962.
8 Bhargava was a representative from East Punjab. Though a congressmember, he was known for his strong critical views against the government and was largely oriented to right-wing politics.
9 Hanumanthaiya was a prominent congressmember from Karnataka, considered to be very close to Nehru.
10 Such faith was reflected in the speeches of Congress Party members like Algu Rai Shastri, among others. See CAD VII: 767.
11 Krishnamachari was a prominent congressmember from Madras and an efficient economist.
12 Ghosh was a representative from Bihar. He argued: 'one expects that so far as the rights of the people are concerned, they should be expressed in clear, simple and straight language, so that a common man when he reads the Constitution can understand exactly and precisely what are his rights and what are the checks to his rights. I do not propose to say that at times of emergencies or grave needs freedom does not require to be checked to a certain extent. I believe in checks and balances, but at the same time, I must say that those checks should be very precise, and clear and should not be couched in ambiguous language and left to courts for decisions'
13 Munshi was one of the most vocal members in the Constituent Assembly. Though a congressmember, his ideas were largely influenced by right-wing ideology.
14 Ismail Sahib was a prominent member of the Muslim League and represented the Madras Presidency.
15 Along with Sardar Hukam Singh, Mann was the other Sikh representative inducted in the Assembly.
16 Volume VII of CAD is full of such instances where leaders of different parties highlighted this issue, especially in the discussions of 1 December 1948.
17 Pant was one of the topmost leaders of the Congress Party and the first Chief Minister of Uttar Pradesh, who later became the Home Minister in Nehru's cabinet.
18 One of the most prominent women leaders in Indian National Congress, Kaur became the Union Health Minister in Nehru's first cabinet.
19 Mehta was a reformist and social activist. She was known for her strong views on the Uniform Civil Code and all forms of reservations except for Scheduled Castes.
20 Trained as a barrister at London, Masani was one of the founding members of Congress Socialist Party in 1934.
21 See Rao (1966–1968, Vol. II: 140, 165, 173, 208). Also see the note of Rajkumari Amrit Kaur, Hansa Mehta and Minoo Masani to the fundamental rights sub-committee dated 14 April 1947 in Rao (1966–1968, Vol II: 162).
22 For example, Naziruddin Ahmad considered the demand for reservations as a result of a post-partition 'fear complex', which was now fast disappearing, and the situation was improving (CAD, Vol. III: 296). Also see Tajamul Husain, CAD, Vol. III: 270; Z. H. Lari, CAD, Vol. III: 283.
23 See Ayyar's Comments on the Draft report on 10, 14 and 15 April 1947 in Rao (1966–1968, Vol. II: 157).
24 Pannikar was a well-known journalist and historian who represented Punjab. For his comments on the subject see Rao (1966–1968, Vol. II: 157). Also see *Proceedings of the Meetings of the Advisory Committee on 21–22 April 1947* in the same volume at page 231.

25 For Rajagopalachari's comments see *Proceedings of The Meetings of the Advisory Committee on 21–22 April 1947* in Rao (1966–1968, Vol. II: 232).
26 Chand was a retired judge of the High Court who represented East Punjab in the Assembly.
27 H. C. Mookherjee was the Vice President of the Constituent Assembly. He was an educationalist and a prominent Christian leader of the Congress Party from West Bengal.
28 It is significant that the Minutes of the Drafting Committee recorded only the conclusions of each meeting but did not record the discussions. However, there is no trace of any such protest even during the discussions on the draft constitution in the Assembly, which makes the case more curious.
29 Tahir was a Muslim representative from Bihar.
30 Karimuddin was a famous criminal lawyer and a congressmember from Central Province.
31 Amendment No. 477 placed on the floor of the house on 2 December 1948. For details see CAD VII.
32 Ayyangar was a lawyer representing the Madras Presidency and became the first Deputy Speaker and later the Speaker of the Lok Sabha.
33 See Patel-Nehru letter dated 3 July 1950 in Patel (1972, Vol X: 358).
34 See *Parliamentary Debates*, Vol. XII (henceforth to be called PD and all references in this chapter belong to same volume, so only the column number will be mentioned), part 2, 17 May 1951, 90067.
35 See *Statements of Objects and Reasons*, appended to the Constitution (First Amendment) Act, 1951.
36 Kamath was a Socialist leader representing All India Forward Bloc.
37 Bharatiya Vidya Bhawan is a central government–funded organization founded in 1938 by K. M. Munshi, a popular Congress leader. See 'Stray Musings', *The Times of India*, 30 September 1956.
38 Nehru wrote to the Chief Ministers: 'There were reports being spread that in Aligarh Gita was desecrated which was wrong and led to mob violence', as quoted in Gupta (2006: 273).
39 'Military Preparedness by India Suggested: Mr. Chatterjee's Address at Mahasabha Conference', *The Times of India*, 12 November 1956; 'Clenched Fist Shown at India: Karachi Protest against Book', *The Times of India*, 22 September 1956.
40 'Protest Must Stop: Bhavan's Book', *The Times of India*, 3 October 1956; 'Agitation is Condemned', *The Times of India*, 7 October 1956.
41 See letter dated 29 September 1956 in Nehru (1990, Vol. 4). Also see, 'Special Letter in Addition to Fortnightly Letter' on page 447 of the same volume.
42 This position was justified by Home Minister Lal Bahadur Shastri in his closing speech on the subject. He said: "Our intention in omitting the explanation is with a view to cast responsibility on the offender to prove that his intentions were not malafide or malicious" (LSD: 6220).
43 See 'Delhi Approves Legislation to End Communalism; Measures Suggested by Home Ministry', *The Times of India*, 3 July 1968; 'Communal Riots: Preventive Steps Favoured', *The Times of India*, 23 June 1968. The recommendations were based on a report prepared by the Sub-committee headed by Andhra Pradesh CM K. B. Reddy.
44 This position was reiterated by several opposition leaders like B. N. Mandal (RSD: 5484); S. K. Vaishampayan (RSD: 5490); Niren Ghosh (RSD: 5511); Z. A. Ahmad (RSD: 5484).

45 See Niren Ghosh (RSD: 5511); Z. A. Ahmad (RSD: 5484); Rajnarain (RSD: 5777–5783).

46 See for example Congressmember Abid Ali representing Maharastra in Rajya Sabha (RSD: 5516–5519); Forward Bloc member Sheel Bhadra Yajee (RSD: 5506–5511).

47 Yajee (RSD: 5506–5511); Shukla (RSD: 5483–5484).

3

PREVENTING RELIGIOUS OFFENCE

Law, Courts and Freedom of Expression

Many commentators on Indian politics opine that 'unlike most western democracies, liberty was neither a political nor a primary social norm' for the post-Independence Indian State (Bhowmik 2009; Mahajan 1998; Mehta 2011). One of the primary challenges before the newly formed state was to balance competing claims of liberty and social tranquillity, and as a response, it endorsed the restrictions on individual freedoms. In fact, the concern for public order 'tilted the balance in favour of policing rather than civil liberties', whereby the state used its executive powers extensively to curtail fundamental rights like freedom of speech and expression in the pretext of public interest (Mahajan 1998; Sorabjee 1976). Government's decision to curb freedom of speech is guided both by the real and imaginary fears of a threat to public order, as well as the pressure exerted by socio-religious groups so that 'social censorship' comes to be linked with 'state censorship' (Dhavan 2008; Eswaran 1992). This made the role of the courts as defender of citizens' fundamental rights especially significant in the post-Independence period. As the final arbitrator of law, the courts in India have the power to define the scope of freedom of speech and expression, and under the reviewing authority assigned by the constitution, the courts can also check the arbitrary actions of the government.[1] If that is the case, how do the courts respond to the competing claims of freedom of expression and religious offence in order to judge whether the government's action is justified under the provisions of 'reasonable restriction'?

Legal practitioners and scholars like Soli J. Sorabjee (1994) and Rajeev Dhavan (2008) have argued that though some High Courts are more prone to allow restrictions of freedom of speech on the pretext of 'offence' and threat to public order, the Supreme Court generally maintains wide protection in its favour. Ratna Kapur (1996), based on her study of case laws, has held that there is no evidence of 'either an overuse of the provisions or a judicial abuse of the power of censorship' on the part of the courts. In fact, she argues, the courts have done an excellent job of protecting minority groups from hatred of the Hindu Right, which according to her was an important objective of India's hate speech laws. Contrary to this opinion, however, Pratap Bhanu Mehta (2008) has claimed that laws on the subject

DOI: 10.4324/9781003369257-4

are so ambiguous that the courts often seem to be upholding any form of censorship by the government, particularly in relation to religiously contentious speech acts, either due to the presumed threat to public order or based on its effect on the religious sensibilities of the followers within the community in question.

This chapter aims to engage with these interpretations based on my study of court cases involving religiously offensive publications. The aim is also to highlight the contemporary debates on the issue and put India's statutory laws in perspective. For analysis, cases both from the Supreme Court as well as different High Courts in India have been used.[2] One of the general limitations with legal studies pertaining to freedom of expression in India has been exclusive dependence on Supreme Court judgements to draw conclusions, overlooking the debates in the High Courts, including their observations. High Court cases are significant because most controversies about contentious publications fall under the category of law-and-order subjects that are primarily dealt with by the High Courts. Few of these cases travel to the level of Supreme Court – only if the constitutionality of any statutory laws is challenged or if review petitions against the decision of High Courts are filed. More importantly, a review of Supreme Court cases reveals that many of these High Court judgements and observations of the judges also play a guiding role in Supreme Court decisions and are referred recurrently in the debates of the courtroom. The analysis of case laws presented in this and the next chapter is derived from study of thirty-two court cases related to contentious books claimed to be religiously offensive during the period 1947–2010. For this a search was conducted on Manupatra Database[3] for the terms '19(1)(a)'; '19 (2)'; '295(A)'; '153(A)'; and 'CrPC 95'. The reason was that these are the sections of the constitutional and statutory laws which deal with the subjects of freedom of speech and expression vis-à-vis the claims of religious offence, including issues like proscription and banning of publications. Following this, I tried to locate the original cases in various official records, like AIR (All India Reporter) and journals published by the Supreme Court and other agencies like the Indian Law Institute, at Delhi, like CriJL (*Criminal Law Journal*), SCC (*Supreme Court Case*), and SCR (*Supreme Court Reporter*). The lists of cases referred here include all cases from the Supreme Court and High Courts on the subject, which were recorded in these documents.

Religious Offence and Restrictions to Freedom of Speech and Expression

According to the Oxford English Dictionary, 'offence' means annoyance or resentment brought about by a perceived insult or disregard for oneself. The expression contains two aspects – an action and an effect. In this work, 'offence' is used to refer to the hurt or wounded feelings produced, either voluntarily or involuntarily, by speech acts, most notably books and other publications. In this context, the idea of 'offence' also implies a relationship between two parties, that is, one who offends (who gives offence) and the offended (who takes offence). The one that gives offence can be either an individual or an object (in the present case books and other publications). At the same time, the offended can be an individual as well as a group (when the offence is experienced by many individuals from the same social group or community).[4] Religious offence, therefore, refers to the hurt generated to the religious sensibilities of individuals or groups, through the invocation of contentious religious subjects like defamation of religion or promoting hatred on the basis of religion. Considering that the injury is caused by speech acts, the subject under examination here is: when should law interfere, if at all, to regulate such speech acts in cases where religious offence is claimed?

There are several advocates of absolute and universal freedom of expression. Asserting this position in relation to religious offence, legal philosopher Ronald Dworkin (2006) opines that everyone has 'the right to ridicule' and no one has the 'right not to be insulted or offended'. He is against the idea that freedom of speech should have limits or that it ought to be balanced against any other good that society aspires to achieve, like the virtues of multiculturalism. Dworkin's views are based on the basic principle of human dignity, whereby he argued that expressing attitudes, opinions, fears and even libel confirmed the speaker's standing as a responsible agent in collective action (2009: vii–viii). But Dworkin's position emphasized the dignity of the 'speaker' and did not take into consideration the dignity of his or her putative target, that is, against whom the speech act was aimed.

Jeremy Waldron (2010), for example, raises this issue and further maintains that 'freedom from censorship of someone who uses hate speech does not outweigh the freedom from defamation of his or her target'. Developing this approach, Waldron provides a liberal defence to hate speech laws. But Waldron's use of 'dignity' is very specific. He defines dignity as the confirmation of *equal membership* in a society – 'basic social standing ... as a proper object of society's protection and concern' (2012: 15). Waldron suggests that the concern for dignity should be distinguished from concern to avoid offence. He argues that the feeling of offence is highly subjective, and it is the 'public nature of hate speech – in time, manner and place – that takes it outside the realm of offense of feelings (2012: 106). The aim of hate speech laws, he contends, should not be to prevent people from being offended. As is visible, neither Dworkin nor Waldron support legal action against religiously offensive speech acts. Dworkin completely rejects any basis whatsoever to restrict freedom of speech, and Waldron's idea of 'hate speech', though it allows some forms of restrictions, does not allow religious insults and offence as a valid and justifiable ground to restrict speech acts.

Perhaps one of the most significant and enduring contributors to the debate over validity of religious offence as a reason for restrictions was John Stuart Mill. Mill in his classic *On Liberty* devised what is popularly known as the 'harm principle'. The central tenet of Mill's idea is that 'the only purpose power can be rightfully exercised over any member of any civilized community, against his will, is to prevent harm to others' (Mill 1978). In case of speech acts, Mill would not support any action solely on the basis of the content of an opinion because he defended 'fullest liberty of professing and discussing, as a matter of ethical conviction, any doctrine, however immoral it may be considered' (1978: 106). For him, the circumstances in which the opinion is expressed could only make a speech act punishable. The corn dealer example that Mill used to explain his argument is also indicative of the difference he would place between 'advocacy' and 'instigation'. 'Instigation' was different from 'advocacy' in that in the case of 'instigation', there is a direct urging to action and the action follows immediately. For example, Mill argued that it was acceptable if someone advocated through print that the corn dealer starved the poor. But when the same view is expressed in front of an angry mob standing outside a corn dealer's home, it can lead to violence and hence harm to the dealer. In this case there appears to be a direct link between the idea advocated and the action of the mob, and hence the speech act was punishable. So, according to Mill, a speech act was only punishable if it was in the form of instigation and resulted in an 'overt act' and 'at least a probable connection can be established between the act and instigation' (1978: 107). Drawing a parallel, it could be deduced that for Mill, even a religiously offensive speech act could be punished only if it was in the form of 'instigation', which means defamation of religion would not constitute a valid crime and could only be punished if, for example, it promotes hatred among the audience and instigates them to harm others as a result. Religiously offensive publications in the form of books or printed articles would similarly escape punishment, according to Mill's standards.

Some critiques feel that Mill's consequentialist argument set the bar too high, and if this principle was taken seriously, it will be difficult to constrain any form of speech. Joel Feinberg (1973, 1985), for example, argued that there were human experiences that might be 'harmless' but still so unpleasant that a demand for legal protection against them would be justified even if it was at the cost of an individual's liberty. Therefore, Fienberg formulated the 'offence principle'. The basic assumption is that offence is less serious than harm, and the offended mental state is a condition different from harm. According to Feinberg, 'offense' takes place when (1) one suffers a disliked or unpleasant state and (2) one attributes that state to the wrongful conduct of another and (3) one resents the other for his or her role in causing that state (1985: 1–2). However, Feinberg was clear that not all such claims could be legally protected at the cost of freedom of speech. Therefore, he derived certain standards for analyzing whether an action in this regard was warranted or could be justified as reasonable. These standards included: (1) the 'extent of offence' standard – in order to allow consideration of the intensity and durability of repugnance produced; (2) the 'reasonable avoidability' standard – to check whether the offensive displays could be easily avoided by the subject; and (3) the 'volenti' standards – to assess whether or not the witness has willingly assumed the risk of being offended (Feinberg 1985: 26–27). For Feinberg, an action against a speech act could be justifiable only if the witness had to face it involuntarily and was in such a position that there was no way in which the displays could be avoided and the 'offence' produced by the display was deeply hurting. This scale could be useful for all kind of offence, including that caused by religiously injurious speech.[5] Feinberg held that the offence principle is dependent on 'cultural standards' that vary greatly from place to place and within each nation 'constantly and rapidly change' (1985: 47). This stress on context-based analysis of the need and nature of law is also supported by political philosophers like Charles Taylor (1989 and Bhikhu Parekh (2012).

Modern democracies have come up with their own sets of laws to restrict freedom of speech and expression according to their specific needs and challenges (Letsas 2012). As discussed in the last chapter, in India, laws were introduced to restrain freedom of expression in the name of preventing the threats it posed to peace and tranquillity in society. The process began with the introduction of the penal codes during the colonial regime. Based on the 'unique' context of India, specific laws were created to take care of the performative dimension of speech, but more specifically, these laws were characterized by a predisposition towards protecting against mental agitation and hurt sentiments in response to loaded words, offensive gestures and transgression of hierarchical order. Gradually newer laws were added to prevent harmful impacts of religiously offensive speech acts, significant among them the addition of section 153(A) in 1898 and section 295(A) in 1927. In the post-Independence period, these laws were adopted as part of the revised penal codes. So, with regard to defamation of religion and incitement of religious hatred, other than the limits drawn under article 19(2) of the constitution, the two older, colonial-era statutory laws became particularly important. Section 295(A) aimed to prevent acts where nuisance is not the physical aspect of a communication, but arises because the message is considered provocative, indecent or denigrating. It prohibits 'deliberate and malicious acts, intended to outrage religious feelings of any class by insulting its religion or religious beliefs'. Though it is not a blasphemy law, it was meant to serve a similar purpose. It does not punish an imputation to god but to the followers, whereby the outrage and hurt felt by the followers is protected. Section 153(A) is aimed to prevent the consequences of a communication that may indirectly bring about harm to others by promoting hatred against any religious group. So, it criminalises the promotion of 'enmity between different groups on grounds of religion, race, place of birth, residence, language, etc.', or 'doing acts prejudicial to maintenance of harmony'. Both these laws form the basis of state action against offenders who indulge in any of the above-mentioned activities. Unlike Dworkin's and Waldron's propositions, where the individual is the unit of analysis, these laws are meant to respond to the threat experienced by a 'group' or 'class' of citizens. Also unlike in Mill's argument, these laws criminalized not just instigation, but any speech act that intended to outrage religious feelings or promote hatred. There is no necessary emphasis on either the consequences of the outrage or the hatred produced. Such laws allow government to criminalize a wide range of activities in the name of protecting the religious sensibilities of the citizens. The 'reasonableness' of government action was to be based on the test about how justifiably the government has used these statutory laws within the limits approved by the constitution. In order to make that judgement, the courts first needed to define the scope of these laws, which could help in understanding when and why religious offence became punishable.

Understanding 'Religious Offence' in the Light of Statutory Laws: A Perspective from Indian Courts

The present section examines what according to the courts is problematic in religious offence that warrants government's intervention either in the form of punishing the agent or in the form of censoring the speech act. Firstly, I discuss the courts' understanding about what makes a publication contentious – whether it is the 'manner' in which the opinion is expressed or the 'matter' contained in the publication. Secondly, I show how the courts further open the interpretation of statutory laws by emphasizing the essential difference between 'punitive' and 'preventive' laws. The subject-matter under consideration here shifts from the publication itself to the judgement of the government officials, thereby expanding their powers to proscribe or forfeit contentious publications without proper examination of the facts.

The Matter versus Manner Conundrum

Debates over legal intervention against freedom of expression include a vital concern about what should be the determining factor in such decisions: is it the substance of the speech or the form of expression? There is a strong belief among scholars that it should be the 'manner' in which the views are expressed and not the 'matter' that should be the basis of analysis. The expression of an opinion can be curbed, it is argued, only to the extent that offence is caused by the manner in which it is expressed (Feinberg 1973; Jones 1980). If the emphasis is shifted from 'matter' to 'manner', it allows the bar to be set higher; it hence creates a more favourable environment for a marketplace of ideas in search of truth by not interfering with people's ability to make judgements about religion, but does not allow the speech act to be deliberately offensive. Thus, it offers a balanced position to those who value freedom of expression but also want to avoid offence (Feinberg 1973). It also helps to maintain a distinction between what people disagree with or disapprove of and what causes offence. One of the extreme positions on this subject is reflected in the 'content-neutrality' doctrine popularized by American jurisprudence (Heyman 2002). The 'content-neutrality' doctrine assumes that the state would not punish or restrict speech acts on the basis of the content or the substance of the expression. Content-neutrality includes both 'subject-matter neutrality' as well as 'viewpoint neutrality', which means that speech acts could not be restricted on grounds of either the matter of the expression or the idea that the matter represented.

However, in the Indian context, the courts have emphasized the need to consider both the 'manner' as well as the 'matter' of the speech. Focus on 'manner' of speech helps in two vital aspects that substantiate the 'reasonableness' of legal intervention: (1) it helps the courts to trace the 'intention' of the accused; and (2) it helps the courts to weigh the intensity of the hurt. An important component of the punitive law under section 153(A) and 295(A) of the IPC is the aspect of *mens rea*, which emphasizes the need to examine the intention of the accused. In both the above-mentioned laws, punishment is justified only if it can be proved that the accused had 'deliberate and malicious' intentions involved in the contentious speech act. Courts analyze the 'manner' in which an idea is represented in order to test for 'deliberate and malicious' intention. They have upheld this reading of law in several judgements. For example, in 1960 the Allahabad High Court heard a case where the government of Uttar Pradesh had ordered the forfeiture of six books written by Baba Khalil Ahmad (*Baba Khalil Ahamad v. State* [1960] A.I.R. 1960 All. 715). The controversy was regarding the character of a historical figure, Muwaiya, who was considered revered by certain Sunni Muslim communities, whereas others thought him to be an evil person. The counsel for the applicant urged that the notification of the government was flawed, as any hurt caused was not intentional and the only aim of the author was to educate the masses about the negative character of Muwaiya and his role in Islamic history as a tyrant and a villain. Counsel also argued that the claims in the books were based on historical facts, and therefore it could not be seen as a deliberate attempt to hurt religious sentiments. The court held that:

> The intention of the writer of a book must be judged primarily by the language of the book itself.... If the language is of a nature calculated to produce or to promote feelings of enmity or hatred, the writer must be presumed to intend that which his act was likely to produce.

The court further remarked that 'even a true statement may outrage religious feelings', and therefore the argument about the content being based on historical facts did not really matter. In order to test whether the books were injurious in the above case, an inquiry into the language used in the publication, with reference to Muwaiya, was therefore considered important. It was reflective of the fact that court believed that the 'manner' in which ideas or arguments are presented become the primary indicator of the intentions of the author.

Secondly, the courts also examine the 'manner' in which the subject of speech is presented to differentiate between the content of speech acts that people disagree with or disapprove of and those that cause offence and are liable to legal intervention. Considering that it is impossible to quantify the feeling of hurt or offence, the courts concentrate on the intensity of offence. One of the primary tests that the courts have endorsed is that of the 'reasonable man' doctrine, which implies that only those speech acts that have the capacity to 'grossly offend' any 'reasonable man' deserve to be restricted (*Shiv Ram Dass Udasin v. The Punjab State* [1954] A.I.R 1955 P H 28). To apply this test, the court maintains that the expression 'outrage' (as used in section 295[A]) needs to be distinguished from feelings like 'wound', 'hurt' and 'injury'. In the *Sujato Bhadra* case, the West Bengal High Court differentiated between 'wounding' used in section 298 IPC and 'outraging' used in section 295 IPC. It held that the expression 'outraging' is much stronger than 'wounding', and that the term 'outrage' means 'to wrong grossly, treat with gross violence or indignity (*Sujato Bhadra v. State of West Bengal* [2006] 39 A.I.C. 239). The expression 'grossly offensive' is a natural extension of this distinction maintained by the courts.[6] Also, the courts have repeatedly asserted that the impact of a speech act should not be judged on the basis of the reaction that is expected out of a believer or an emotional person; rather the effect is 'to be judged from standard of [a] reasonable, strong minded, firm and courageous' person (*State of Maharashtra & Ors. v. Sanghraj Damodar Rupawate & Ors.* [2010] Civil Appeal of 2010 [Arising out of S.L.P. {C} No. 8931 of 2007]).[7]

The most important signifier in each of the above-mentioned tests is the language used to express the opinion, since this is considered to be an explicit indicator of both – the intention of the accused as well as the intensity of the hurt caused. Based on the emphasis on the 'manner' of expression in general, and language in particular, a study of courts' judgements provides some understanding about how they perceive the idea of religious offence. The courts have held that 'rational criticism of religion couched in restrained language' (*Lalai Singh Yadav v. State of Uttar Pradesh* 1971 CriLJ 1773) or 'doctrinal disagreement' (*Zac Poonen v. Hidden Treasure Literature* [2001], 2002 CriLJ 481) could not be considered an offence under law. However, even if the criticism of the religion is based on truth claims, the use of vile and insulting language would make the speech act eligible for punishment and prohibition (*Henry Rodrigues and Anr.* 1962 CriLJ 564). The courts went so far as to argue that if the writing in question was not intended to insult other religions or to promote hatred among different religious groups, then proselytizing writings could also not be restricted (*Ramlal Puri v. State of Madhya Pradesh* [1970] AIR 1971 MP 152). The emphasis on language to decipher the intention, however, provides an extremely subjective tinge to the analysis. It further highlights the moralizing aspect of courts' behaviour, whereby they dictate what form of expression is allowed or disallowed in a civil discourse.

It would be wrong to conclude, however, that the courts in India depend only on the 'manner' of expression or the language used in the publication to judge its legality. In different cases courts have also emphasized the need to look into the 'matter' or the content of the publications. It is maintained that in several instances, though the publication may not contain offensive language, the matter itself might be volatile and thereby attract legal injunction. Two primary reasons can be attributed to this approach: (1) the extensive scope of statutory laws, especially section 153(A) of the IPC, and (2) difficulty in deriving clear clinical tests to maintain the manner-matter distinction to contemplate religious offence. As discussed above, the emphasis on the 'manner' of speech acts helps in judging the intention of the author as well as the intensity of the 'hurt' caused by the speech. However, the statutory laws governing legal intervention to speech acts in India include section 153(A), where the subject under analysis is whether a speech act 'promotes or attempts to promote, on grounds of religion ... disharmony or feelings of enmity, hatred or ill-will' between different religious communities. In order to judge whether a publication falls under this category, the courts cannot solely depend on the 'manner' of the expression but are also required to analyze the content or the 'matter'. Consider, for example, the case of *Babu Rao Patel* in the Supreme Court, where the court was considering the constitutionality of section 153(A). An additional question under analysis was whether political writing or historical truth could attract the provisions under section 153(A) (*Babu Rao Patel v. State of Delhi* 1980 A.I.R. 763). The case was regarding the arrest of Babu Rao Patel after two of his articles – 'A Tale of Two Communalisms' and 'Lingering Disgrace of History' – were published in the political magazine edited by him called *Mother India*. These articles were considered to be a deliberate and malicious attempt to promote feelings of enmity and hatred among Hindus and Muslims. It appeared in the Supreme Court in the form of special appeal from the plaintiff after the High Court had refused to quash the arrest order.

In the first article 'A Tale of Two Communalisms', Patel discussed Muslim communalism and argued that communalism in India was an instrument employed by political minorities. The central thesis of his article was that Muslims were a 'violent race' with a 'radical tradition of rape, loot, violence and murder'. The second article, 'Lingering Disgrace of History', was written as a protest against the naming of Delhi roads after the Mughal Emperors, whom he calls 'lustful perverts, rapists and murderers'. He extended his criticism to argue that:

> From Mohammad Ibn Qasim, who landed in India in June 712 AD with 6000 Muslim cut-throats, to Mohammad Ali Jinnah, who cut the ancient cradle of a peace loving human race into three bleeding

> birds in August 1947, we have had 1235 years of bloodstained history in which our life has been constantly punctuated by endless raids, rapes, loots, arson and slaughter. (As quoted in the judgement of *Babu Rao Patel v. State of Delhi 1980* A.I.R. 763)

After discussing various atrocities and tyrannies of the Mughals ending with Aurangzeb, he wrote:

> To have a street named after this Mughal bastard in New Delhi, the capital of India, is not only a disgrace to the Hindus but a raging insult to the brave community of Sikhs. Had the Muslims been insulted thus, they would not only have burnt every house on the road named after the tyrant but also set fire to the whole damned city. The Muslims know how to guard their traditions.

In the Supreme Court, A. K. Sen, the counsel of the appellant, argued that if the articles were seen as a whole, it would be visible that 'A Tale of Two Communalisms' was no more than a political thesis, and the second article, 'Lingering Disgrace of History', was no more than a protest based on historical truths. It was contended that none of the articles attacked any religion, and so there was no question of promoting and attempting to promote feelings of enmity, hatred or ill-will between different religious groups. But the court rejected these arguments and held that both the articles were deliberately and maliciously written to promote feelings of enmity, hatred and ill-will between the Hindu and Muslim communities, and this, the court maintained, 'cannot be done in the guise of political thesis or historical truth'. The method applied by the court to reach this conclusion is indicative of its approach. The court discussed the content of each article in detail, citing important sections and highlighting possible interpretations. Based on an extensive analysis of the 'matter' contained in the articles, the court concluded that the possible implication of the publication was well within the scope of 153(A) and required action by the government. As we can see, both the subject-matter as well as viewpoint expressed in the publication together played a significant role in examining the consequences of the articles under controversy.

However, the pressure of statutory law is not the only reason why the courts include as part of their analysis the 'matter' of speech acts. They face extreme difficulty in maintaining a principled distinction between the 'matter' and the 'manner' of the speech act, in relation to religious offence. Can an expression be held to be offensive to the religious susceptibilities of the followers only if vile or insulting language is used to denigrate religious beliefs, a revered personage or a basic religious value system? The courts have held that freedom to criticize religion is allowed only if the criticism pertains to the practices of that religion and does not extend to its principles or basic tenets (*N. Veerabrahmam v. State of Andhra Pradesh* [1959] A.I.R.

1959 A.P. 572). Also, any criticism or questioning of the character of a religious personage or of a religious text is clearly prohibited (*Baba Khalil Ahamad* A.I.R. 1960 All. 715; *P. Ramasami* 1964 1 MLJ 147). The courts have held that even if the language used in the publication is neither aggressive nor outrageous, commentaries on these subjects have the potentiality to offend the religious sensibilities of the followers of any religion as well as promoting hatred among different religious groups. The use of restrained language or the claims of historical truth do not make the publication any less volatile, nor do they decrease the intensity of harm that such publications can cause. In such cases the reference point for the courts is the probable impact such expression could have on the religious followers.

The case of *Master Aman Preet Singh*, heard at the Punjab High Court in 1996, is reflective of this complexity. A Public Interest Litigation was filed by Master Aman Preet Singh, a class XII student of a school under the Central Board of Secondary Education (CBSE) for issuance of appropriate directions for deleting remarks alleged to be derogatory to Guru Gobind Singh (the tenth Guru of Sikhs) contained in a history textbook prescribed for Class XII students called *Modern India* (*Master Aman Preet Singh and Others v. Government of India and others* [1996] AIR 1996 PH 284). The book was written by historian Bipan Chandra and published by the National Council of Educational Research and Training (NCERT). The applicant had claimed that the chapter on Guru Gobind Singh presented the Guru in a bad light, noting in particular a reference to him being an employee of Bahadur Shah, a Mughal king. It was alleged that such references were contrary to facts and opposed to the teachings and writings of the Guru and hence 'offensive' to the Sikhs. In this case, the primary complaint was not about the 'manner' in which the subject was discussed or about the language being vile or insulting but about the content itself. A historical claim about the life of the Sikh guru (even though duly supported by historical evidence) came under controversy.

The respondents, including the publisher and the author, rejected the charge that the section deemed offensive in any way hurt the religious sentiments of any person. It was argued to be a fact based on historical research. They forwarded three arguments in favour of their position: (1) the contentious section was extracted out of context and the chapter as a whole aimed to situate the Sikh religion in perspective and to stress the popular, egalitarian and socially radical character of the Sikh religion founded by Guru Nanak; (2) the authenticity of the objectionable remarks was a matter of 'legitimate historical debate'; it was maintained that many historians disagreed with the view expressed and the truth content could only be extracted by historians alone 'by discussing it in a spirit of historical objectivity on the basis of acceptable historical evidence'; (3) the writer's view in this chapter was based on historical writings of eminent historians like Joseph Davey Cunningham (*History of the Sikhs*), William Irvine (*Later Mughals*), Sir Gukul Chand Narang (*Transformation of Sikhism*) and also upon a

Gurmukhi script, *Panth Parkash*, written by Bhai Gian Singh and a Persian work, *Umdat-ul-Twarikh*.

The court, however, remained unimpressed by the arguments of the respondents. It upheld the petition and ordered the removal of the offensive passages. It held:

> A Guru who is respected, revered and worshipped and is admitted to have fought against Moghul emperor throughout his life and sacrificed all that which was precious to him cannot be permitted to be projected to students to be an employee of Moghul emperor as the same is likely to hurt the religious feelings of the community.

The court approached the case as a question about protection of secular values of the Indian polity rather than as an infringement of freedom of speech and expression. It maintained that freedom of speech and expression could not be treated as a licence to infringe the rights or faith of others. In fact, it claimed that 'the State is under a constitutional obligation to preserve and protect the interests of Sikh Community', and therefore, 'the respondent/authorities are under an obligation to refrain from becoming a party to such controversial writing, which may ultimately hurt the feelings of the Sikh community as a whole or a part of it'.

Most significant was the observation of the court on the claim about historicity. This case was an explicit example of the blurring of the manner-matter distinction in relation to the impact of a publication. As there was no complaint about the form of expression or the language used, the decision was based strictly on the content or subject of the writing. The fact that the subject was related to a 'controversial' historical episode in the life of Guru Gobind Singh was considered reason enough to restrict the publication in the name of protecting the values of secularism. The subject-matter expressed was seen as an insult to the Guru, and though the language was neither abusive nor libellous, it was thought to be potentially offensive to the religious sensibilities of the followers of Guru Gobind Singh. The court also overlooked the fact that any kind of historical enquiry necessitated the free flow of arguments based on historical evidence. On this latter point the court held: 'The writings about religious Gurus cannot be permitted to be justified on the basis of disputed and debatable historical truths, lest it may destroy the very secular fabric of the Constitution'. Given that the author had never claimed that his views had unanimous acceptability among historians, while at the same time had shown that his statement was not bereft of historical evidences supported by several other historians, he had arguably allowed space for a view that it was aimed neither at denigrating any religious personage nor at hurting religious sentiments. But contrarily, the court suggested that 'self-restraint is expected in matters like religion, particularly when they are apprehended to affect the sentiments of a section of the society, forming part of the Indian polity'.

The above discussion shows that while interpreting statutory laws, the courts provide a very wide definition of religious offence, and this is reflected in their consideration of both 'matter' as well as 'manner' of speech acts that are seen as requiring government action. Only a restrained language and non-interference in critical aspects of religion, according to the courts, could be justified while dealing with the subject of religion. The immunity such a position provides to several aspects of religious belief, from attack or criticism, places constraints on the free exercise of freedom of speech and expression, even historical research on the subject.

Extending the Reach of Law: Separating 'Punitive' and 'Preventive' Actions

While adjudicating cases concerning contentious publications, the courts have maintained a distinction between 'punitive' and 'preventive' laws. The punitive laws like section 295(A) and 153(A) of the IPC can be used to punish authors/publishers who produce religiously offensive publications or publications that incite communal hatred, whereas the preventive law, like section 95 of the CrPC, can be used to proscribe or forfeit contentious publications. Section 95 of the CrPC empowers the government to declare any printed material forfeited which 'appears to the State Government to contain any matter the publication of which is punishable under section 124(A) or section 153(A) or section 153(B) or section 292 or section 293 or section 295(A) of the Indian Penal Code' by notification, 'stating the grounds of its opinion'. A look at the provision under section 95 would suggest that it is concomitant to the crime defined under the punitive laws, that is, the powers conferred upon the authorities to forfeit or proscribe can be used only if the conditions mentioned under other laws like section 295(A) or 153(A) are fulfilled. However, the courts have highlighted at least three important aspects in which the provisions are not only defined differently but also allow wider latitude for state action in order to prevent the circulation of publications containing religiously offensive subject-matter.

Firstly, the courts have maintained that the reference of various IPC laws in section 95 is only a description of the kind of offence required to be prevented and that the use of section 95 is not dependent on the tests mentioned for other statutory laws. Initially, some High Courts held that the law expected that cases be examined based on the tests suggested under sections 153(A) and 295(A) and only if a violation was deduced under these clauses could the action of the government to forfeit a publication be justified. This included tests such as *mens rea*, as required in the punitive laws.[8] The approach of the courts seems to have departed from this position significantly after the *Nand Kishore Singh* case. In this case, the Patna High Court argued that 'it would be somewhat fallacious to mathematically equate the proceedings under Sections 95 and 96 of the Code with a trial under Section 295-A of the Penal Code with the accused in the dock (*Nand Kishore Singh v. State of Bihar* AIR 1986 Pat 98). It held that the law under section 95 was essentially preventive in nature and to require the government be satisfied of the deliberate and malicious intention before using it was like defeating the very purpose of section 95. Also, the statute did not specify that it should be 'proved' to the state government or that the state government is 'satisfied' that all requirements of punishing section are established. All that the section expected was that it should 'appear' to the state government that the offending publication would come under the relevant section of the law. In this case the court also made it explicit that the 'clear and present danger' doctrine, as used in the US, cannot be applied in the Indian case.

This interpretation of law was significant for many reasons. On the one hand, it meant that the state government could proscribe a publication, without being satisfied about the tests like 'deliberate and malicious intention' of the author or publisher in the said case; nor was the government required to defend its decision in the courts on such grounds. On the other hand, it also allowed the state government to act towards pre-emption of the threat posed by the controversial publication. Broadly, the courts allowed a wider space for government's intervention on contentious publications, much wider in latitude than in cases under punitive laws. This interpretation of section 95 was upheld in several subsequent cases, most notably including the Supreme Court's observations in the *Sri Baragur Ramachandrappa* case and in the *Sangharaj Damodar Rupawate* case.[9]

Secondly, within the application of preventive laws, courts expect the government to spell out the 'grounds of opinion'.[10] A close analysis suggests that the courts insist that the 'ground of opinion' should include at least the citation of the offending passages (*Mohammad Khalid v. The Chief Commissioner, Delhi* [1967] A.I.R. 1968 Delhi 13) and the noting of the communities whose susceptibilities were allegedly hurt by the speech act (*Harnam Das* 1961 A.I.R 1662) as well as the 'conclusion of facts' (*Sanghraj Damodar Rupawate* Civil Appeal of 2010 [Arising out of S.L.P.(C) No. 8931 of 2007]) which led the government to forfeiture of the publication. The ground of opinion formation helped judges to understand the 'application of mind' by the authorities. The courts emphasized the importance of mentioning the grounds on which the opinion of the government was based in order to avoid arbitrary action by the government (*Lalai Singh Yadav* 1977 AIR 202),[11] and a failure on the part of the government to mention the ground of opinion could become the reason for cancellation of the notification of forfeiture (*Lalai Singh Yadav* 1977 AIR 202; *M/S Varsha Publications* Cri LJ 1446).[12] However, the courts have made this test lenient and subjective by reducing the details expected by the officials to spell out in a notification. There was the threat that the objectionable content, if declared in the notification explicitly, would ultimately be made available in the public sphere and thereby defeat the very objective of forfeiture or ban. In *Nand Kishore Singh* case, the Patna High Court took cognizance of this problem and brought some clarity on the issue. It opined:

> The declaration of forfeiture is consequently not required to be an exhaustive or self-contained document incorporating all the offending material as also each and every fact on which it is based. Any such detailed recitals or contents in a notification are neither mandated by statute nor precedent and would perhaps be incongruous in the nature of the notification envisaged by the statute.... It is amply sufficient if on the grounds of opinion, that is, the conclusions of fact being duly stated, the Government's opinion arrived at there from is clearly exhibited that the publications come within the mischief of the law.

As to mentioning the grounds of opinion, the courts held that though it was important, it did not need to include detailed exposition of the subject-matter but should exhibit the link between the conclusion of facts and the decision by the government. This is not an exception, as the courts have been consistently citing this case in order to check the validity of the notifications. The detailed notification was mandated in order to ascertain that the officials had conducted a thorough examination of the contentious publication before acting against it. The exemption pronounced in *Nand Kishore Singh*, therefore, protected the authorities from this mandatory procedure, making it easier for them to act against a contentious publication, even without a survey of the publication in question. It made it possible that the decision of authorities to act be guided more by the form of opposition or threat to public order that such publication would have attracted, and less by the content of the publication.

Thirdly, courts also held that in cases where any person appealed to the High Court against the forfeiture order, the onus of proof fell on the aggrieved, that is, it is for the petitioner in such cases to prove that the book does not contain anything disallowed in the section under which the order was passed. This followed from an interpretation of law under section 96(1) of the CrPC, which deals with the application in the High Court against forfeiture. Section 96(1) states:

> Any person having any interest in any newspaper, book or other document, in respect of which a declaration of forfeiture has been made under section 95, may, within two months from the date of publication in the Official Gazette of such declaration, apply to the High Court to set aside such declaration on the ground that the issue of the newspaper, or the book or other document, in respect of which the declaration was made, did not contain any such matter as is referred to in sub-section (1) of section 95.

Therefore, in order to challenge the order of forfeiture, the applicant would have to show that: (1) the publication in question did not contain anything 'which will offend or outrage the religious feelings of any section of the society' (*Baragur Ramachandrappa* [1998] CriLJ 3639); (2) there did not exist any intention on the part of the author to do so (*Sanghraj Damodar Rupawate* Civil Appeal of 2010 [Arising out of S.L.P.{C} No. 8931 of 2007]); and (3) the opinion of the government to proscribe the publication could not be sustained. This was in complete contradistinction to the requirements of punitive laws where the state government was expected to defend its decision to prosecute an individual by presenting evidence that not only proved the commission of offence but also pointed at 'deliberate and malicious' intention involved in the act.

Considering all these aspects together shows that if the state government follows the technical requirements, the probability of its action being upheld by the courts is quite high. It is far easier for government authorities to proscribe and forfeit a contentious publication than to punish (under statutory law) an individual attached to that publication. This also reveals the court's attitude towards the balance that it was expected to maintain between freedom of expression and claims of religious offence. Its interpretation of statutory laws provides wide space for the government's action against publications that are charged with defaming religion or promoting hatred against any religious groups. This is further confirmed by the difference the courts maintain between punitive and preventive law. The claim of freedom of expression becomes weaker with respect to controversial publications because courts do not intervene against censorship or proscription of such material in the name of public interest if the procedural aspect of law is not violated. The threat perception of government agencies becomes an important guiding point, and the interpretation of the preventive laws by the courts helps it to justify its prompt action.

The above section analyzed how courts interpret statutory laws, including the tests and doctrines they use to adjudicate on the subject of publications claimed to be religiously offensive. But an important question that still needs to be considered is why courts provide such a broad definition of religious offence, thereby making government's action justifiable in a wide range of cases.

Restricting Freedom of Expression: Courts and the Justifications for Legal Intervention

There is some general consensus that limitations to freedom of expression are acceptable if there are fears of disturbance to public order. Yet there is much less agreement on how to judge whether a specific speech act is in fact a threat to public order, and therefore deserving of prohibition. Mill's differentiation between 'advocacy' and 'instigation', as discussed earlier in this chapter, was indicative of this tension. That idea became more explicit in Justice Holmes's famous advocacy of the 'clear and present danger' doctrine that dominated American jurisprudence on freedom-of-speech questions during the last century. Justice Holmes in the *Schenck* case argued that it was largely a matter of 'proximity and degree'. He held:

> The question in every case is whether the words used are used in such circumstances and are of such a nature as to create a clear and present danger that they will bring about the substantive evils that Congress has a right to prevent.
>
> (*Schenck* 249 U.S. 47)

This approach was further fine-tuned during his dissent in the *Abrams* case, where he was joined by Justice Brandeis. In this case, Holmes opined that there should not only be 'clear and present' danger but rather the danger should be imminent and only if a direct relation could be established between the intentions of the actor and the consequence of the act would it be reasonable to punish such acts (*Abrams v. Unites States* [1919] 250 U.S. 616). In other words, it is argued that there should be a direct consequential relation between the speech act and the threat to public order.

In the Indian case, public order as a valid limitation to freedom of speech and expression was inserted in the constitution through the First Amendment in order to create a balance between 'individual freedom' and 'social freedom' as explained by Nehru in the *Statements of Objects and Reasons* for the Constitution (First Amendment) Act, 1951. The Supreme Court in its various judgements has refined the definition of the term 'public order', thereby drawing out its scope and limitations, especially when the claim of public order is used by the government to restrict freedom of speech and expression. In the *Superintendent, Central Prison, Fatehgarh* case the court defined public order as the absence of disorder involving 'breaches of local significance' (*Superintendent, Central Prison, Fatehgarh v. Ram Manohar Lohia* [1960], 2 SCR 84). The state of public order was marked as the orderly state of society or community 'in which citizens can peacefully pursue their normal activities of life'. Judges accepted that 'public order' was a wide term that might include minor 'law and order' aspects or major issues like the threat to state security such as attempts to overthrow it, and therefore asserted that the usage of the term should be precise. Emphasizing precision, the court in the *Dr. Ram Manohar Lohia* case referred to a set of three concentric circles with 'law and order' and 'security of state' in its outer- and inner-most circles, with public order in the middle (*Dr. Ram Manohar Lohia* 1966 AIR 740). The court opined that 'an act may affect law and order but not public order' and that not all cases of public disorder pose a threat to the security of the state. In the *Arun Ghosh* case, the court further asserted that the disturbances of public order needed to be distinguished 'from acts directed against individuals, which do not disturb the society to the extent of causing a general disturbance of public tranquillity'. 'It is the degree of disturbances and its effect upon the life of the community in a locality' that would determine, according to the court, 'whether the disturbance amounts only to a breach of law and order' (*Arun Ghosh v. State of West Bengal* [1969] 1970 3 SCR 288). Since the constitution of India devolves the power of maintaining law and order to the state government, it is the prerogative of the state officials to decide when a condition resembles a public-order problem and also to determine the possible ways to handle the situation. However, in order to justify its action against freedom of speech, the government was required to show (1) the speech act under question had caused or was likely to cause actual disturbance of a local significance and (2) the speech act should not only affect one or few individuals but the larger community.

Public Order and the Issue of Religiously Offensive Publications

The threat to public order posed by religiously offensive publications became the reason for the birth during the colonial period of most statutory laws that govern the freedom of speech and expression even today. In the post-Independence phase, the controversial religious content of political speeches and the printing press were thought to be playing a major role in promoting enmity and instigating violence among different communities and were therefore considered eligible for regulations.

But how and when does religious offence lead to public-order problems, and when is the government justified to act in such cases? In the context of independent India, the judiciary was expected to balance the claims of social cohesion with those of individual liberties. The fear was that the government in power could use the threat of public order for political purposes, thereby restricting freedom of speech and expression unreasonably. Contrarily, there was also fear that even small misjudgements on the part of authorities could lead to a severe public-order problem. So, courts were expected to draw the line between freedom of expression as a fundamental right to be freely enjoyed by all citizens and its misuse that threatened public order. In this regard, Pratap Bhanu Mehta (2008) is critical about the role of the judiciary. He argues that since the fundamental right to expression can be regulated on grounds of 'maintaining public order' legally, courts generally tend to allow regulation of any 'insult' to religion. This, according to him, is made possible because courts read the public-order exception in articles 19 and 25 so broadly that whenever a restriction is said to be associated with public order, they do not pursue any further questions. In the process, as Mehta argues, courts also assume that every attempt to insult religion tends to disrupt public order. This analysis of the judiciary's role, though suggestive, is not free from limitations. While Mehta's conclusion that the judiciary refrains from allowing private judgement to impede the 'legitimate purposes of the state that can be publicly justified', especially in relation to religious discourse, might be correct, his analysis of the cases to reach the conclusion is inconclusive and does not adequately do justice to the judiciary's position.

Let us consider two cases, one related to criminal prosecution for vilifying religious personage, the second related to the ban and forfeiture of a book. These examples help us to analyze the judiciary's role in questions of public order from different dimensions. In the first case, *Ramji Lal Modi*, a case that Mehta also cites, the government's action directly impacted freedom of speech and expression as well as an individual's personal freedom. In the second case, *Lalai Singh Yadav*, the government's action was limited to proscription of the controversial publication.

Case 1: As early as 1957, the Supreme Court was faced with the questions concerning an 'insult to religion' and its impact on the public-order situation. While testing the constitutionality of section 295(A) of IPC, in *Ramji Lal Modi*, the court dealt with the subject in great detail. In August 1952, a cartoon appeared in a popular Hindi daily published from Allahabad, Uttar Pradesh, *Amrit Patrika*, which caricatured the Prophet Mohammed in the form of a donkey. The state witnessed protests from the Muslim community, which turned violent in many instances. *Bandhs* and demonstrations were organized, despite prohibitory orders from the government (*The Times of India*, 14 August 1952). Repeated apologies by the editor, the publisher and the director-in-charge of the newspaper did not help to pacify the situation (*The Times of India*, 6 October 1952). It was only after government's decision to prosecute the newspaper that the situation was controlled. In the month of November, when the case was still fresh, Ramji Lal Modi, the editor and publisher of a monthly magazine called *Gaurakshak* (a magazine published to serve the cause of the Cow Protection Movement), wrote an article in the November issue questioning the protests by the Muslims. On the one hand, the article questioned the rationale behind such reactions, and on the other hand, it launched a scathing attack on the basic tenets of the Muslim religion, including popular beliefs about the Prophet. Fearing threats to law and order in the polarized communal context, the government ordered the prosecution of Ramji Lal Modi under sections 153(A) and 295(A) of the IPC. In the Sessions Court of Kanpur, the judge acquitted him of the charges under section 153(A) but found him guilty under 295(A), and thereby sentenced him to 18 months' rigorous imprisonment. Modi then appealed against the judgement before the High Court, but the court held that the article was published with a deliberate and malicious intent to outrage the religious feelings of the Muslims and hence was punishable.

The accused then approached the Supreme Court with two separate applications, one claiming a stay on the High Court order and the other, under article 32 of the constitution, urging that section 295(A) was *ultra vires* and void inasmuch as it interfered with the petitioner's freedom of speech and expression (*Ramji Lal Modi* 1957 AIR 620). The Supreme Court rejected the application for a stay and dismissed the other application, thereby upholding the action taken against Modi. During the trial, the counsel for the appellant argued that it was only in the 'interest of public order' that a 'reasonable restriction' to freedom of speech and expression could be justified, and therefore, the likelihood of public disorder 'should be a matter of proximate and not remote consideration'. He substantiated these arguments using the Supreme Court's observations in the *Romesh Thapar* and *Brij Bhushan* cases and insisted that in the present case, there was no direct threat of public disorder. Secondly, he maintained that insults to religions and religious beliefs may or may not lead to public disorder, and therefore there was always a sense of ambiguity attached to the practical implications of section 295(A), which was dangerous if allowed to curtail a fundamental right. The Court rejected both these submissions and held that section 295(A) was well within the scope of article 19(2), which set reasonable restrictions to freedom of speech and expression. The observations of the court were significant for future cases. On the first submission, the court held that after the First Amendment, Romesh Thapar's and Brij Bhushan's cases were no more relevant because the First Amendment had significantly changed the nature and scope of article 19(2). The court differentiated between two significant phrases: 'for the maintenance of' and 'in the interest of'. According to the court, the addition of the phrase 'in the interest of' public order had significantly widened the scope of article 19(2), and therefore, even if some action by the government might not be justified on the grounds of directly maintaining public order, it might still be important in 'the interest of public order'. Chief Justice S. R. Das pronounced: 'If ... certain activities have a tendency to cause public disorder, a law penalising such activities as an offence cannot but be held to be a law imposing reasonable restriction "in the interests of public order", although in some cases those activities may not actually lead to a breach of public order.' The court also rejected the claim that freedom of speech and expression could be restrained only if the threat to public order was proximate and imminent. Countering the second proposition, the court did not believe that there was any sense of ambiguity in law. It held that 'deliberate and malicious' intention was the sine qua non of section 295(A), and therefore only those acts of insult to religion or religious beliefs that were carried out with deliberate and malicious intention were punishable. Deriving a direct connection between the calculated tendency of an 'aggravated form of insult' and 'public order', the court held that such intentional vilification, aimed 'clearly to disrupt the public order and the section, which penalises such activities, is well within the protection of cl. (2) of article 19'. It meant that if government could successfully show that an act was 'deliberately and maliciously' aimed at insulting religion or religious beliefs, it would be assumed to be a threat to public order and hence punishable under law. Based on these arguments, the court held Ramji Lal Modi guilty and rejected his application.

Significantly, in the unrecorded trial of the editor and the publisher of *Anand Patrika*, who were prosecuted by the state under section 295(A) for publishing the cartoon of Prophet, the accused were acquitted by the Allahabad High Court due to the failure by the prosecution to produce enough evidence to prove that the act was done with 'deliberate and malicious' intention.[13] The contrast in both cases is evident of the court's differing approach. It is significant that the reactions to the publication of the cartoon were directly responsible for a law-and-order situation in Uttar Pradesh. The acquittal of the editor and publisher of the newspaper hinted that for criminal prosecution, it was necessary to establish a link between the intentions of the accused and the reaction of the members of religious community who claimed a feeling of 'offence'. In Modi's case, the fact that his essay was in reaction to events surrounding the publication of the cartoon helped to establish deliberate and malicious intention. The same did not apply to the editor or publisher of *Amrit Patrika*, who had continuously pleaded it to be a case of ignorance and had also publicly apologized for the same. So, it can be concluded that though the court believed that government could act based on its assessment of public-order problems and it did not compulsorily include the 'clear and present danger' test, the prosecution of individuals under criminal law required authorities to prove presence of deliberate and malicious intentions.

The above analysis hints at two important aspects of the court's position on the subject of criminalizing speech acts that contain religiously offensive subjects. First, courts allow for action if there was an aggravated form of insult, presuming that such utterances had every chance to flare up into a public-order issue. At the same time, it did not explain what could be included as an aggravated form of insult or how it is to be differentiated from insults of a general kind, which could not be punished. The reluctance of the courts to examine or provide clear directions left it largely to the prerogative of government officials to decide when to act. Secondly, the actors in these cases could be held guilty only if deliberate and malicious intention was proven. Considering the fact that the intention was to be derived from the content and language of the publication, the court tried to distance the justification of government's action from its implication for an individual's personal liberty. The only justification required for the government's action is the presumption of public-order problems. Whether prosecution in the case was legally justified or not could be left for the judiciary to decide later. Arguably, such a position enables government officials to act on the presumption of public-order threats without taking into account the reasonability of such action vis-à-vis freedom of speech and expression. This approach of the judiciary has even more serious implications in cases involving proscription or banning of the books in a territory.

Case 2: The second case is related to the proscription order of the book *Sachchi Ramayana*.[14] The case was about the Uttar Pradesh government's appeal in the Supreme Court against the Allahabad High Court's decision to strike down a government order banning *Sachchi Ramayana* or *Ramayana: A True Reading*, originally written by radical Tamil social reformer Periyar, later translated and published by Lalai Singh Yadav, a resident of Uttar Pradesh. It was a polemical text questioning the sacredness of different characters of the revered epic. Contemplating a threat to public tranquillity, the Intelligence Department sent copies of the book to Kanpur police to enquire if any action could be taken. The Magistrate then decided to forfeit all copies from Lalai Singh Yadav. Later, formal orders of forfeiture of all the copies of the book, both in Hindi as well as the English language, were notified through the *Gazette* of Uttar Pradesh on 8 December and 20 December 1969 under section 99 (A) of the CrPC.[15] The government claimed that by treating the main characters of the epic with disdain, the author and publisher had offended the religious sentiments of a majority of Hindus. However, in the notification issued for proscription, officials had not mentioned the grounds for the opinion formation, and the High Court held the notice insufficient because it did not clearly state why government believed the publication fell under section 295(A). It maintained that until an offence qualified under the tests of section 295(A) of IPC, section 99(A) of CrPC did not apply, and hence the order was struck down. The Uttar

Pradesh government approached the Supreme Court against the judgement. Though the Supreme Court upheld the decision of the High Court, it was essentially on technical grounds, and as the judgement mentions, it was not reflective of the view of the judges 'on the merits of the book or its provocative vitriol' (*State of Uttar Pradesh v. Lalai Singh Yadav* [1976] 1977 AIR 202).

In the unanimous judgement written by Justice V. R. Krishna Iyer, the approach of the court on the question of the proscription of a contentious publication under the threat of a public-order situation is discussed in great depth. Firstly, the Court made it absolutely clear that the decision to ban or forfeit a controversial publication was a legitimate power in the hands of the government and 'whoever violates by bombs or books societal tranquillity will become [a] target of legal interdict'. Secondly, it was maintained that though the 'clear and present danger' test, as popularized in American jurisprudence, was not relevant for Indian conditions, extreme caution was required on the part of the government in its judgement of how to safeguard social tranquillity. Thirdly, reiterating the views of the court in *Ramji Lal Modi*, the judges recognized a clear relationship between religious offence and public disorder. It held: 'Hatred, outrage and like feelings of large groups may have crypto-violent proneness and the State, in its well-grounded judgment, may prefer to stop the circulation of the book to preserve safety and peace in society.... The actual exercise will depend not on doctrinaire logic but practical wisdom'. The practical wisdom of government was to depend on a number of factors including the context and content of the publication. As mentioned earlier, the court rejected the application on technical grounds; however, it also pointed out that if the state government thought that the peace of the state would be disturbed by the book under consideration, it could reissue a fresh notification, keeping in mind the essential legal requirements. So, though the judgement was in favour of the publisher of the book, the court hinted that the technical aspects aside, the government was well within its legitimate capacity and powers to order proscription under the perception of a threat to public order.

Both the above cases had some significant similarities and differences. It is clear that the Supreme Court in both the cases held that government's intervention was justified and was constitutionally protected under article 19(2) if it was seen to be 'in the interest of public order'. The significance of the phrase 'in the interest of' was made explicit by the court's reference to the First Amendment, whereby the phrase was introduced to the constitution. This was in contradistinction to Mehta's assumption that the fundamental right to expression

Court reasoned that 'in the interest of public order' has a larger connotation and implications for government's action than 'for the maintenance of public order', as it allowed for intervention even if there were no direct threats to public order. Thereby courts also seemed to have rejected the application of the 'clear and present danger' doctrine in the Indian context as in the US. Furthermore, the two judgements also revealed that, unlike Mehta's proposition, the court did not base its judgement solely on the government's claims of a threat to public order. In the first case, the court held that the prosecution of an individual also required that 'deliberate and malicious intention' was proven. In this way, the court balanced an individual's personal liberty with the threat posed to public order by the contentious publication. In the second case, the court emphasized the importance of mentioning in the notification order the grounds on which the officials had based their opinion, which could reflect the application of mind by the government in making the decision to forfeit or ban a particular publication. Therefore, in such cases the threat to public order, though an important condition, was not considered as a sufficient claim for justifying the government's action under 'reasonable restriction'. However, under the looming threat to public order and the government having cogent reasons to believe it, the court held that it was totally justified in acting against the publication or the person responsible for it.

Secularism and the Protection of the Right to Conscience and Religion

One of the main dilemmas attached with laws against religious offence has centred on the role of state – concerning the scope and limitations of state intervention in such subjects. For example, a very strong justification in favour of blasphemy laws has been that it is the duty of state to preserve morality in society. This was especially true about societies where blasphemy laws were used to protect from insult the religion of the majority. For example, one of the strongest advocates of blasphemy laws in Britain, Lord Devlin justified the presence of blasphemy laws on grounds that morals and religion were intrinsically related and enforcement of morals in society was the duty of state. Therefore, according to him, the state was duty-bound to protect religion from attacks (Devlin 1965: 23–25). But in the changed context of multicultural societies, this position faced challenges from different quarters. One school of thought argues that restriction of freedom of speech and expression on the pretext of religious offence had lost its moral justification. For example, George

Letsas (2012) believes that the fact that each religious system is based on a set of 'particularities' represented in the form of doctrines, symbols or figures requires that any protection of religion would mean forcing people to accept the ethical ideas and ideals that they might not have contemplated or have been familiar with. This, according to Letsas, should not be the role of the state, and therefore any law like blasphemy could not be supported (2012: 255–257). Other critics, like Peter Jones (1980), argue that 'the protection of religion for moral purposes ceases to be feasible in a multi-religious society' because it would be detrimental to the idea of a secular state to prefer and protect a certain conception of a good life represented by the religion of the majority, and on the other hand, if the state 'tried to avoid that inequity by protecting all religions it would be supporting contradictory beliefs and beliefs which had different moral consequences' (1980: 133). So, it was asserted that the state should either not indulge in restricting freedom of expression in the name of religious offence or it should look for a more potent justification to legitimize its action, like the threat on public order. However, there were others who believed that the law of blasphemy should be extended to protect all religious subjects. It was argued that the changing nature of societies, whereby they were becoming multi-religious and plural, required a secular state to extend such protections to followers of all religions. For example, Lord Scarman, who favoured the expansion of the common law crime of blasphemy to protect the religious feelings of non-Christians in Britain, urged during the *Lemon* case[16] that the common law be changed by legislation to protect the sensibilities of all religious groups (*Whitehouse v. Lemon* [1979] 2 WLR 281). Scarman cited the example of India to build a case for the need for protection of all religions in a plural society. He said:

> In an increasingly plural society such as that of modem Britain it is necessary not only to respect the differing religious beliefs, feelings and practices of all but also to protect them from scurrility, vilification, ridicule, and contempt....When Macaulay became a legislator in India, he saw to it that the law protected the religious feelings of all. In those days India was a plural society: today the United Kingdom is also.... My criticism of the common law offence of blasphemy is not that it exists but that it is not sufficiently comprehensive.
>
> (As quoted in Post 1980: 312)

Britain abolished the offences of blasphemy and blasphemous libel from its common law in 2008 by the Criminal Justice and Immigration Act, 2008.

Looking at the history of laws against religious offence in India, one can conclude that ever since it got codified under the colonial state, it was meant to protect followers of all religions. But the question about how a secular state should behave in a multi-religious and plural society still remains a puzzle. Unlike many Western democracies, where the principles of secularism expected an approach of neutrality from the state on the issues concerning religions, in India it was expected to maintain what Rajeev Bhargava has famously called 'principled distance'. On the one hand, it meant equal treatment of all religions and non-interference in matters internal to religion; on the other hand, on subjects that affected the public in general, it had every right to assert its authority. Protection of the right to freedom of religion as guaranteed under article 25 also became a constitutional as well as a moral duty for the state to uphold in India's multi-religious society.

But how was the state expected to behave when freedom of religion was threatened by publications that vilified and insulted religious beliefs, symbols and practices? In its various judgements, courts have considered instances where freedom of speech and expression clash with other constitutional guarantees, including freedom of conscience and the right freely to profess, practice and propagate religion. It has been observed that courts in such situations attempt to preserve a balance based on two premises: first, as discussed earlier in the chapter, courts hold that wounding religious susceptibilities of other religious denominations could lead to disruptions of public order; and second, courts opine that freedom of conscience and religion needs to be protected, and it is the duty of the state to create an environment where this right can be freely enjoyed. One of the earliest examples of this attitude of the court was reflected in the *N. Veerabrahmam* case. The Andhra Pradesh High Court in this case was considering the constitutionality of section 99(A) and ban of the book *Bible Bandaram* – which was claimed to be a rationalist critique of the Bible (*N. Veerabrahmam v. State of Andhra Pradesh* [1959] A.I.R. 1959 A.P. 572). The author had pointed at incongruities and inconsistencies in the Bible, raised doubts about its authorship, and made certain controversial claims like, for instance, because nobody can be born of a virgin, Jesus was a product of an adulterous union and the Immaculate Conception theory was a cover-up. Introducing a balanced approach, the court held: 'People are at liberty to write books without offending deliberately the religious sentiments of other citizens who are as much entitled to certain freedoms as the petitioner himself.' Rejecting the argument from the counsel for the petitioner that the book was based on rational and free thinking and was therefore eligible for protection under article 19(1)(a), the court defined the boundary of such claim by arguing that free thinking did not 'involve freedom to make scurrilous attacks on the religion and religious beliefs of other sects with impunity'. 'It is not free-thinking to abuse and insult other religions', the court observed. Deliberating the subject further, judges held that 'no citizen could claim a right to insult the religion or religious beliefs of another section of the population'. They maintained that it was the duty of the state to ascertain that citizens are able to exercise freedom of religion and conscience, and according to the court, section 99(A) of the CrPC as well as section 295(A) of the IPC were legitimate powers in the hands of the government to ensure such protection for the rights of all its citizens. The emphasis on protecting freedom of conscience and religion was based on the understanding that though freedom of speech and expression was important, it did not enjoy any special status and hence needed to be balanced with competing claims based on other fundamental rights. In the final section of the judgement, the court observed that 'all the citizens of India are guaranteed freedom of religion and freedom of conscience by our Constitution and each one has a right to pursue his own way of attaining salvation, unhampered and without interference from others'. This attitude of the court provides both moral and legal protection to freedom of conscience and religion against freedom of expression. By recognizing that freedom of religion should be 'unhampered and without interference', courts provided certain immunity to religions against criticism.

This perspective is further reflected in the way courts determine what constitutes legitimate criticism when it is directed against religion. So, for example, courts have proved to be lenient against criticism of religious practices but at the same time have made explicit that any insult or vilification of a religious personage and criticism of religious texts and beliefs could not be allowed. It was based on the perception that a criticism or insult of a religious personage and of religious texts amounted to interference in the faith of others, something that could not be allowed in a secular and plural society like India. This position of the court was reiterated in the Supreme Court's judgement in the *Sri Baragur Ramachandrappa* case, where the court observed:

> [N]o person has a right to impinge on the feelings of others on the premise that his right to freedom of speech remains unrestricted and unfettered. It cannot be ignored that India is country with vast disparities in language, culture and religion and unwarranted and malicious criticism or interference in the faith of others cannot be accepted.
>
> (*Sri Baragur Ramachandrappa & Ors. v. State of Karnataka & Anr* [2007] 5 S.C.C.11)

The court emphasized that secular values needed to be protected, and the state was duty-bound to act if such values were threatened, even if it was done under the garb of freedom of expression. This position provides a justifiable reason for government's intervention by warranting a restriction on freedom of expression in cases where it is found to interrupt free exercise of the right to freedom of religion. Government's action is also justified, according to courts, in cases that include acts of vilification or wounding religious susceptibilities of followers of any religion, as they have a tendency to lead to disruption of public order. 'If there is no law authorising the executive to take necessary action ... there will be disorder in society and bitter feelings and even hatred between various sections of society which is not conducive to the maintenance of order', the court observed in the *N. Veerabrahmam* case. This was another ground on which section 99(A) was considered well within the limitations set by article 19(2) to the freedom of speech and expression. This aspect was further elaborated by Justice Krishna Iyer in the *Lalai Singh Yadav* case. He maintained that in a country like India, the secular state was obligated 'to create conditions where the sentiments and feelings of people of diverse or opposing beliefs and bigotries are not so molested by ribald writings or offensive publications as to provoke or outrage groups into possible violent action'. Justice Iyer believed that state was expected not only to protect society against breaches of peace but also to prevent the causes of such a state of order. This essentially involved proscribing publications which were deeply offensive to the religious sentiments of any section of the population. He said:

> [P]ublic power comes into play not because the heterodox few must be suppressed to placate the orthodox many but because every-one's cranium must be saved from mayhem before his cerebrum can have chance to simmer. Hatred, outrage and like feelings of large groups may have crypto-violent proneness and the State, in its well-grounded judgment, may prefer to stop the circulation of the book to preserve safety and peace in society.
>
> (*State of Uttar Pradesh v. Lalai Singh Yadav* [1976] 1977 AIR 202)

This principle of balancing counter-claims about fundamental rights along with the assumption of a threat inherent in the misuse of freedom of speech and expression allowed space for state governments to ban books that insulted or even criticized religions.

Conclusion

The decisions and observation of the courts show sensitivity towards protecting the religious sensibilities of citizens from being affronted by religiously offensive publications. In the process, courts allow wide latitude for government intervention both in its punitive as well as preventive actions. This reading of the court's attitude departs from Sorabjee's and Dhavan's studies, whereby they held that courts in general and the Supreme Court in particular has put a strong defence in favour of freedom of speech and expression. A point to note in this comparison is that both Sorabjee (1994) and Dhavan (2008) talk about freedom of speech and expression in general, and this study concentrated only on religiously offensive publications. Though Sorabjee's and Dhavan's arguments may be more generally valid, my own analysis of publications that defame religion or promote religious hatred certainly qualifies their more general claims. In fact, courts seem to maintain that there are some subjects that cannot be discussed even in mild and non-harmful language. These include criticism or insult of religious personage or denigrating religious texts or sacred beliefs. This gives some kind of covert immunity to religion from criticism, a point also made by Mehta (2008: 332). In the name of maintaining public order and protecting the ethos of secularism, the claims of religious offence have generally received a much more favourable response from the courts than do the claims of freedom of expression.

Notes

1 As Samuel Walker (1994) has shown in the case of the US, courts played a defining role in determining the scope of freedom of speech. Though the laws in India do not allow the same liberty to the courts, their role is still significant. The courts in India are expected to limit their role to checking whether the state action is based on procedure set by law rather than the 'due process' doctrine followed by American courts.

2 I have used cases from High Courts across different states of the country depending upon the importance of such cases and whether they deal exactly with the subject under discussion here, that is, religiously offensive publications.

3 Manupatra is a digital legal database which includes all the reported judgements of the Supreme Court and High Courts in India, along with Central and State Acts, Central Rules, Pending Bills in the Parliament, and Notifications of various Central Ministries.

4 Many scholars present 'offence' as a subjective experience (Collini 2010; Melville 2009). However, recently scholars like Lorenz Langer (2014) have argued that though a subjective experience, it has the potential to mobilize similar experiences of hurt.

5 Cohen-Almagor argues that 'the offence to sensibilities argument in and of itself can serve as grounds for restricting freedom of expression in extreme cases when the offense is severe and the target group cannot avoid being exposed to the offence' (2005: 107).

6 Courts have also used other expressions like 'aggravated form of insult' in the *Ramji Lal Modi* case or 'aggravated form of criticism' in the *R. V. Bhasin* case. But the intention in each of these expressions is to argue that not all forms of insult or claims of hurt can be taken into consideration while employing section 295(A). The expression 'grossly offensive' is also used by courts in several other cases like *Shiv Ram Dass Udasin* and *N. Veerabrahmam*.

7 This test was first introduced by Justice Vivian Bose in *Bhagwati Charan Shukla v. Provincial Government* A.I.R. 1947 Nagpur 1, where he held that the impact of words 'must be judged from the standards of reasonable, strong-minded, firm and courageous men, and not those of weak and vacillating minds, nor of those who scent danger in every hostile point of view'. Thereby this became an important test in Indian jurisprudence.

8 For example, in the *N. Veerabrahmam* case, the court held that 'it is only insults to religion or religious beliefs that are deliberately and maliciously made that would bring into play section 99-A criminal procedure code'. This position was reiterated in the *Baba Khalil Ahamad* case. This position continued till the *M/S*

Varsha Publications case. But since the Patna High Court's observation in *Nand Kishore Singh* case, courts have changed their position on the subject.

9 In the *Sri Baragur Ramachandrappa* case, the court agreed with the interpretation in *Nand Kishore Singh* and held: 'It will be seen that section 95 and section 96 of the code when read together are clearly preventive in nature and one designed to pre-empt any disturbance to public order. At the same time, we find that section 95 does not by itself create a criminal offence and the reference to the various sections of the penal code is merely description of the kind of offence which need to be prevented by a declaration under section 95.' This position was reiterated by courts in different cases like *R. V. Bhasin* and *Sanghraj Damodar Rupawate*.

10 In fact, courts have indicated that its only role in cases regarding forfeiture and proscription is to judge on the basis of notification whether or not the action of the government falls within the scope of 'reasonable' restrictions. See *Harnam Das v. State of Uttar Pradesh* (1961), 1961 A.I.R 1662.

11 Justice Krishna Iyer held: 'If you laze and omit, the law visits the order with voidness and this the State Government must realize especially because forfeiture of a book for a penal offence is a serious matter, not a routine act to be executed with unconcern or indifference. The wages of neglect is invalidity, going by the text of the Code. These considerations are magnified in importance when we regard the changeover from the Raj to the Republic and the higher value assigned to the great rights of the people.'

12 Courts argued that since the law allowed the victim to challenge the decision of forfeiture or ban in the High Court (under section 96 of the CrPC), it was important for the victims to know the reasons for proscription, in order to defend their position. Also, in order to decide the case, the court needed to be informed as to 'which communities were alienated from each other or whose religious beliefs had been wounded according to the Government, or why the Government thought that such alienation or offence to religion had been caused'. These details, according to court, were necessary for it to reach to a conclusion on the subject.

13 Though the judgement was not recorded, the case was closely followed in the press owing to the public-order situation it had created. See, 'Hooliganism Breaks Out Again in Kanpur: Government Decides to Prosecute Hindi Paper', *The Times of India*, 14 August 1952; 'Case against Newspaper: Police Official's Deposition', *The Times of India*, 6 October 1952; 'Allahabad Editor Acquitted: Muslim Feelings Not Wounded', *The Times of India*, 23 April 1954.

14 It was translated and published by Lalai Singh Yadav after seeking permission from Periyar. It was published at Ashok Pustakalaya: Jhinjhak, Uttar Pradesh in 1969.

15 This information was given by the then–Health Minister of UP, Krishnanad Rai, on the floor of the UP State Legislative Assembly. See *UP State Assembly Debates*, 21 May, 1969, vol. 279, part 3: 323.

16 It was a blasphemy case in the UK regarding a poem published in *Gay News* which was considered to be denigrating the image of Christ.

4

LAW AND LEGAL PROCESS AS HURDLES

In May 2015, PEN Canada and the International Human Rights Programme, University of Canada's Faculty of Law, produced a report titled *Imposing Silence: The Use of India's Laws to Suppress Free Speech* (2015). The report argued that 'vague overboard laws' and a 'corrupt inefficient justice system' have given rise to an environment in India where free speech can easily be censored. It further discussed the regulatory framework used by government officials, individuals and social and religious groups to curtail freedom of expression. The report looked at various aspects of the legal process that account for the diminishment of freedom of speech in India. Issues ranging from the filing of criminal charges and civil suits, the role of the police and judicial corruption, and questions as to the competence of the judiciary to hear cases on the subject were examined. On the one hand, the report discussed the limiting attitude of Indian law and the judicial process, and on the other hand, based on a comparative analysis with international legal provisions, it criticized India's position in protecting the freedom of speech and expression. The report also forwarded a list of suggestions, which included issues such as reform in the police and judiciary and scrapping as well as amending significant statutory laws. The sentiment embodied in the report has also been reflected earlier by scholars like Lawrence Liang (2004) and Sohini Ghosh (2004), among others, who believe that the real threat to freedom of speech and expression in the Indian context emanates from the 'slippery slope'[1] effect produced by the legal provisions. They recommend repealing of laws like section 153(A) and 295(A) in order to prevent misuse. For example, Liang (2012: 1) argues that 'once you have a law that allows for the making of legal claims on the basis of charged emotional states, you begin to see the emergence of cases that steadily cultivate a legal vocabulary of hurt sentiments'. It is in this sense that Ahmed notes that attempts to 'regulate wounded attachments and religious passions' through law may 'conversely constitute them'. Such legal construction of offence, Ahmed argues, gives space to 'social groups to organize in order to ensure the state take cognizance of blasphemous events and practices' (2009: 177). Though the slippery slope argument forwarded by these scholars holds strong ground, it fails to explain how it was

DOI: 10.4324/9781003369257-5

a unique phenomenon attached to laws governing freedom of speech and expression. Any law could be misused in a situation where the executive was not sensitive to its usage. Further, the criticism of law forwarded by these scholars does not take into account the responsibility of the judiciary as interpreter of law in drawing the boundaries of the legal discourse. The analysis therefore suffers limitations.

In this chapter, I highlight the operative and functional inadequacies attached to the legal process, including the role of the judiciary that impacts free speech cases. Lacunae in the procedural and functional aspects of the working of law together contribute in strengthening the role of non-state actors in cases related to censorship. These weaknesses have inspired the claimants of hurt sentiments to approach the legal route as a means to censor free speech. On the other hand, the labyrinth of law and legal process produces an environment of fear and confusion for authors/publishers. Their struggle to defend freedom of speech and expression is set back due to the insecurities and uncertainties surrounding the legal process and system. It may even result in their surrender to the demands of censorship by non-state actors, in order to escape the long and exhausting legal process. The fissures in the law and legal process, therefore, act as constraints upon the free exercise of the freedom of speech and expression.

The Procedural Dimensions of the Legal Process as a Hurdle to Freedom of Speech and Expression

Procedural dimensions here refer to the process through which cases related to contentious publications arrive in courtrooms, as well as the procedural aspects related to the functioning of courts. Three aspects have particular relevance for freedom of speech and expression, and these directly or indirectly act as hurdles in its free exercise: (1) spurious charging and overcharging; (2) the tendency to file cases against the author/publisher in different parts of the country; and (3) the delay in administering justice. The first two aspects are related to the pre-courtroom phase. However, even after the case reaches the stage where the formal legal process begins in the courts, it takes a long period of time to deliver judgement, making the legal process itself a hurdle. All these together contribute to making the process tedious and demoralizing, thereby dissuading actors from seeking legal recourse when their freedom of expression is curtailed by either state or non-state actors.[2] On the contrary, the legal process becomes an easy option for non-state actors to harass the author/publisher and force them to agree to their demands for censorship.

Spurious Charging and Overcharging

The phenomenon of spurious charging and overcharging is related to vagueness of the law as well as the tendency among government authorities to react under pressure and act in order to avoid immediate threats to public order. Spurious charging refers to instances where police register cases under different sections of laws without being sure about the legal validity of such laws in the courts. Overcharging includes framing multiple accusations in a single case. It may result in charges being framed against authors and publishers under sections of law which might not even be relevant in that case. The vagueness in constitutional and statutory laws governing freedom of speech and expression (as discussed in Chapter 1) leaves the authorities unsure about which laws could be justifiably invoked in a particular case. To add to it, the pressure exerted by different socio-religious groups claiming hurt to their sentiments by the publications creates an environment of uncertainty, leaving it to the legal prerogative of the officials to decide upon the relevant sections to be invoked, and to register a First Information Report (FIR) accordingly. As many legal scholars have also noted, an important facet of statutory laws governing freedom of speech and expression in India is that the kind of offences that fall under their purview are 'cognizable' and 'non-bailable' (Bhatia 2016: 139–145; Narrain 2016a: 41–42). This means that officials do not require any form of prior approval either from the state government or the judiciary to act in such cases. Further, the 'non-bailable' nature of the offence ensures that the accused has to face trial and can only be granted bail after the matter is debated in the court. So, the investigation and opinion of the officer on duty becomes central in such cases, which have a high possibility of being guided by the pressure asserted by the complaining parties/groups. Legal commentators have observed that police use these provisions as tools to avoid any kind of altercation in the public-order situation arising due to contentious publications. At the same time, it also ensures that even if charges against the publication and the author/publisher do not stand in the court of law, the accused party could still be found guilty under some section of the law (Dhavan 2008: 145). As my reading of cases also suggests, in most cases where criminal charges were invoked, officials charged the authors/publishers of being guilty under multiple sections of the penal codes. Generally, section 153(A) was invoked together with sections 295(A) and 298 of the IPC and section 95 of the CrPC. It was left to the judiciary to decide whether the charges fell within the legal brackets defined by any of those provisions. Further, as criminal charges against the author/publisher and notification for forfeiture of their publication formed two separate cases, the accused publishers/authors had to appear for trials in both these cases separately. The criminal charges fall under the category of 'cognizable' and 'non-bailable' offense, so appearance before the court is compulsory, whereas in cases of forfeitures, it remains the prerogative of the author/publisher to approach the court under section 96 of CrPC if they want the notification to be revoked. This means extra expenditure both in terms of time and resources for the authors and publishers to defend their position.

The Liberty to Lodge a Case against the Book or Author/Publisher in Any Part of the Country

The Code of Civil Procedure (CPC), 1908, under section 19 allows that a case may be instituted either in the jurisdiction in which the defendant resides or carries on business or where the tort was committed. This means that a publication in India could be accused of the hurting sentiments in any part of the country, and on that basis, a complaint could be lodged with the local police station of that area or a case could be filed in the local court, irrespective of the place where the author/publisher resided or where the work was published. So, if an author resided in Delhi, and such complaint or case was lodged against him/her in Mumbai, he/she would have to appear before the local courts in Mumbai for hearing. Take for example, the case of historian D. N. Jha's book *Holy Cow: Beef in Indian Dietary Conditions*. Even before the book was officially released, it became controversial due to its subject matter.[3] Jain Seva Sangh, a Hyderabad-based organization dedicated to the propagation and protection of Jainism, filed a civil suit against the author and CB Publishers, the publisher of the book, in a civil court at Hyderabad. The author, who was a professor at the University of Delhi, had to travel to Hyderabad to appear in the court to defend his position.[4] Similarly, in the controversy over NCERT textbook on history (discussed in a previous chapter, the petition was filed in Punjab and Haryana High Court, and historian Bipan Chandra, who was one of the respondents in the case and was based in Delhi, had to appear before the court at Chandigarh each time he was summoned. This legal provision therefore becomes a source of harassment. At times, as has been demonstrated by legal scholar Rajeev Dhavan (2008: 173), this legal provision is used consciously by non-state actors to put pressure on the author/publisher to either delete the controversial portions of the publication or withdraw the entire publication in order to escape the tedious legal process.

The Issue of Delay in Judgements

The amount of time each case takes in the Indian judicial process has been a significant concern for the justice delivery system.[5] In case of contentious publications, this delay also means that the relevance of the publication declines with time. In order to understand the delay in the courts, I examined a data set of 32 cases related to both punitive and preventive laws that appeared in High Courts and the Supreme Court during 1947–2010 (as explained in the introduction to Chapter 3) (see Table 4.1). These cases were related to publications that were deemed controversial owing to their comments on religious subjects. From the table given below, which indicates the date, month and year (based on availability) of government notification or registration of the case, and the date on which the respective High Court or Supreme Court delivered the final judgement in the case, it is clear that

Table 4.1 List of cases, primary statutory laws invoked in each case, year of issuance of notification, date of delivery of final judgement and time taken by courts in each case

S.No.	*Case*	*Section of IPC/ CrPC (Primary Charge as Invoked in Court)*	*Year of Notification/ Order of Arrest*	*Date of Final Verdict at High Court*	*Date of Final Verdict at Supreme Court*	*Total Time Taken in High Court*	*Total Time Taken for Judgement If Case Reaches Supreme Court*
1.	Shiv Ram Dass Udasin *v.* The Punjab State	99(A) {equivalent to 95 of current CrPC}	29/02/1952	05/04/1954	Not Applicable	2 years, 2 months	Not Applicable
2.	Ramji Lal Modi *v.* The State of UP	295(A) IPC	12/12/1952	25/10/1956	05/04/1957	3 years, 10 months	4 years, 4 months
3.	Harnam Das *v.* State of Uttar Pradesh	99(A) CrPC	30/07/1953	07/05/1957	27/04/1961	3 years, 10 months	7 years, 9 months
4.	N. Veerabrahm-am *v.* State of Andhra Pradesh	99(A) CrPC	23/03/1958	12/03/1959	Not Applicable	1 year	Not Applicable
5.	Baba Khalil Ahmad *v.*The State	99(A)	1956 (Only year mentioned)	20/04/1960	Not Applicable	4 years	Not Applicable
6.	The State of Mysore *v.* Henry Rodigues and Another	295(A)	January 1959	11/10/1961	Not Applicable	2 years, 9 months	Not Applicable
7.	Public Prosecutor *v.* P. Ramasami	295(A)	February 1961	16/10/1963	Not Applicable	2 years, 8 months	Not Applicable

8.	Mohammad Khalid *v.* The Chief Commissioner, Delhi	99(A)	27/11/1959	10/12/1962	02/03/1967	3 years, 1 month	7 years, 4 months
9.	Sant Das Maheshwari *v.* Babu Ram Jadoun and others	Writ petition under article 226	27/03/1961	06/02/1968	Not Applicable	6 years, 11 months	Not Applicable
10.	Ramlal Puri *v.* State of Madhya Pradesh	99(A) CrPC	28/09/1970	24/12/1970	Not Applicable	3 months	Not Applicable
11.	Chinna Annamalai *v.* The State of Tamil Nadu	Writ petition	12/02/1971	24/02/1971	Not Applicable	1 month	Not Applicable
12.	Babu Rao Patel *v.* State of Delhi	153(A) IPC	March 1968	14/08/1973	21/02/1980	5 years, 5 months	11 years 11 months
13.	State of Uttar Pradesh *v.* Lalai Singh Yadav	99(A) CrPC	08/12/1969	19/01/1971	16/09/1976	1 year, 2 months	6 years, 9 months
14.	Lalai Singh Yadav *v.* State of Uttar Pradesh	99(A) CrPC	26/08/1970	14/05/1971	Not Applicable	9 months	Not Applicable
15.	M/S Varsha Publications Pvt. Ltd. *v.* State of Maharashtra and Others	95 CrPC	31/07/1982	03/05/1983	Not Applicable	8 months	Not Applicable

(Continued)

Table 4.1 (Continued)

S.No.	*Case*	*Section of IPC/ CrPC (Primary Charge as Invoked in Court)*	*Year of Notification/ Order of Arrest*	*Date of Final Verdict at High Court*	*Date of Final Verdict at Supreme Court*	*Total Time Taken in High Court*	*Total Time Taken for Judgement If Case Reaches Supreme Court*
16.	Nand Kishore Singh and etc. *v.* State of Bihar and another	95 CrPC	29/10/1983	04/09/1984	Not Applicable	11 months	Not Applicable
17.	Chandmal Chopra *v.* State of West Bengal	Writ petition for proscription under sec 95 CrPC	March 1985	24/11/1987	Not Applicable	2 years, 8 months	Not Applicable
18.	Master Aman Preet Singh and others *v.* Govt. of India and others	PIL (Public Interest Litigation) for removal of content	January 1996	19/04/1996	Not Applicable	4 months	Not Applicable
19.	G. Jairaj and others *v.* State of Karnataka and others	Writ petition to apply section 95	June 1994	25/07/1997	Not Applicable	3 years, 1 month	Not Applicable
20.	Baragur Ramchandra-ppa and others *v.* State of Karnataka and another	95 CrPC	27/03/1997	16/04/1998	02/05/2007	1 year, 1 month	10 years, 2 months
21.	The Trustees of Safdar Hasmee Memorial Trust *v.* Govt. of NCT of Delhi	95 CrPC	21/08/1993	16/07/2001	Not Applicable	7 years, 11 months	Not Applicable

22.	Zac Poonen *v.* Hidden Treasure Literature	295(A) IPC	1998	27/07/2001	Not Applicable	3 years	Not Applicable
23.	Yashwant Venilal Sanghvi *v.* Sahdevsinh Dilubha Zala	295(A) IPC	January 2004	16/08/2004	Not Applicable	1 year, 7 months	Not Applicable
24.	Sujato Bhadra *v.* State of West Bengal	95 CrPC	28/11/2003	22/09/2005	Not Applicable	1 year, 10 months	Not Applicable
25.	State of Maharashtra and others *v.* Sanghraj Damodar Rupawate and others	95 CrPC	20/12/2006	26/04/2007	09/07/2010	4 months	3 years. 7 month
26.	R. V. Bhasin *v.* 2 Marine Drive Police Station	95 CrPC	09/03/2007	06/01/2010	Not Applicable	2 years, 8 months	Not Applicable
27.	Prasad Jacob (US citizen) *v.* State of Kerala	153(A) IPC	29/03/2010	06/04/2010	Not Applicable	1 month	Not Applicable
28.	Manzar Sayeed Khan *v.* State of Maharashtra	153(A) IPC	23/02/2004	06/05/2004	05/04/2007	3 months	3 years, 2 months
29.	Hulikal Nataraju *v.* State of Karnataka	PETITION-153(A) IPC	27/02/2006	13/09/2010	Not Applicable	4 years, 7 month	Not Applicable

(Continued)

Table 4.1 (Continued)

S.No.	*Case*	*Section of IPC/ CrPC (Primary Charge as Invoked in Court)*	*Year of Notification/ Order of Arrest*	*Date of Final Verdict at High Court*	*Date of Final Verdict at Supreme Court*	*Total Time Taken in High Court*	*Total Time Taken for Judgement If Case Reaches Supreme Court*
30.	Father C. R. Prabhu *v.* State of Jharkhand and another	PETITION-153(A) IPC	11/06/2010	09/04/2013	Not Applicable	2 years, 10 months	Not Applicable
31.	Maninder Singh and another *v.* State of Punjab and another	295(A) IPC	09/09/2010	02/08/2013	Not Applicable	2 years, 11 months	Not Applicable
32.	Piara Singh Bhaniara *v.* State of Punjab and another	95 CrPC	27/09/2001	11/11/2008	Not Applicable	7 years, 2 month	Not Applicable

on an average it took 2.43 years for the High Court to deliver judgement in all such cases, with an average of 2.35 years in cases under section 96 of the CrPC[6] (which is related to challenges against proscription orders of the state), and an average of 3.06 years for cases under section 295(A) and section 153(A) (both related to criminal charges against the author or the publisher). The time taken by the High Court varies from 1 month in a case to 7 years, 2 months. Similarly, if the case is further appealed in the Supreme Court, the average time taken for final judgement on the subject since the registration of case is 6.87 years. This data clearly reflects that the legal process is exhausting. The fact that in each case, the judgement of the court finally arrives after several rounds of hearings, where both plaintiff and accused need to be present, means that it is a constant source of difficulty for the author or publisher who wishes to defend himself/herself or his/her work. This process requires both – the expenditure on advocates who argue the case in the courts, as well as the loss of valuable time for the author/publisher, since he/she has to be present in the courts for the hearings – which as my evidence indicates, can continue for years.

The Functional Dimensions of the Legal Process as a Hurdle to Freedom of Speech and Expression

The issues discussed in the previous section are not unique to cases related exclusively to freedom of speech and expression, but form part of the legal process in general. The attempt is to show how these issues impact the author/publisher against whom the accusations are filed or who seeks to defend their publication against government's action. In the present section, I highlight the functional dimension of courts that act as impediments against cases related to contentious publications. Two aspects that have direct bearing on the discourse of freedom of expression include (1) low importance rendered to cases related to freedom of speech and expression by courts and (2) inconsistency in judgements, which creates confusion regarding precedent and a high degree of subjectivity.

The Court's Interest in Free Speech Cases

Abhinav Chandrachud (2012) in a study of free speech cases in the Supreme Court shows that these cases don't fall under 'high priority' status on the docket of the Supreme Court of India. Chandrachud undertook a quantitative study of 107 cases related to freedom of speech and expression under section 19(1)(a) until November 2011. His conclusions were based on a set of structural and behavioural observations related to the treatment of these cases in the apex court. Structural observations included aspects such as instances where the Chief Justice formed part of the judgement bench and the size of the panel that heard the cases. As is the general trend, the Chief Justice forms the panels for each case and includes himself in those panels that hear the cases of highest priority.[7] Chandrachud's study shows that Chief Justices have formed a part of the panel of judges in only 40.1 percent of cases related to free speech. The possibility that the Chief Justice forms a part of such a panel has significantly declined over the years – from 85.7 percent during the 1950s down to just 3.8 percent during the period 2000–2010. Similarly, Chandrachud shows that the size of the panel for hearing such cases is extremely small, and at most times it was a two-member bench that heard cases related to free speech (in 44.8 percent of cases). Constitutional benches of five or above are a rarity in such cases.[8] These observations conform to Nick Robinson and others' (2011) assessment about the size of Supreme Court benches in all cases related to constitutional subjects. While scholars tend to agree that the smaller size of benches could also be due to the increasing number of cases, they are unanimous in the view that whenever a particular case is held to be important, it is referred to a larger bench. The behavioural observations that Chandrachud gleans in his study include aspects like the judges' voting patterns in each case and the registry of concurring and dissenting opinions. A large degree of homogeneity and a smaller number of dissents or concurrence statements is traced back to the idea that the degree of deliberation is less compared to other cases and also seen as an indication that other judges concur with the senior-most judge's views, who is most often responsible for writing the judgement on behalf of the bench. Chandrachud shows that in 51.4 percent of case related to freedom of speech and expression, the senior judge writes the judgement on behalf of the bench, and only in 15.8 percent of cases do we find evidence of concurring judgements by other judges; in only 10. 2 percent cases were dissenting opinions registered. These findings of Chandrachud are indicative of the importance the apex court attaches to free speech cases. I applied a similar method to test if the conclusions reached were in conformity with studies of scholars like Robinson and Chandrachud. However, the data set – which included both Supreme Court as well as High Court cases – differed from studies by Robinson and Chandrachud because they examined only cases heard in the Supreme Court. Further, my study focused on only cases related to contentious publications on religious grounds, unlike Robinson, who provides a detailed study about constitution benches in the Supreme Court, or Chandrachud, who worked with all cases related to article 19(1)(a) of constitution.

My research suggests that Chandrachud's and Robinson's observations were indeed applicable even to free speech cases. For example, in the 32 cases (as reflected in Table 4.2), the Chief Justice formed part of the bench only six times, once in the Supreme Court and five times in High Courts. However, the conclusions about the size of the Court benches differ from other studies. Section 96 makes it mandatory that any case where the proscription notification of the government is challenged, a bench of three High Court judges will hear such pleas, and therefore most of the cases in the study consisted of three judges. But in other cases, the benches consisted of

Table 4.2 List of cases along with size of bench, presence of chief justice and whether it included opinion of judges other than the one who wrote the judgement[9]

S.No.	*Case & Year of Controversy*	*Sections of Statutory Laws Invoked*	*Size of Bench of Judges Hearing the Case*	*Was the Chief Justice a Part of the Panel? (Yes/No)*	*Whether Judges Other Than the One Writing Judgement Registered Their Concurrence/ Dissent?*
1.	Shiv Ram Dass Udasin *v*. The Punjab State (1954)	Section 99(A) (Currently section 95)	3	No	Yes. Only agreement, no explanation
2.	Ramji Lal Modi *v*. The State of UP (1956)	Section 295(A) IPC	5	Yes	No
3.	Harnam Das *v*. State of Uttar Pradesh (1957)	Section 99(A) (Currently section 95)	5	No	Yes. Each judge expressed his/her opinion and explanation
4.	Harnam Das *v*. State of Uttar Pradesh (1961)	Section 99(A) (Currently section 95)	3	No	No
5.	Baba Khalil Ahmad *v*. The State (1960)	Section 99(A) (Currently section 95)	3	No	Yes. Only agreement, no explanation
6.	N. Veerabrahmam *v*. State of Andhra Pradesh (1959)	Section 99(A) (Currently section 95)	3	Yes	Yes. Each judge expressed his/her opinion and explanation
7.	The State of Mysore *v*. Henry Rodigues and Another (1961)	Section 295(A) IPC	2	No	No
8.	Mohammad Khalid *v*. The Chief Commissioner, Delhi (1967)	Section 99(A) (Currently section 95)	3	No	No

(Continued)

Table 4.2 (Continued)

S.No.	*Case & Year of Controversy*	*Sections of Statutory Laws Invoked*	*Size of Bench of Judges Hearing the Case*	*Was the Chief Justice a Part of the Panel? (Yes/No)*	*Whether Judges Other Than the One Writing Judgement Registered Their Concurrence/ Dissent?*
9.	Public Prosecutor *v.* P. Ramasami (1963)	Section 295(A) IPC	1	No	NA
10.	Sant Das Maheshwari *v.* Babu Ram Jadoun and others (1968)	Section 295(A) IPC & Section 95	2	No	No
11.	Babu Rao Patel *v.* State of Delhi (1973) (in High Court)	Section 153(A)	1	No	NA
12.	Babu Rao Patel *v.* State of Delhi (1980) (in Supreme Court)	Section 153(A)	2	No	No
13.	State of Uttar Pradesh *v.* Lalai Singh Yadav (1976)	Section 99(A) (Currently section 95)	3	No	No
14.	Lalai Singh Yadav *v.* State of Uttar Pradesh (1971)	Section 99(A) (Currently section 95)	3	No	No
15.	Ramlal Puri *v.* State of Madhya Pradesh (1970)	Section 99(A) (Currently section 95)	3	No	Yes. Each judge expressed his/her opinion and explanation
16.	Chinna Annamalai *v.* The State of Tamil Nadu (1971)	Section 99(A) (Currently section 95)	3	No	No
17.	M/S Varsha Publications Pvt. Ltd. *v.* State of Maharashtra and Others (1983)	Section 95	3	Yes	No

(Continued)

Table 4.2 (Continued)

S.No.	*Case & Year of Controversy*	*Sections of Statutory Laws Invoked*	*Size of Bench of Judges Hearing the Case*	*Was the Chief Justice a Part of the Panel? (Yes/No)*	*Whether Judges Other Than the One Writing Judgement Registered Their Concurrence/ Dissent?*
18.	Nand Kishore Singh and etc. *v*. State of Bihar and another (1984)	Section 95	3	Yes	Yes. Each judge expressed his/her opinion and explanation
19.	Chandmal Chopra *v*. State of West Bengal (1987)	Section 95	2	Yes	Yes. Each judge expressed his/her opinion and explanation
20.	The Trustees of Safdar Hasmee Memorial Trust *v*. Govt. of NCT of Delhi (2001)	Section 95	3	Yes	No
21.	G. Jairaj and others *v*. State of Karnataka and others (1997)	Section 95	2	No	No
22.	Baragur Ramchandra-ppa and others *v*. State of Karnataka and another (1998) (in the High Court)	Section 95	3	No	No
23.	Sri Baragur Ramchandra-ppa and others *v*. State of Karnataka and another (2007) (in Supreme Court)	Section 95	2	No	No
24.	Master Aman Preet Singh and others *v*. Govt. of India and others (1996)	Section 95	2	No	No

(Continued)

Table 4.2 (Continued)

S.No.	*Case & Year of Controversy*	*Sections of Statutory Laws Invoked*	*Size of Bench of Judges Hearing the Case*	*Was the Chief Justice a Part of the Panel? (Yes/No)*	*Whether Judges Other Than the One Writing Judgement Registered Their Concurrence/ Dissent?*
25.	Zac Poonen *v.* Hidden Treasure Literature (2001)	Section 295(A), 505, 508 IPC	2	No	No
26.	Piara Singh Bhaniara *v.* State of Punjab and another (2008)	Section 95	1	No	No
27.	Sujato Bhadra *v.* State of West Bengal (2005)	Section 95	3	No	Yes. Each judge expressed his/her opinion and explanation
28.	Yashwant Venilal Sanghvi *v.* Sahdevsinh Dilubha Zala (2004)	Section 295(A), 505, IPC	1	No	NA
29.	Manzar Sayeed Khan *v.* State of Maharashtra (2007)	Section 153, 153(A), 34 IPC	3	No	No
30.	State of Maharashtra and others *v.* Sanghraj Damodar Rupawate and others (2010)	Section 95	2	No	No
31.	Hulikal Nataraju *v.* State of Karnataka (2010)	Section 153, 153(A) IPC	1	No	No
32.	R. V. Bhasin *v.* 2 Marine Drive Police Station (2010)	Section 95	3	No	No

(Continued)

Table 4.2 (Continued)

S.No.	*Case & Year of Controversy*	*Sections of Statutory Laws Invoked*	*Size of Bench of Judges Hearing the Case*	*Was the Chief Justice a Part of the Panel? (Yes/No)*	*Whether Judges Other Than the One Writing Judgement Registered Their Concurrence/ Dissent?*
33.	Prasad Jacob (US citizen) *v.* State of Kerala (2010)	Section 153(A) IPC	1	No	No
34.	Father C. R. Prabhu *v.* State of Jharkhand and another (2013)	Section 153(A) IPC	1	No	No
35.	Maninder Singh and another *v.* State of Punjab and another (2013)	Section 295(A) IPC	1	No	No

either one or two judges, with only two instances where the case was sent for hearing to a bench consisting of five members (both times in the Supreme Court in years 1957 and 1961). So, Chandrachud's observation that the sizes of benches hearing free speech cases are usually small is also borne out by my own findings. Similarly, his points about behavioural aspects were equally valid. It was found that only in five instances (all in the High Courts) did judges other than the one who wrote the judgment register their concurrence, and in only two instances (both in High Courts) did the other judges dissent. In only five such cases where the opinion was registered, it was supported by a detailed explanation of the judges' position. The list of cases where concurrence by other judges was registered includes: *Nand Kishore Singh*, *Shiv Ram Dass Udasin*, *Baba Khalil Ahmad*, *N. Veerabrahmam* and *Sujato Bhadra*. Out of these, in *Shiv Ram Dass Udasin* and in *Baba Khalil Ahmad*, only the concurrence of the other judges was registered, without any explanation. The two cases where a dissenting opinion was registered included one in the Andhra High Court by Justice Bheemshankaran in the *N. Veerabrahmam* case, and another in the Supreme Court by Justice Das Gupta in the *Harnam Das* case. In all other cases, judges preferred either to remain silent or were completely convinced by the opinion of the judge who wrote the judgement and his grounds for forming that opinion. The statement of concurrence or dissent is important because it helps us to understand why judges agreed or disagreed with the judge who pronounced the judgment. It can add to the description of the case and also suggest grounds on which the judgement was arrived. A complete silence on the part of other judges does not contribute to analysis of the judgement in any way, and also indicates that other judges might not have taken equal interest in the case as the judge who was expected to write the judgement on their behalf. So, based on earlier studies like those of Chandrachud and Robinson, and their appositeness to my own analysis, it is indicative that cases related to freedom of speech and expression do not invite particular interest from the judiciary.

The Problem of Conflicting and Confusing Precedents

One of the pressing problems related to the courts' position on freedom of speech and expression cases has been the issue of conflicting and confusing precedents. The 'doctrine of precedent' expects courts to provide a legal framework for individuals to plan their lives and take decisions based on settled laws. Absence of a settled precedence related to law invokes a context of confusion and doubt. Further, lack of coherence also undermines the rule of law whereby two litigants are not treated equally. This makes the operation of the law unequal and uncertain (Mehta 2005). The conflicting precedents in higher courts also cascade to lower courts and have significant impact on the decisions taken at the level of lower courts. Confusion and indeterminacy tend to produce two lines of precedents, which lead to unpredictability of outcomes of the cases. In the present section, I focus on this aspect of the courtroom and discuss the broad themes around which cases related with contentious publications are dealt with in the courtroom. The aim is to highlight the inconsistencies in judgements and their impact on freedom of expression.

The debates and decisions of courts on various cases of censorship can be categorized into two types. Firstly are the cases where the court looks into the procedural aspects as mentioned in section 95 of the CrPC. These include an examination of the operative part of the government's action as well as the scrutiny of the grounds on which the action was based. Secondly are cases where the court examines the validity and applicability of government's action in the light of the publication in question. This includes an evaluation of state government's order based on the evidence presented. It largely revolves around the questions of 'intention' of the author or *mens rea*, the nature of the subject dealt with in the book, and the assessment of the method employed in making sense of the book's contents. On all these above-mentioned grounds, courts have exhibited diverse opinions which have resulted in similar books meeting different fates. This has only served to increase ambiguity about a settled position. A more detailed analysis will show the range of variance.

The Operative Part of Government's Action

Courts have generally held that it is the prerogative of state government to decide whether a publication falls under the prohibitive sections or not. Making its position clear in this respect, the court in the *Sri Baragur Ramachandrappa* case held that as section 95 was preventive in nature, government could take action if it pre-empted any danger to public order and there was no need for the actual occurrence of such incidents. This attitude is also reflected in the cases of *Nand Kishore Singh* and *R. V. Bhasin*. But this freedom has been questioned in other cases citing section 95 of CrPC that warranted government issuance of notification for any ban or forfeiture. In such cases the content of the notification was closely examined to look at the 'application of mind' in the decision. But even in these cases there has been diverse opinion about what such notifications should contain. In different cases proscription and forfeiture orders were set aside, citing different reasons. For example, in the *Sanghraj Damodar Rupawate* case, the Supreme Court held that it was important to mention the grounds on which government formed the opinion for forfeiture. It maintained that the notification should also include a 'conclusion of facts' on which opinion was arrived so that courts could evaluate those facts to check the applicability of the decision (*Sanghraj Damodar Rupawate* Civil Appeal of 2010 [Arising out of S.L.P. {Cl No. 8931 of 2007]). However, in the *Mohammad Khalid* case, the Supreme Court had held that mere opinion or grounds of opinion were not enough. The objecting communities as well as the objectionable passages should also be clearly mentioned in order to substantiate the basis of such opinion formation, and any absence of such reference could lead to such notification being set aside (*Mohammad Khalid* A.I.R. 1968 Delhi 13). Quite contrarily, in the *N. Veerabrahmam* case and *Nand Kishore Singh* case, respective High Courts opined that though opinion should be mentioned, an absence of grounds of opinion cannot be reason for not proscribing the book. In each case it was argued that section 99-D (96 of the current CrPC) mandated the courts 'only to examine the correctness of any such order made by the government' based on evaluation of the content of the publication and not to determine the content of notification.[10] Therefore, it was held that mentioning the grounds of opinion could only be an indicative and not a conclusive aspect of the notification order. The above discussion highlights the absence of any set precedent in examining government's order for forfeiture of contentious publications.

The Evaluative Aspects of the Government's Decision

A second set of cases included those where courts evaluated the government's order in light of evidence. An important requirement of statutory laws like section 153(A) and 295(A) that govern freedom of expression in India is the presence of 'deliberate and malicious intentions' on the part of the author/publisher. Though courts broadly agree on the necessity of this clause, there are divergent views about how intentions could be extracted and what tests are to be employed for such examination. For example, in some cases, courts seem to hold that the whole book and not isolated passages should be taken into consideration while making sense of the intentions of authors/publishers (*Sujato Bhadra*, 39 A.I.C. 239; *Nand Kishore Singh*, A.I.R. 1986 Pat. 98). However, in other cases it was maintained that this did not prevent the state from taking decisions based on portions or isolated passages, the validity of which could be later judged by the court (*Sanghraj Damodar Rupawate*, Civil Appeal of 2010 [Arising out of S.L.P. {C} No. 8931 of 2007]).

On the question about how to gather the intention of author/publisher, in the *N. Veerabrahmam* case the Andhra High Court opined that 'intention of the author has to be gathered primarily from the language used'. It was similar to the position of Allahabad High Court in the *Baba Khalil Ahmad* case, which had ruled that if language was problematic, there was no need to look for any other evidences and that no defence could stand for vituperative and offensive language (*Baba Khalil Ahamad*, A.I.R. 1960 All. 715). In the *Sanghraj Damodar Rupawate* case, the court extended the test to examine the content of offending passages as well as their import. So, if passages were drawn from 'folklore, tradition or history something in extenuation could perhaps be said for the author', the judges held. In *Nand Kishore Singh* case, the court maintained that along with language, and the import of offending passages, the audience to which the publication was catered to should also be kept in mind. Similarly, in the *R. V. Bhasin* case the Bombay High Court reiterated that the recognition of the audience for whom the publication was written and published was equally important to identify the intentions of the author. Interestingly, in the *Nand Kishore Singh* case, the court had explicitly maintained that no other external evidence should be considered while judging the intention of the author/publisher. However, in the *Sujato Bhadra* case, the court's observations were drawn extensively from the external context about which the book had referred. The significance of external circumstances was also upheld in the *Manzar Sayeed Khan* case, where the Supreme Court held that the circumstances in which a book was written and published were one of the critical indicators of the author's intention (*Manzar Sayeed Khan v. State of Maharashtra* [2009] 12 S.C.C. 157). It would appear, therefore, that there are no fixed criteria about how to make sense of the intentions of the author, even though these are seen as an important aspect of law.

Further, in several cases courts have held that if intentions were proven to be deliberate and malicious, even the claims of truth and history could not be used as excuses to defend offensive writings. For example, in the *Sanghraj Damodar Rupawate* case, the Supreme Court observed:

> If the writing is calculated to promote feeling of enmity or hatred, it is no defence to a charge under section 153(A) of the IPC that the writing contains a truthful kind of past events or is otherwise supported by good authority. Adherence to the strict path of history is not by itself a complete defence to a charge under section 153(A) of the IPC.

Quite contrarily, the Bombay High Court argued in the *M/S Varsha Publications* case that these sections should not be extended so far as to affect historical research or writings criticizing religions. The court held:

> Different considerations will prevail when we are to consider a scholarly article on history and religion based upon research with the help of a number of reference books. It will be very difficult for the State to contend that a narration of history would promote violence enmity or hatred. If such a contention is accepted a day will come when that part of history which is unpalatable to a particular religion on the pretext that the publication of such history would constitute an offence punishable under S. 153A of the I.P.C.
>
> (*M/S Varsha Publications*, Cri LJ 1446)

Another test courts use to examine the validity of government's decision of proscription or forfeiture is that of 'reasonability'. It is based on the perception that impact of any publication should not be judged on the basis of reactions of a believer or an emotionally invested person; rather, the effect is 'to be judged from standard of reasonable, strong minded, firm and courageous' (*Sanghraj Damodar Rupawate*, Civil Appeal of 2010 [Arising out of S.L.P. {C} No. 8931 of 2007]). So, only works which are considered 'grossly offensive to reasonable man' should be eligible for proscription or forfeiture (*Shiv Ram Dass Udasin*, A.I.R 1955 P H 28). However, in the *Baragur Ramachandrappa*, case the Karnataka High Court made it explicit that 'we are concerned with [the] impact of the book on the minds of ordinary people with religious beliefs and not discerning intelligentsia'. Also, in the *Baba Khalil Ahmad* case, the court opined that if the content was insulting to some sacred figure, it naturally led to a feeling of offence for its followers and hence the content itself should be the guide in the subject.

The above discussions show that the jurisprudence relating to ban and forfeiture of publications has been chaotic, to say the least, and leaves considerable room for subjectivity of judges (Dhavan 2008: 145). In similar cases, courts have employed quite different yardsticks and have come up with starkly opposite and irreconcilable conclusions. Such inconsistency has significant consequences, both in terms of principles as well as practice. Its impact on the principle of precedents has already been discussed. In practical experience, it encourages non-state actors to exert pressure on government officials to issue ban orders. In the absence of a clear mandate on the subject, the magistrate and other officials consider it better to act against the publication, the validity of the action being left to be decided later in the court. Dhavan views this as 'problem solving' politics, whereby, the government 'solves' the problem of social pressure by imposing the ban, and the court later provides the 'legal' solution by taking decision on the ban (2008: 144). The lack of clarity in the judiciary's position also encourages non-state actors to file criminal cases against authors/publishers in the hope that the court's verdict could run in their favour. From the perspective of the author/ publisher, both these strategies are particularly intimidating. There is a constant fear of loss of civil liberty, punishment, and even imprisonment. Add to this the tiring legal process including the duration for a verdict, which may take decades, and the whole experience in itself can be like a punishment. Even after all that, one can never be sure about which side the court's decision would go. The tough and exhaustive legal battle in the judiciary, where free speech cases are not high in the docket of cases and which works in the context of a lack of conclusive precedent, can have a lasting impact on the experience of authors/publishers defending their freedom of expression (Liang 2012; Narrain 2016b). This also creates an environment of fear and uncertainty where authors/publishers often choose to desist from such engagement and instead give in to the demands of protesting groups either by removing controversial sections or by pulping the publication itself. The case of Wendy Doniger's *The Hindus* is an explicit example of this phenomenon.

Pulping of Wendy Doniger's *The Hindus: An Alternative History*: A Case Study

On 10 February 2014 the district court in Delhi accepted the settlement agreement between Penguin Books India Pvt. Ltd. and Dina Nath Batra[11] of Shiksha Bachao Abhiyan Samiti. After a legal battle that lasted four years, the publishers of the book, in an out-of-court settlement, succumbed to the demands of Batra. Penguin agreed to 'recall and withdraw' all copies of the book from Indian territory with immediate effect. It also promised that it would pulp all the 'recalled/withdrawn/unsold copies of the book' at their own cost. In return Batra agreed to withdraw all civil/criminal cases/complaints filed against the author or the publishers of the book.[12]

The ordeal surrounding Doniger's book *The Hindus* began in 2010 when Saraswati Research and Education Trust started an online petition claiming that the book contained factual errors about the historical past as well as vilification of Hinduism.[13] It highlighted 16 factual errors, including distortion of maps, mistakes in historical accounts and bibliographic inaccuracies among others. It also cited eight passages which it claimed to be highly derogatory, defamatory and offensive to Hindus. These concerns were reiterated in a legal notice sent by Batra to the author and publishers of the book in the same year.[14] He charged the author and publishers of the book of consciously misrepresenting the Hindu religion by quoting passages from religious books out of context, distorting facts and providing wrong information. He further claimed that the author also promoted obscenity and vulgarity through images and writings in the books, which were aimed to vilify Hinduism. Doniger's approach to the question of religion, Batra argued, was that of a 'woman hungry of sex' and the book was written with a 'Christian missionary zeal and hidden agenda to denigrate Hindus and show their religion in poor light'. The notice asked the author and the publisher to seek an 'unconditional apology', 'withdraw the said objectionable parts from book' and 'undertake not to offend the religious sentiments of the Hindus in future'. Failing that, he warned 'legal action under section 153, 153(A), 295(A), 298, 505(2) of IPC' would be initiated and that he would further ask Hindus to 'boycott the books published by Penguin Books India Pvt. Ltd'. When no action was taken in response to the legal notice, Batra took the author and publishers to court and filed several civil and criminal suits against them.[15] After battling the court cases for more than four years, the publishers finally decided to give in to Batra's demands.

The settlement agreement was criticized by several scholars and intellectuals as surrender by the book company to radical conservative forces, thereby weakening the battle for freedom of speech and expression.[16] But here I am concerned with only the debates surrounding legal aspects of the case. Penguin's submission to legal pressure generated by Batra indicates the complex role that law and the legal process play in the discourse of censorship. On the one hand, it highlights how law and the legal process could be used as legitimate tools for censorship by those claiming hurt sentiments, and on the other hand, it also shows the vulnerability experienced by authors and publishers when such pressure is exerted. In the process, the practical limits of the theoretical debates surrounding freedom of speech and expression were clearly exposed.

The Role of Law and the Legal Process in Penguin's Surrender

It was not the first time that Dina Nath Batra was using a legal route to censor historical work he considered objectionable. In 2008, Batra on behalf of Shiksha Bachao Andolan Samiti (SBAS) moved to the Delhi High Court, requesting it to issue orders to University of Delhi to remove A. K. Ramanujan's essay titled *Three Hundred Ramayanas: Five Examples and Three Thoughts on Translation* from its history syllabus taught at the undergraduate level.[17] Judges at the High Court decided not to interfere in the subject as it was an internal matter of the university and also because, according to them, the court lacked the capacity to judge academic matters. The plea was therefore rejected. But Batra filed another civil suit in the Supreme Court. Hearing the matter in July 2010, the Supreme Court asked the university to set up an expert committee competent to look into the matter. This eventually led to the removal of the essay from the syllabus.[18]

So, Batra had previous experience with how to use legitimate legal means to enforce censorship. Unlike the violent mob that threatened authors or vandalized bookstores, Batra claimed to be a law-abiding citizen, and expressed it to be his legal right to raise objections and bring it to the notice of the government and judiciary if anything denigrating his religious beliefs was published and circulated. Batra's legal counsel, Monika Arora, justified his act in an article written in *Organizer*, the mouthpiece of RSS. Arora argued that the Indian constitution did not allow for unlimited freedom of speech and expression and that 'reasonable restrictions' could be imposed, which were to be defined on case-to-case basis by the judiciary (*Organizer*, 23 February 2014). She claimed that Batra was right in bringing such cases to the judiciary and left it upon the judges to take decision about the future of such controversial publications. It is evident that people like Batra use law as a potent weapon in their battle against publications they consider hurting their religious sentiments. In fact, just after his success in the Doniger case, Batra reportedly sent similar legal notices to other publishers regarding other books that he thought were offensive to Hindus.[19]

An equally important aspect related to such incidents of censorship is the effectiveness of legal methods. When the case of settlement between Penguin and Batra became public, legal scholars and practitioners criticized the company for succumbing to legal threats and presented two sets of arguments about why the step was completely unnecessary. On one hand, some scholars argued that provisions of Indian law under which civil and criminal charges were registered did not even apply to the case. It was therefore liable to be summarily rejected by the courts. Noorani claimed that Batra was able to win the battle 'with a toy gun' (*Frontline*, 4 April 2014). He and other commentators like V. Venkatesan (*Frontline*, 7 May 2014) believed that Penguin did not receive the right legal guidance on the subject because, as Noorani held, 'the High Court is there to ensure such a dismissal even if the District Judge or the Magistrate or the police did not follow the law. If not the Supreme Court would have surely done that'. They opined that instead of surrender, Penguin should have continued the legal battle. Another set of legal scholars, like Saurav Datta, claimed that if Penguin would not have given up, it would have been assured of a legal victory, if not in the lower courts than at least in the Supreme Court (*DNA*, 4 March 2014). To substantiate his point, Datta used cases from the Supreme Court where it had handed judgements in favour of authors/publishers in similar cases.

The issues raised by both sets of commentators are significant, but the arguments that were offered by either do not seem convincing. One of the primary limitations of their analyses is that it completely overlooks Penguin's point of view. Further, these arguments, especially in the context of Penguin's action, missed some important facts. Take, for example, Datta's claim that 'the courts have [a] long tradition of protecting freedom of speech by upholding the right to express divergent and alternative views on religions even if they rile a majority of believers'. It was hailed and cited uncritically by various other scholars and journalists.[20] Datta's conclusions, however, are based on selective analysis of court cases, and suffer from a severe misreading of facts in cases that he cites as evidence for his conclusions. In the last chapter, I have shown how courts in India have favoured proscription of books claimed to be offensive to religious sentiments of different communities, and therefore Datta's position that Penguin was assured of a legal victory if they would have continued the legal battle is far from reality. Even if one agrees that criminal charges could not stand in the court of law as it would have been difficult for the counsel of the plaintiff to show 'deliberate and malicious intentions' of the author/publisher, nevertheless the civil suit could still go against them. Further, as discussed earlier in this chapter, given the fact that courts have been inconsistent in terms of doctrines used to decide each case, it is quite difficult to predict whether or not the courts would have upheld the criminal charges.

Coming back to arguments of legal scholars like Venkatesan and Noorani, we see that though it is difficult to comment whether Penguin was misled by its legal advisors, it is clear that its fear was more than just about court's position on criminal charges levelled against the author and the company. This is evident from the statements released by Doniger and Penguin India Ltd. in response to the criticism they faced after the settlement agreement. It was maintained in both responses that uncertainty over interpretation of section 295(A) was one of the primary reasons for their out-of-court settlement with Batra. Doniger called statutory laws 'the true villain' in the case, as they threatened to 'jeopardize the physical safety of any publisher, no matter how ludicrous the accusation brought against a book'.[21] The company feared that 'the Indian Penal Code, and in particular section 295(A) of that code, will make it increasingly difficult for any Indian publisher to uphold international standards of free expression without deliberately placing itself outside the law'.[22] The concern was not only with the vague and broad language used in such a law but also the ambiguity over its probable interpretations in the courts. Doniger and her publisher, Penguin, were equally worried about the ambiguity of the legal process. Doniger argues that in Indian context 'if you got the wrong judge ... you'd be convicted just for publishing a statement that you had good reason to believe might well offend someone'.[23] Penguin, on its part, pointed out that it was obligated to respect the law of land, 'however intolerant and restrictive those laws may be', but at the same time, it was also committed to protect its employees from threat and harassment. Therefore, it maintained that the decision to settle the matter after four years of legal battle was justified. Although the act was seen by many legal commentators as surrender to radical forces, the reasons forwarded by the company point to insecurities that the author/publisher faced in the absence of robust institutional structures for protection of their freedom of speech and expression.[24]

Doniger's was not an isolated incident where legal notices from groups claiming hurt sentiment had forced significant changes in the attitude of publishers. For example, in September 2008, while a case was filed in the Delhi High Court to order the removal of A. K. Ramanujan's essay from the history syllabus being taught at undergraduate level, the SBAS also served a legal notice to Oxford University Press (OUP), India, the original publisher of the essay in an edited volume, asking them to stop printing the essay.[25] The OUP not only apologized for the fact that the essay had hurt religious sentiments of Hindus, but also gave assurance that the essay was no more in print, nor did the publishers have any intentions of reprinting it.[26] Also, in case of James Laine's book *Shivaji: Hindu King in Islamic India*, the publishing house had promised, even before the case reached court, to stop printing and withdraw the publication from market due to fear of legal action against it.[27] Similarly, in case of D. N. Jha's book *Holy Cow: Beef in Indian Dietary Tradition*, the publisher, CB Publishers, refused to publish the book, due to fear of further prosecution or controversy, even after the civil court in Hyderabad lifted its stay on the publishing of the book.[28] The concern guiding each such publisher's decision to withdraw or pulp a book is almost the same, that is, to protect themselves from entering the vortex of a legal process which harms their interest both financially as well as in the form of intimidation through criminal charges against its employees.

Conclusion

It is evident from above discussion that both law and legal process can act as hurdles in the free exercise of freedom of speech and expression by creating an environment of fear of retribution. This eventually encourages what Cook and Heilmann call 'public self-censorship'. Public self-censorship is a phenomenon where the censor and the censee are two different agents 'and where the censee censors him or herself in response to this external censor' (Cook & Heilmann 2013: 186–187). Cook and Heilmann differentiate 'public self-censorship' from 'private self-censorship' based on absence of an external censor in the later case: the censor and the censee therefore being the same agent. In the case of Doniger's book, it was explicitly a case of self-censorship, where the publisher decided to pulp the book, without any such direction from either governmental institutions or the judiciary. However, in this case there were two sources of external censors. First of all, there was Dina Nath Batra, who threatened by filing civil suits and criminal charges against the author and the publisher; and second, law and the legal process played the role of another censor by creating an atmosphere of uncertainty and prolonged distress. As the external sources were not situated in any form of government order for a ban or the judiciary's pronouncement in the case, it cannot be seen as a classic case of censorship. The role of law and legal process as external sources for censorship in this case cannot be put into the same bracket of overt forms of censorship[29] (Cook & Heilmann 2013: 180–183), as it had less to do with the stated position of the law in the constitution or statutory books or even the settled interpretation of the law by the judiciary, and much more to do with the ambiguity produced by the language of the law as well as the fluctuating position of the judiciary in such cases. In Doniger's case, the decision to pulp the book by Penguin as the censee was a response to its interaction with external sources of censorship. This phenomenon precisely reflects the pressures exerted by law and the legal process in the struggle for freedom of speech and expression in the Indian context.

Notes

1 The idea of a 'slippery slope' has been an important argument for claiming extreme freedom in relation to speech and expression. It assumes that if laws are made to constrain such freedom, they can be misused in different ways to hurt the core of the value enshrined in freedom of speech and expression.

2 Dhavan uses the phrase 'process as punishment' to explain how the long legal process harasses authors/publishers/painters who are targeted by the socio-religious groups, who in the name of hurt sentiments create hurdles for their freedom of expression (Dhavan 2008: 223). The sense of alienation from the legal process is reflected in the fact that some authors/publishers, as in Wendy Doniger's case (discussed later in the chapter) agree for an out-of-court settlement of the issue with the non-state actors.

3 The book discussed, with the help of historical evidence, how beef had been an essential component of Indian dietary habits since ancient times; and this practice, he argued, was present among all religions, including Hinduism, Jainism and Buddhism. Before the book was released, a Member of Parliament from the BJP, R. S. Rawat, wrote to the union Home Ministry demanding a ban on the book and the arrest of the author and publisher. See, 'Book on Beef Eating Runs into Trouble', *The Hindu*, 9 August 2001.

4 Sheela Reddy, 'A Brahmin's Cow Tales', *Outlook*, 17 September 2001. The court issued a temporary stay on the publication of the book. Though the stay was lifted after a year of judicial process, the publisher, fearing further controversy, and prosecution, refused to publish the book. As a result, Jha had to look for another publisher, and the book was published later by London-based Verso publishers, under a new title, *The Myth of the Holy Cow*.

5 This is not unique to cases related to freedom of expression. There have been various reasons cited for such delay, like the number of judges in the judiciary, among others. For details on such concerns, see Law Commission of India's 77th Report titled *Delay and Arrears in Trial Courts*, November 1978, available at lawcommissionofindia.nic.in/51-100/report77.pdf (last accessed 28 June 2018. Also see Robinson [2011: 27] and Chandrachud [2011: 71–78]).

6 Note that the maximum time allowed for a complainant to file a case against the government's notification for forfeiture is two months from when the notification order is made public.

7 Robinson and others argue that the apex court in India is 'Chief Justice–dominant' and highlights the important role that the Chief Justice plays in the court (2011: 31).

8 As article 145(3) of the Indian constitution suggests, the 'minimum number of Judges who are to sit for the purpose of deciding any case involving a substantial question of law' has to be five.

9 The data set is of 32 cases. However, the difference in serial number is because in three cases, I have also included the data of the same cases appearing both in the High Court as well as Supreme Court. Years mentioned in table are according to the year the final judgement was delivered.

10 This position was also upheld by Justice Das Gupta in his dissenting note in the case of *Harnam Das*, 1961 A.I.R 1662.

11 Dina Nath Batra is a retired schoolmaster who now heads Shiksha Bachao Andolan Samiti (SBAS), an organization that claims to be dedicated to protecting Indian values and reforming the Indian education system. It is considered to be very close to the RSS.

12 The copy of the settlement agreement was widely available. The one here is taken from, www.outlookindia.com/article/penguin-to-withdraw-the-hindus-an-alternative-history/289467 (last accessed on 27 June 2018).

13 The online petition was started by Saraswati Research and Education Trust and addressed to the CEO and the president of Penguin Group. It was launched on the website www.petitiononline.com. However, the website has not been functional since 30 September 2014. But the content of the online petition and the attached letter can be found at www.outlookindia.com/article/the-book-promotes-prejudices-and-biases-against-hindus/289472 (last accessed on 27 June 2018).

14 Legal notice sent by Dina Nath Batra to Wendy Doniger, Penguin Group (USA) Inc. and Penguin Books India Pvt. Ltd., dated 3 March 2010 and Ref. No. 254/LN/0310 is available at www.outlookindia.com/article/your-approach-is-that-of-a-woman-hungry-ofsex/289468 (last accessed on 27 June 2018).

15 Batra pursued two forms of legal pressure building – civil and criminal. He filed a complaint under criminal charges at Hauz Khas Police Station on 29 April 2010 and another in 2013. On 19 March 2010 he also brought a civil suit in the Saket District Court at Delhi (No. 360 of 2011).

16 There were diverse reactions on the episode. Some commentators claimed it to be another case of an attack on the freedom of expression by radical fundamentalist forces. See Kenan Malik, 'Changing Landscape of Free Speech', *The Hindu*, 12 February 2014; Ratna Kapur, 'Totalising History, Silencing Dissent', *The Hindu*, 15 February 2014; 'Narrowing Horizons: Withdrawal of Doniger Book Highlights Sway of Taliban-like Forces in India', *The Times of India*, 13 February 2014. However, most commentators believed that it was surrender by the company against such forces that was an important matter of concern. The incident was followed by several public statements signed by scholars and academicians criticizing Penguin for the act. See for example, 'Statement on Withdrawal of Wendy Doniger's Book Issued by Centre of Historical Studies, JNU', available at kafila.org/2014/02/21/chs-jnu-statement-on-the-wendy-doniger-issue/ (last accessed on 27 June 2018); 'SAHMAT Statement on Wendy Doniger's Book', available at www.sacw.net/article7666.html (last accessed on 27 June 2018); Sridharan and Cerulli (2014: 274–276).

17 See *Dina Nath Batra v. University of Delhi Laws* (DLH) 2008-7-180, decided on 19 July 2008. Also see A. A. Mahaprashta, 'The Rule of Unreason', *Frontline*, 5 November 2011.

18 'Delhi University Scraps Ramanujan's Essay on Ramayana', *Deccan Herald*, 13 October 2011.

19 On 3 March 2014 Batra sent legal notice to Aleph Books demanding that the book company should withdraw another book by Wendy Doniger, titled *On Hinduism*. See 'Doniger's Book *On Hinduism* Put on Hold', *The Indian Express*, 11 March 2014. In May 2014, he also sent a legal notice to an academic publisher to halt the release of Megha Kumar's book *Communalism and Sexual Violence: Ahmedabad since 1969*. See 'Another Publisher Forced to Censor Textbooks', *The Hindu*, 3 June 2014.

20 See, for example, Sethi & Sengupta (2014: 290–299); Pallavi Polanki, 'Censorship by Other Means, Dinanath Batra Shows the Way', available at www.firstpost.com/india/censorship-by-other-means-dinanath-batra-shows-the-way-1560243.html (last accessed on 27 June 2018).

21 See Wendy Doniger's statement released by PEN India, available at www.outlookindia.com/article/i-do-not-blame-penguin-books-india/289473 (last accessed on 27 June 2018).

22 See 'Penguin India's Statement on *The Hindus* by Wendy Doniger', available at http://www.penguinbooksindia.com/en/content/penguin-india%E2%80%99S-statement-%E2%80%98-hindus%E2%80%99-wendy-doniger (last accessed on 27 June 2018).

23 See Wendy Doniger, 'India: Censorship by the Batra Brigade', *New York Review of Books*, 8 May 2014, www.nybooks.com/articles/archieves/2014/may/08/india-censorship-batra-brigade/ (last accessed on 27 June 2018).

24 This concern was also reflected by commentators like Pratap Bhanu Mehta and Shivprasad Swaminathan. Mehta held that the courts have consistently failed to protect liberal values like freedom of speech and expression and therefore have led to the silencing of 'liberal India'. See Pratap Bhanu Mehta, 'Silencing of Liberal India', *The Indian Express*, 12 February 2014. Swaminathan on a similar line showed that if the potential benefits are pitted against the hazards, the authors and the publishers ought to prefer some form of censorship in order to protect themselves from the distress surrounding legal actions. See Shivprasad Swaminathan, 'Scribblers, Scholars in the Same Boat', *The Hindu*, 25 February 2014.

25 SBAS served a legal notice to Oxford University Press in relation to the book edited by Paula Richman (1991).

26 In the Supreme Court the advocate of the publisher assured the court about this in 2010. See 'When a Department Let the University Down', *The Hindu*, 3 November 2011.

27 James Laine's book *Shivaji: Hindu King in Islamic India* was banned in Maharashtra after some Hindu groups from Maharashtra protested against it. Later the Supreme Court lifted the ban. See *Sanghraj Damodar Rupawate* Civil Appeal of 2010 (Arising out of S.L.P. [C] No. 8931 of 2007).

28 The author and the publisher faced several threats during the controversy. Jha's property was also vandalized by unknown assailants. For complete reporting of the events, see Sheela Reddy, 'A Brahmin's Cow Tales', *Outlook*, 17 September 2001.

29 Overt forms of censorship here refer to the censorship imposed by state institutions directly. Normally laws limiting freedom of expression form part of the tools used by the state to regulate speech acts. However, in cases like those mentioned here, laws do not act directly to restrict free speech.

5

NON-STATE ACTORS AS CENSORS

The Legal Position

The last two chapters discussed the attitude of courts in India towards freedom of speech and expression in general, and with regard to contentious publications in particular. It was observed that lacunae largely associated with the functioning of the courts and the ambiguities reflected in its judgements have proved counter-productive for defenders of free speech. It has resulted in not only creating an atmosphere of uncertainty and fear among authors/publishers but has also acted as a source of encouragement for people demanding censorship of publications, based on their claims of religious offence. It can be claimed that the institution of the judiciary, which was established by constitution makers as the ultimate defender of civil and fundamental rights of the citizens – especially freedom of speech and expression – has allowed curtailment of this important right in the garb of legal language and constitutional interpretations. Though some judgements seem to uphold freedom of expression, courts' general attitude of defining the limits of freedom of expression vis-à-vis public order or other values that it considered important for Indian society has resulted in producing a public context which cannot be considered favourable for free exercise of freedom of expression.

This chapter shall examine cases related to censorship where government, the judiciary and non-state actors interact. The process through which social forces collude with state power often renders subordinate the role of courts in the politics of censorship. To highlight this aspect, I focus on two types of cases: (1) cases where the use of statutory laws like the Customs Act renders an immunity to the decision of government and (2) cases where the prevailing atmosphere forced the author/publisher to censor controversial writing regardless of the fact that court had found nothing objectionable in the text and hence revoked the official ban on the book. In each of these cases we see an active role played by non-state actors (which include socio-religious groups as well as political parties). Although the main arena of contestation between claims of religious offence and freedom of expression remained outside the courtroom, demands of censorship predominantly used the language of law as its legitimizing source.

 DOI: 10.4324/9781003369257-6

Trivializing the Role of the Court in the Politics of Censorship

The role of courts in censorship is significantly limited by the existence of laws that protect the executive's decisions from judicial scrutiny. For example, the Customs Act[1] is one of the notable laws that government uses to prevent import of any publication that it presumes will create problems in the country or that may be in bad taste according to the government. Historically, this law has been used to stop the import of propaganda material, political manuscripts and also publications on religion which, according to the government, have the potential to create unrest among any section of the population.[2] In many such cases, the government's act goes unnoticed as it does not become part of the popular discourse nor does the news get appropriate mediation. As early as 1956, Nehru's government decided to ban the import of Aubrey Menen's *Rama Retold*, which was believed to contain material that could hurt the sentiments of the Hindus in the country.[3] The use of the Customs Act to prevent entry of any publication in the territory of India reflects a paternal attitude on behalf of the state, where it decides for its citizens which material is readable and which could instigate sharp reactions. One of the significant cases of censorship where the Customs Act played a role was the ban on Salman Rushdie's *Satanic Verses*. The banning of *The Satanic Verses* raised several moral and normative questions about religious offence and freedom of expression, which became the subjects of intense debates within political theory. However, here I primarily discuss the debates on the subject from the perspective of law and the role played by non-state actors.

Banning The Satanic Verses *and Public Debate over Law*

Much before the formal launch of the book, there were apprehensions about the probable impact it could have on Indian readers. Khushwant Singh[4] advised the publishers of the book, Viking Penguin, not to publish the book in India as he feared that the content of the novel, especially satirical references to the Prophet and his wives, would not be received in good spirit by the country's Muslim audience. Before the launch of the book, an interview with the author, Salman Rushdie, along with some extracts from the book were published in two popular journals.[5] Syed Sahabuddin, the Member of Parliament (MP) from the Janata Party, along with other prominent Muslim representatives like Khurshid Alam Khan[6] brought the interviews of Rushdie and the extracts published in *India Today* to the notice of the government.[7] They feared that the book might create communal disturbances in the country and therefore requested that the book be banned. The Rajiv Gandhi government felt that the concerns were reasonable and hence the ban order was passed on 5 October, 1988 under section 11 of the Customs Act, which prevented any import of the book into India.[8]

The call for the ban incited controversy. It was argued that government had succumbed to demands of Muslim politicians and showed disregard for freedom of expression and misuse of the legal provisions. Some legal luminaries argued that the Customs Act did not contain any provision to ban a book on the basis of religious insults. For instance, Soli Sorabjee remarked that the law 'curiously does not impose any ban on books which insult religion or offend religious sentiment of the people, as have been erroneously assumed in some quarters'.[9] However, an official statement by the government maintained that the ban under section 11 of Customs Act (1962) was a 'pre-emptive step' to avoid 'misrepresentation' of passages of the *Satanic Verses* for 'political purposes', which it feared could lead to a public-order problem. It further held that the order did 'not detract or otherwise reflect on the artistic or literary worth of the book or its author'.[10] The government presented it as a judgement based on public-order concerns rather than on the merits or contents of the book and held that although a ban under the Customs Act was immune from any challenge in the judiciary, the decision could be justified in the public realm as pragmatic and well within the constitutional limits set for freedom of expression under article 19(2).[11]

The decision to ban the book initiated a public debate about the state of freedom of speech and expression in India. One section raised issues about the intentions of government, as it appeared that it had succumbed to pressure from some Muslim politicians.[12] The demand for the ban was raised by influential Muslim legislators and ministers, like Shahbuddin and Khurshid Alam Khan, and government was accused of responding to such demands simply to distract public attention, as well as to regain the confidence of India's Muslim population, which was lost due to its position in the Ayodhya case.[13] As a result, it was claimed by those who opposed the ban that the decision of government was arbitrary and it lacked cogent justification for imposing the Customs Act.[14] Though it was not the first time that a book was banned in India, the case of Rushdie attracted international attention owing to polarized reactions on the subject the world over. This included a fatwa by a Muslim cleric in Iran for beheading Rushdie, and an explicit position taken by governments across countries like Britain of not banning the book despite pressure from Muslim communities.[15]

On the contrary, the supporters of the ban invoked both moral as well as legal arguments. They appreciated the role of government in the entire episode and lauded it for protecting the constitutional spirit of secularism and multiculturalism.[16] Support for the ban was broadly based on three sets of arguments. The first argument was that the vilification of religious personalities contained in the book could hurt religious sensibilities. Sahabuddin argued that insulting the respected figures of Islam could not be a part of satire, and any act of casting aspersions on such pious symbols could not be tolerated. He commented:

> You depict the holy Prophet ... as an imposter and you expect us to clap for you. You have the diseased mind and the evil pen to situate the wives of the holy Prophet ... the mothers of the community, in a brothel and you expect the Muslims to prove your power of imagination.[17]

The second argument was that the book could ignite religious sensibilities, and could lead to rioting and communal disturbances. This was in contradistinction to Rushdie's belief that 'no book can cause riots'.[18] This claim was effectively rebutted by Khushwant Singh, who remarked that Rushdie was 'naïve' to think that way because Indian history was full of cases where hurt sentiments had led to communal mobilization culminating in violence and riots.[19] The third argument forwarded in support of the government's action was about violations of Indian laws. It was argued that the demand for the ban as well as the government's decision were not based on abstract principles or force; rather, they had firm support from within the legal structure of the country and were therefore justified. Salman Khurshid, a prominent Congress leader and also a lawyer, charged Rushdie with defying 'Indian laws relating to obscenity and religious practice'.[20] Laws under the IPC were quoted along with the Customs Act to convey the point that if Rushdie had been present in India, he could even be convicted under sections 295(A) and 153(A).[21] So, overall the book was found objectionable by those supporting the ban of the book on three grounds: it was considered to be 'a crime against human decency'; 'an insult to Islam'; and 'an offence under Indian law'.[22] Two lessons from the episode are significant. Firstly, it exposed the limits of courts when laws like the Customs Act are invoked by government. Though it was claimed that the book violated the law, the validity of the claim could not be tested as such laws provide immunity to government orders from being challenged in courts. Secondly, it had shown that government could be forced to order a ban on publications in the name of hurt sentiments and threats to public order. This aspect was crucial as it threw light on the role of non-state actors in censorship.

The binary created between freedom of expression and protecting the interest of religious communities in the name of the state's role in a multicultural society persisted even after *The Satanic Verses* episode. In fact, in certain cases the binary became more acute with a more direct role of non-state actors. This phenomenon was visible when Taslima Nasreen, the Bangladeshi author, was physically attacked, and under pressure from socio-religious groups, she agreed to delete controversial portions from her novel *Dwikhandito* regardless of the fact that the High Court had found nothing objectionable in it. This case not only uncovers the complexity of censorship debate in the Indian context but also shows how censorship has often become a tool for instrumental politics among the stakeholders.

The Curious Case of Dwikhandito *and the Role of the Courts*

The book *Dwikhandito* was the third volume of Nasreen's autobiographical series and discussed the author's multiple sexual relationships with some of the most prominent authors and poets both in Bangladesh and India during her youth. It first came to public scrutiny when the West Bengal High Court passed an injunction on the publication, sale, marketing and circulation of the book after a defamatory suit was filed by Syed Hasmat Jalal, one of the figures with whom Nasreen had claimed sexual relations in the book. The government of West Bengal banned the book only a week after this injunction order. Some Muslim organizations like Jamiat Ullema-e-Hind and All India Minority Forum (AIMF) had also complained about the book. They had claimed that certain passages contained insults against the Prophet and Islam.[23] Justifying the ban, Chief Minister of West Bengal, Budhadeb Bhattacharjee, said, 'I've read the book, not once but several times. I've discussed the contents with 25 people who matter and have finally decided to proscribe it.'[24] The government argued that if the book were not banned, 'it could ignite communal tension'.[25]

As in Rushdie's case, criticism of the government's decision came from those who believed that it had submitted to the demands of extremists. Some critics believed that the reaction of government was not based so much on fear of communal violence as on Nasreen's reference to sexual relationships with prominent personalities of Bengal, who as it happened were also close to the Left Front government leaders of Bengal.[26] Nasreen expressed shock at the ban order. She argued that there was nothing 'in the relevant pages of the book that might cause riots'. 'Also'. she pointedly asked, 'is it correct to underestimate Muslims so much? Are Muslims so ignorant, illiterate, intolerant, and convertible when faced with any kind of criticism about their religion?'[27] However, government had decided to ban the book, and the decision was actively supported by other major political parties. They believed that the book contained perversions of the teachings of the Quran and hence would give sustenance to anti- Islamic views. Further, it was claimed that adjectives used for the Prophet were not in good taste.[28]

A human rights activist from Kolkata, Sujato Bhadra, appealed the ban in the High Court. After almost two years, the court lifted the ban from the book, on 22 September 2005. The court's observations were crucial. It held that the intention of author, 'who herself profess[es] the same religion has to be gathered from the context of the book'.[29] It further maintained that though the book contained harsh language against the Prophet, there was no deliberate and malicious intent on the part of the author of *Dwikhandito* to outrage the religious feelings of any class of citizens of India because 'the insult to religion was not the central theme of the book, read as a whole'. It also opined that if the insult to religion is in good faith in 'his/her endeavour or object to facilitate some measure of social reform by administering such a shock to the followers of the religion, as would ensure notice being taken by any criticism so made would not attract the mischief of section 295(A)'. As the author was dealing with the specific situation in Bangladesh 'which was a theocracy and not India, which is a secular country', the court did not find any deliberate or malicious intent to hurt religious sentiments of Indian citizens. Though the court came to the defence of Nasreen's freedom of expression, one might see it as a case of 'overindulgence' with the text. For example, the court overlooked the insulting references to the Prophet because it believed that the subject of the book itself was not based on them. Further, the emphasis laid on the context rather than content was questionable, as it did not say anything about the possible fate of the text if the narrative was based in the Indian context. The observation that the author was dealing with a situation specific to Bangladesh, 'which was a theocracy and not India, which is a secular country', gives an impression that the court would have dealt with the book differently if it discussed a similar situation in India. The judgement of the court was therefore largely prescriptive. In the absence of a principled position, as discussed in earlier chapters, it remained open to interpretation in other cases. The stress placed upon the context also seemed to imply that the court did not believe that freedom of expression could be an absolute right. However, once the court held that there was nothing objectionable in the book and rejected the ban order against it, legality of her book was established beyond doubt. The state government also did not pursue the case further by either filing a review petition or pleading at the Supreme Court.

Muslim Groups and Nasreen's Submission

The controversy reignited four years later, in August 2007, during the release of the Telugu translation of another novel, *Shodh*, when Nasreen was physically attacked by a group led by three legislators of the Majlis-e-Ittehadul Muslimeen (MIM). The attackers justified their act by arguing that she could not be allowed in Hyderabad because of her objectionable writings against Islam and the Prophet.[30] The anger was primarily with respect to *Dwikhandito* which was first published in 2003 and had remained controversial since then. Interestingly, Nasreen also wrote a few articles in *Outlook* magazine in January 2007, where she criticized Muslim society for imposing a restrictive way of life on women, especially by insisting on *purdah*, and also on the Quran for enjoining such impositions. The issue caught the attention of Muslim organizations all over India, and Muslim organizations in Kolkata organized a protest against her visa extension. There was a general feeling that her attack on Islam and other religious symbols had consistently demeaned Muslims. Protests culminated into city-wide rioting on 21 November 2007.[31] Responding to the situation, government planned her secret escape to Rajasthan, and from there she was later shifted to Delhi, where she stayed in a safe house for 110 days before leaving for Sweden.[32]

In the context of charged Muslim sentiments, no political party was in a position to explicitly support Nasreen. It was the ruling Left Front government of West Bengal that decided to deport Nasreen, and the Congress-led central government provided the required logistics. The state government defended its action by maintaining that they respected individual freedom and rights, 'but it does not mean a person can hurt the sentiments ... and abuse religion'.[33] Jyoti Basu, the top leader of the ruling CPI(M) commented, 'No Muslim will stand the way she criticized the Quran and the Prophet. That is why we banned her book *Dwikhandito*.'[34] A statement was issued in the Parliament on 28 November 2007 by the Minister of External Affairs, Pranab Mukherjee, who made it clear that though government would continue to provide shelter to Ms. Nasreen, it was expected that the 'guests will refrain from activities and expressions that may hurt the sentiments of our people'.[35]

Consequently, Nasreen asked her publishers to withdraw the controversial parts from *Dwikhandito*. She issued a note that said:

> I have withdrawn some parts of my book *Dwikhandito*. Some said parts of the book were hurting the sentiments of the people. I hope after its withdrawal, there would be no more controversies.... The decision to withdraw these parts from *Dwikhandito* is to prove that I never wanted to hurt the people's sentiments.[36]

This decision was seen as an apology and welcomed by different parties, including non-state actors that were involved in the controversy.[37] Siddiqullah Chaudhary, General Secretary of the Jamiat Ullema-e-Hind, one of the prominent Muslim organizations involved in the controversy, said: 'This is a good step and we are happy that good sense has prevailed. If she had taken this step before, then a lot of conflict could have been avoided.'[38] Even Jyoti Basu issued a statement expressing that she could return to Kolkata.[39] Given the surrounding political circumstances, Nasreen's decision to delete controversial portions from her book was seen by authors, journalists and other members of the civil society, who only a few days earlier had organized a massive rally in Kolkata in her support, as forced censorship and a setback to the struggle for freedom of expression.[40]

The events leading to Nasreen's decision to herself delete controversial sections raises some important issues regarding censorship. The incidents at Hyderabad and Kolkata in 2007, which themselves qualified as crimes, produced a context where the legality of the book, even when pronounced by the court, was of no rescue to the author. The sentiment of hurt made visible in the streets of Kolkata was silenced with an act of self-censorship, where the court had no authority to sit on judgement.

This was not an isolated case in the history of censorship in India. There were other cases as well where the court in its legal submissions found nothing wrong with a publication, but social pressures forced the author to censor his/her writing. Another notable case was the withdrawal of *Agnipariksha* (The Test on Fire) from public circulation by its author, Acharya Tulsi, a Jain monk, in 1970. In September 1970, Acharya Tulsi, a respected and popular Jain preacher, reached Raipur[41] to stay at the Anuvrat Ashram[42] during the holy period of *chaturmasa*.[43] During one of the sessions of a discourse on 16 September, he referred to his work *Agnipariksha*, which was recently published and was based on Jain version of Ramayana. He was particularly referring to some episodes where the character of Sita[44] was questioned. This caught the attention of some orthodox Hindus, who claimed that such references had offended their religious sensibilities and demanded apology from the spiritual leader. Later it was argued that certain couplets were vulgar and profane and were designed to cast aspersions on Sita's character. The confrontation rapidly escalated, and there were demands for banning the book and Acharya's exit from Raipur. The following months saw a massive campaign against Acharya, led by Sanatan Dharma Sabha, a prominent Hindu organization in the area. The Sabha observed an 'anti-acharya week' during which massive protest demonstrations were organized and *hartals* (strike) and *bandhs* (closure) were held. Effigies of the Jain leaders and copies of the book were also burnt in Raipur.[45] Though the state government tried to control the situation, protesters defied the prohibitory orders and violated section 144,[46] which was imposed in the city. There were also reports about some individuals sitting on fast, demanding a ban of the book.[47]

Acharya Tulsi promised an unconditional apology if anyone could show mistakes in what he had said. He also maintained that the book did not contain any vilification as claimed by the protestors, but only an interpretation of the story as present in Jain tradition. He even offered to leave Raipur if that would restore peace. Under pressure from the protestors and in view of the fact that the law-and-order situation was continuously deteriorating, with reports coming in of demonstrations taking violent forms in several instances, state government issued notification for banning of the book and forfeiture of all copies available under section 99(A). The protestors had succeeded in preventing circulation of book in Madhya Pradesh.

The publisher of the book and its sponsor approached the court against forfeiture and ban orders of state government. The full bench of the Madhya Pradesh High Court heard the case and delivered its judgement on 24 December 1970. The court set aside the impugned order, arguing that grounds on which state government had based the order of forfeiture did not exist. The Advocate General representing the case argued that couplets used in the book were objectionable, as they hurt the sentiments of Sanatan Hindus. The applicants on the other side argued that the order contradicted their fundamental right to freedom of expression and freedom of religion as guaranteed under article 19(1)(a) and article 25 of the constitution.

The court maintained that the state had every right to interfere with fundamental rights, as both – freedom of expression and freedom of religion – were conditional to public order.[48] However, after a close reading of the controversial couplets, the court concluded that it could not find anything 'grossly offensive or provocative matter', nor did the court 'visualize any deliberate and malicious intention on the part of the author to outrage the religious feelings of Sanathani Hindus'. Both these basic requirements to charge a work under section 295(A) were found to be absent. Delivering the judgement, Justice Tare noted:

> People may have their own views and it cannot be denied that there have been different versions of Ramayana through the ages which have been prevailing at least for more than 2500 years and it may be that different people might give a version which might serve their purpose. But a propagandist version, which does not come within mischief of the law, can in no case be considered to be objectionable.[49]

The court, therefore, came to the rescue of the book against the order of the state government, and its comments on freedom of expression and freedom of religion were truly significant. The court held that such rights were subject to government's understanding of the situation at a practical level. Hence, though the order of forfeiture was set aside, the right of the state government to act in the way it did was upheld. Yet, even after the forfeiture notification was quashed by the High Court, the author decided to withdraw the book from public circulation, as it had initiated conflict among different groups, which was not his motive in writing the text.[50]

The act of censorship in cases of Nasreen and Acharya Tulsi cannot be captured through its conventional lens of understanding. There is no doubt that government was involved in banning the texts, but it is equally true that courts had come to the rescue of the author/publisher. So, the decision either to remove controversial passages of the book or the text from public circulation does not qualify as a fit case of state censorship. It also does not fall into the category of what modern theories of censorship have called 'new censorship' – a concept derived from the writings of Foucault and Bourdieu (Post 1998: 1). The category of 'new censorship' equates the phenomenon of state censorship with all other forms of censorships like that of the market (Post 1998: 4). Consequently, the analytical rigour of the concept of censorship is diluted as it becomes extremely difficult to locate the agency of the censor in such acts of censorship. But in the above-mentioned cases, the censors can be identified clearly. The decision of the authors remains primary in both cases. So, it can be seen as a case for self-censorship. But it is important to view such self-censorship as a consequence of interrelated events rather than arising from the independent judgement of the authors. In the cases of Nasreen and Acharya Tulsi, the pressures exerted by different non-state actors, including political parties, created an atmosphere where the act of censorship occurred. The dominance of a particular discourse defined what could or could not be allowed in the public sphere. This type of censorship is closely related to the category of 'public self-censorship' discussed in Chapter 4, where the censee decides to censor him/herself, but the main agent enforcing the decision stays outside the agent.

In the cases of Nasreen and Acharya Tulsi, the interplay between state and non-state actors is also clearly visible. Interventions by non-state actors compelled state agencies to respond, and as a result authors/publishers seem to be caught in a web of censorship that tests their potential to fight back. In such cases, courts are the only institutions to which the author/publisher can turn for respite. However, if the authority and views of courts are undermined in strategic ways, as occurred in these two cases due to fear of social forces, in practice the scope of freedom of speech and expression is severely limited. Political willingness to respect the position of court becomes crucial. In the above cases, even though the courts held that the publications did not contain anything objectionable according to law; government did not do enough to protect the publications from harm caused by the actions of non-state actors. In fact, it colluded with the non-state actors at different moments, as visible in the case studies. However, it cannot be claimed that government cannot resist the attack on publications. If government wants, it can restrain attempts by non-state actors to impose their will when the court has pronounced its judgement in a case. A clear example of this was the controversy in the *Sachchi Ramayana* case.[51] The text *Sachchi Ramayana* was banned in Uttar Pradesh in 1969, after which the Supreme Court held the notification order null and void on technical grounds. When the demand for its banning resurfaced in 2007, a demand led by the opposition parties in the Legislative Assembly, the Bahujan Samaj Party (BSP) government under the leadership of Chief Minister Mayawati used the court order as pretext to counter the demands.[52]

In the Indian context, the act of censorship is predominantly devised by means of an instrumental logic for the government. The legal landscape related to censorship gives primary importance to the judgement of the government in using laws. It is expressed both in the provisions of statutory laws as well as court judgements. It is assumed that the state, being the custodian and protector of law and order, would take fair decisions based on the merits of the case. However, as has been evident in the cases discussed in this chapter, the state has emphasized the need to protect the sentiments of different communities from hurt, primarily because there is a feeling that these emotions could result in public-order issues. It is further visible that collective mobilization in the name of hurt sentiments has the capacity to exert pressure on the state to act against a controversial publication. This pressure could either be asserted through public display of hurt sentiments, which includes protest and demonstrations (as in the case of Nasreen), or through the channels of political leadership (as in the case of Rushdie), or through threats of causing disruption to public order, including the use of violence (as in the case of Acharya Tulsi). The ambiguity that was reflected in the state's relationship with communities gives identity-based claims to censorship precedence over the individual's freedom of expression. Political mobilization of religious sentiments, a phenomenon that developed during the anti-colonial movement, continued in the times of electoral politics, after India became independent.[53] In the context of growing constraints developed by the pressure of highly competitive electoral democracy, no political party, either in government or in opposition, takes the risk of not attending to the claims of hurt sentiments as presented by socio-religious groups or other non-state actors (Dhavan 2008: 151; Jaffrelot 2010: 305). As there is no way in which the claim of hurt sentiments can be quantified – either in terms of the actual number of people hurt by the offensive publication, or the nature of the hurt caused – there is a constant fear that such controversy might take larger shape and affect the fortunes of political parties by diminishing their electoral support. Therefore, these parties prefer to act on claims raised by socio-religious groups about religious offence rather than to protect the individual's freedom of speech and expression.

The role of non-state actors discussed in this chapter appears to be essentially against freedom of speech and expression. It seems that non-state actors impose their will by exerting pressure, either on the state agencies or directly upon the author/publisher. But are all forms of intervention by non-state actors unjustified, or against the ethos of a democracy, where freedom of expression is held to be an important value?

The Debates over Censorship in India and the Role of Non-state Actors

A significant concern for scholars of free speech in India is the role of non-state actors (Bhowmik 2003: 3148–3152; Ghosh 2004: 453; Liang 2004: 439; Noorani 1999: 2898). Non-state actors, especially socio-religious groups, resort to both legal as well as extra-legal methods to exert pressure on the government to act against a publication (Ghosh 2016: 60). This includes mobilization and protests against a text,[54] its author[55] or publication house,[56] public burning of a book,[57] or even a physical attack on the author.[58] The legal recourse includes filing writ petitions against the author or the publication house or against the book itself. In fact, legal practitioners and scholars like Dhavan (2008) and Noorani (1995) maintain that in India free speech faces a much bigger threat from social censorship than state censorship. However, there are two significant problems with regard to this understanding about the role of non-state actors in censorship. First, there is a general tendency among scholars to relate the phenomenon of vocal and explicit forms of intervention by non-state actors (which includes the use of violent means) quite tightly with the period of growth of Hindu nationalism, especially in the late 20th century (Bose 2006; Ghosh 2004; Kapur 1996). Second, these scholars consider any form of intervention by non-state actors, either legal or extra-legal, as unwarranted. Unfortunately, these estimations are based on overly broad generalizations. For example, even if we were to agree with the claim about the connection between explicit forms of intervention exhibited by non-state actors and the rise of Hindu nationalism in the late 20th century, it does not explain convincingly some crucial aspects attached to social censorship: (1) considering that Hindu nationalism is not a new phenomenon in India, it fails to explain why social censorship took the shape it did, in the later part of 20th century; and (2) it also fails to explain why it did not remain a Hindu nationalist agenda, as we see similar kind of mobilization and protests in response to Taslima Nasreen in West Bengal and in the Akali's response[59] to the interpretations of Adi Granth in Punjab. As we have seen earlier, in Chapters 1 and 2, intervention by non-state actors on claims of religious offense is not at all a new phenomenon. Group mobilization on the subject of hurt sentiments was witnessed even before independence, particularly in the late 19th and early 20th centuries, and has since then remained a social reality in India. In fact, scholars like Gilmartin (1991) have shown how mobilizations of these kinds formed an alternative 'public' during colonial rule. Analysis of censorship after Independence also gives a similar picture, where claims of hurt sentiments were not only used to exert pressure on government to censor controversial texts but were also considered as a legitimate and democratic form of engaging with the government.[60] Nor is it the case that these mobilizations and protests were always non-violent in nature. Examining the controversy over the book *Living Biographies of Religious Leaders* (as shown in Chapter 2) and *Agnipariksha* (as discussed earlier in this chapter) reveals that explicit or even violent forms of intervention by non-state groups are not a late 20th century phenomenon, and they also cannot be directly linked to the growth of Hindu nationalism, as claimed by most scholars.[61]

The second issue is whether all forms of intervention by non-state actors is symptomatic of depleting space for democratic values. One mistake that scholars who hold this view arguably commit is to assume the primacy of freedom of speech and expression, over all other rights.[62] Further, these studies use a teleological approach to judge the intentions of non-state actors based on the consequences of such interventions, that is, the use of litigation or protest by any non-state actor as means to impose their viewpoint. It is argued that even if non-state actors take the legal route, it leads to harassment of the author/publisher and, therefore, restricts the exercise of freedom of speech and expression.[63] Some of these assumptions and conclusions need reassessment. First, as courts have held in their various judgements, freedom of speech and expression does not enjoy any primacy over other rights, including the right to religion, and therefore courts have maintained that it is the duty of state in a multicultural and secular society, like India, to balance conflicting claims based on such rights.[64] Second, on the subject of intervention by non-state actors, the practice of demonstrating or protesting against a publication claimed to be offensive or demanding the state act against such publications needs to be differentiated from other modes of expressing dissent, like those involving any form of violence, which is legally prohibited in any democratic set-up. Both these roles should be viewed differently, even if both have a tendency to restrict the scope of freedom of speech and expression, as the two modes of intervention by non-state actors exhibit a marked difference in both form and content.

There are primarily two ways in which non-state actors intervene through the legal structure. The first is by registering formal complaints in the local police station against contentious publications or mobilizing and demonstrating against the publication to express their hurt sentiments, in order to exert pressure on the state officials to act. The second mode of engagement is by filing petitions against such publications or taking part in the judicial process by filing affidavits in the court supporting the government's decision to seize or forfeit contentious publications. Although in each of these forms of participation, non-state actors play a dominant role, the ultimate decision of censorship rests with the courts. Note that even if state authorities register a formal complaint and decide to act against the publication in question, the author/publisher or any other affected party can under section 96 of CrPC approach the court against such action, and the judiciary can then decide the legality and validity of such action by state authorities. The primary responsibility to act in such cases is that of state authorities, and they are expected (as reflected in various observations of the courts) to act rationally, judging the situation based on the principles of proportionality.[65] However, even if state authorities falter in their decision-making, there is the judiciary to take the final call on such acts of censorship. Therefore, harassment caused to an author/publisher in the process is to be attributed to laws and legal process, as discussed in this chapter, rather than intervention by the aggrieved groups.

Forms of intervention that include using legal mechanisms or even use of protests and demonstration to attract the attention of the government authorities against contentious publications are considered – both by the state as well as the judiciary – as democratic and legitimate rights of citizens. However, there is an important caveat attached to this formal recognition of the democratic rights: such protests and demonstrations should not be violent in any form. The position of the state is reflected in the reaction of Prime Minister Nehru and other leaders during the controversy of the *Living Biographies of Religious Leaders*.[66] Though most leaders deplored the use of violence in the protests that followed the controversy, they were not critical of the subject of the protest itself. Not only Nehru, but even K. M. Munshi,[67] against whom most of the protests were directed, recognized that the claim of religious offence by the protesting Muslims was of a genuine concern. Therefore, the book was set aside as soon as the demands were raised without any form of engagement with the subject-matter under contention. Nehru, in his fortnightly letter to the Chief Ministers wrote:

> I can understand people objecting to some passages in that book and drawing attention to them. But, there was something much deeper, and it was obvious that mischief was afoot and had been deliberately organized. The offending passages were broadcast in cyclostyled papers by the very persons who objected to them.[68]

The real concern of the leaders was about the continuation of the protests, even after the demand for removal of the book was accepted. A clear demarcation was being proposed between claiming democratic rights, like the right to protest and demonstrate, and the illegal use of violence or incitement to violence for the purpose.

The position of the judiciary on the subject of the use of a legal route by non-state actors to express their grievances can be gathered from courts' interpretation of statutory laws, particularly section 95 of the CrPC, which deals with the power of the government officials to proscribe or forfeit controversial publications.[69] Courts have insisted that government officials should mention in the notification (issued for seizure or forfeiture of such publication) the details about the groups or communities offended, the reason for them to feel offended and how the officials reached a rational conclusion that forfeiture of the publication was necessary. The nature of the complaint registered or protests and demonstrations organized by the socio-religious groups in order to attract the attention of state officials towards their grievances are legally recognized by courts as valid grounds on which officials could justify their decision to act against the controversial publication. It can therefore be argued that these forms of intervention are held by courts as an important indicator for officials to form a conclusive opinion about whether action is required in a particular case or not.

On the other hand, the use of violence and threats to cause disturbance to public tranquillity as a means to impose censorship by non-state actors does severely limit the scope of freedom of speech and expression. As evidence suggests, these threats or use of violence have regularly forced authors and publishers to succumb to demands of non-state actors, even after courts held that the publication did not contain anything that could be legally considered offensive.[70] The use of both these means is illegal[71] and against the values of democracy. Courts have also been vigilant about non-state actors' use of threats and violence to impose censorship. They have held that the threat of disruption of public order by such groups is a violation of law and should be strictly dealt with by law-enforcing agencies.[72] Further, courts have also taken serious note of the fact that state authorities relent to the demands of non-state actors, and act erroneously at times under pressure from these groups, as in the case of threats to public order. In the *S. Rangrajan* case,[73] the Supreme Court held that the state could not plead its inability to contain violent protestors. It is the duty of the state, the court maintained, to protect freedom of expression from attack from such groups. This position was reiterated in the court's judgement in *M/S Prakash Jha Productions* case.[74] Recently, in the *S. Tamilselvan* case, related to Perumal Murugan's book,[75] the Tamil Nadu High Court raised serious objections on the way state authorities, in an attempt to maintain peace, relented to the pressure exerted by protesting groups. Though it maintained that it was the duty of state authorities to maintain law and order in their area, a 'threat to peace' could not be used as a reason for compromising anyone's freedom of speech and expression. It also noted that 'merely because a group of people feel agitated … it cannot give them a license to vent their views in a hostile manner, and the state cannot plead its inability to handle the problem of a hostile audience'. The court has also specified a preferred procedure to be followed by state authorities while dealing with any controversial publication, if the claims about it being offensive are raised by socio-religious groups. Three points of the preferred guidelines are indicative of the approach of court: (1) 'There is bound to be a presumption in favour of free speech and expression as envisaged under article 19(1)(a) of the Constitution of India unless a court of law finds it otherwise falling within the domain of a reasonable restriction under article 19(2) of the constitution of India. This presumption must be kept in mind if there are complaints against publications, art, drama, film, song, poem, cartoons or any other creative expressions'; (2)'the state's responsibility to maintain law and order would not permit any compulsion on the artistes concerned to withdraw from his/her stand, and non-state players cannot be allowed to determine what is permissible and what is not'; and (3) 'The state has to ensure proper police protection when such artistes come under attack from a section'. The court has clearly stated that non-state actors cannot define the limits of a constitutional right, such as the right to speech and expression, and that courts are the sole authorities to decide what constitutes 'reasonable restrictions' as defined by the constitution. In the cases discussed above, it is clear that courts have exhibited a zero-tolerance approach towards the use of violence or a threat to public-order disruptions by these groups. They have further established that though it is the duty of state to maintain public order, freedom of expression of any artist or author cannot be compromised in the name of a threat to public order and that the state should deal strongly with groups that threaten disruption to public peace. It is evident from the above discussions that the two forms of intervention by non-state actors – legal and extra-legal – are essentially different in their form and content. It also has a different impact on the legal space defined for the freedom of speech and expression. In the previous form of intervention, courts are able to intervene and determine the reasonability of the action by state authorities; whereas the later form of intervention is not only illegal, the non-state actors take upon themselves to determine the permissibility of an expression.

This distinction also helps to respond to the claims of the scholars on censorship, who believe that the presence of statutory laws governing freedom of expression allows non-state actors to impose their will, by harassing the author/publisher, and on this basis, they demand that all such laws be repealed (Ghosh 2004; Liang 2004).[76] Such claims are largely based on an assumption about the 'slippery slope' tendency of laws. On the one hand, it assumes that all claims of religious offence are essentially targeted against the author/publisher and hence against the democratic values of freedom of speech and expression, and on the other hand, there is the assumption that if statutory laws are removed, it will end the arbitrariness attached to censorship due to the intervention of socio-religious groups. However, both these assumptions seem to be faulty. The assumption that all the claims of religious offence are ploys to impose the viewpoint of the non-state actors seems to overlook or ignore that some of these claims may actually be genuine. The only institution that can judge these aspects is the judiciary, and scrapping laws will only limit the powers of the courts to intervene. As Saba Mahmood (2009) and Tariq Modood (2005) have shown, some religious beliefs and practices define the identity of the religious communities, and if these beliefs or symbols are denigrated, they will feel offended. These feelings can take the form of demonstrations and protests, and in the absence of legal recourse, there are increased possibilities that these forms of expression of grievances turn aggressive.[77] Further, removal of statutory laws would also increase the arbitrary role of state officials. These officials could use other available laws to their discretion and could proscribe publications or arrest authors/publishers at will, in the name of preventing issues related to public order. After all, repealing laws governing freedom of expression does not disarm the officials of powers to act in such situations. So, unlike the assumptions of the scholars discussed above, repealing statutory laws may prove counter-productive and may, in fact, add to the threats to freedom of speech and expression and its free exercise.

A significant exception, however, are laws like the Customs Act, which was used by the government to ban import of publications like *Satanic Verses*, as the nature of these laws puts such bans beyond the purview of the judiciary. In cases like that of *Satanic Verses*, if non-state actors are able to exert pressure on government, they can get a publication banned, and even the judiciary cannot come to rescue these publications. Though this exception is significant and requires a rethink on the part of lawmakers, repealing all statutory laws is not the solution to intervention by non-state actors. The right approach would be to argue for more vigilant government machinery and a system of judiciary that is able to restrain mala fide intentions of non-state actors, and at same time take care of genuine grievances.

Conclusion

The examples of *The Satanic Verses*, *Dwikhandito* and *Agnipariksha* indicate that role of courts is made ineffective in the politics of censorship, where on the one hand, use of laws like the Customs Act places government's decision outside the purview of the court's interference, and on the other hand, the general atmosphere of violence and threat renders even positive interference by courts meaningless. Furthermore, provisions restricting free speech in Indian context (like section 295[A] and 153[A[) are classified as cognizable offences. This means that authorities can arrest suspects without judicial sanction. At the same time, there have been cases where government takes the role of mediator between conflicting claims (those of religious offence and freedom of expression) and reaches for an out-of-court solution while the case is still sub-judice.[78] Though government is well within its power to look for amicable solutions, it indicates the limits of court's intervention in such matters. The Tamil Nadu government's position during the controversy related to the movie *Viswaroopam*[79] is one such example. The problem is that in an attempt to find solutions, government often manages different claims in such a way that freedom of expression is compromised. The settlement, though claimed to be 'amicable', opens doors for more possibilities to assert the claim of hurt religious or communitarian sensibilities leading to a virtual curb on authors'/artists' freedoms. So, considering these cases, can we conclude that the role of the courts is of no use, and does not contribute at all in our understanding of freedom of expression in India? There are two ways to look at this issue. One approach is provided by Gautam Bhatia (2016), where he argues that a study of the role of court remains important as laws are used or misused because the laws exist, and despite several constitutional challenges, courts have not ruled against these laws. So, we need to understand why these laws are considered important by the courts. Secondly, Bhatia is optimistic about a situation when law and practice 'is not as cavernous' as in present times. So, it is essential for those future situations that a critical understanding of the application of these laws is understood. Another way to look at the subject is that though courts have not controlled the direction of free speech debate in India, they have always remained an important stakeholder, and their observations have guided the debates outside. Lack of consistency and procedural complexities, as discussed in the last chapter, remain a problem, but the authority of court has in many cases protected the fundamental right of expression from attack of both state and non-state actors. It is therefore an important institution, which still enjoys the confidence of citizens as the protector of their fundamental rights. This in itself is a reason good enough to not dismiss the role played by courts in the debates around censorship and free speech.

On the subject of intervention by non-state actors in the process of censorship, the two forms of interventions – one that follows the legal route and the other that is extra-legal, and includes use of threat and violence – need to be viewed differently. Both of these interventions are different in form and content. To consider both as unwarranted in a democracy would be to close all doors for even genuine expression of grievances. This distinction helps us to be more sensitive regarding the concerns of religious communities, about offensive publications, and at the same time, ensure that proper judicial scrutiny takes place before any form of censorship is enforced. It would further help in reducing arbitrariness in the process of censorship, a complaint that scholars on censorship in India consistently make, particularly with regard to the involvement of non-state actors.

Notes

1 Section 11 of the Customs Act allows for prohibition of import of any material, including publications, for maintenance of public order, standards of decency and morality and also for any other purpose conducive to the interest of public order.

2 Books whose import to India was banned under the law included *Pakistan-Pasmazarwa Pashmanza* (1950); *Cease Fire* (1950); *What Has Religion Done for Mankind* (1954); *Captive Kashmir* (1958); *The Heart of India* (1959); *Nine Hours to Rama* (1962), among others. Some of these were considered demeaning to the image of India, and others were material for political propaganda. The list of books to be banned from import owing to their commentary on religion included the likes of *Marka-e-Somnath* by Maulana Muhammad Sadiq Husain and Sadiq Siddiqui (1952), *Ayesha* by Kurt Frischler (1963) and *Early Islam* by Desmond Stewart (1975), among others.

3 Aubrey Menen's *Rama Retold* was one of the earliest books to be banned in independent India in 1955 on this ground. Menen's was a satirical work and dealt with the characters of Ramayana in a very different way than as in the popular discourse.

4 Singh was a well-known literary figure in India. The publishers of *The Satanic Verses*, Penguin, approached him for comments on the book six months before its formal release.

5 The interview with Madhu Jain was published as 'My Theme Is Fanaticism', *India Today*, 15 September 1988; Interview with Sharbani Basu was published as 'Of Satan, Archangels and Prophets', *Sunday*, 18–24 September 1988.

6 Khurshid Alam Khan was a minister in the Rajiv Gandhi government and a prominent Muslim leader of the Indian National Congress.

7 'The Day After', *Sunday*, 6–12 November 1988.

8 'Book Banning, Philistinism and Freedom of Expression', *Frontline*, 15 October 1988. Interestingly, *Satanic Verses* was released on 26 September 1988 in the UK, and advance copies had reached India soon afterwards. However, the government's notification only prevented the importation of copies of the book to India and did not say anything about the copies that had already reached Indian territories. So, even today, possession or reading of the novel in India is not legally banned.

9 Soli J. Sorabjee, 'Ban on Rushdie's Book: A Pernicious Precedent', *The Indian Express*, 14 October 1988.

10 Official statement as presented in 'Book Banning', *Frontline*, 15 October 1988.

11 This argument was also forwarded by Buta Singh, the Minister of Home Affairs. While answering one of the queries on the subject in Rajya Sabha, he justified the ban by arguing that 'the contents of the title were likely to be detrimental to the maintenance of public order'. Though legislator B. Satyanarayan Reddy had also asked about the objectionable material found in the book, the Minister chose to evade the question. See *Rajya Sabha Debates*, 3 November 1988, pp. 41–42.

12 Rushdie wrote an open letter to Rajiv Gandhi in this regard, which appeared in several news dailies. See Appignanesi & Maitland (1989: 42–45). He believed that the step of the government was senseless as his work was about a secular person's view on the ideas of religion and revelation. See '"A Senseless Step," says Rushdie', *The Times of India*, 8 October 1988.

13 Ayodhya is the place in Uttar Pradesh where it is claimed that Rama the Hindu deity was born. At the site of his birth, it was claimed that Babar, the Moghul king, had forcefully constructed a mosque after destroying an age-old temple. The Union government of Rajiv Gandhi had decided to open the doors of the deserted part of the temple so that prayers could be offered by Hindus. It created an atmosphere of tension that culminated in the destruction of the Babri Mosque by Hindu groups in 1992.

14 It was reported in several foreign newspaper of the time. For example, *The Independent*, under the title 'Rushdie Novel Banned in India' on 6 October 1988 reported: 'The Indian government, bowing to pressure from Muslim groups, yesterday banned Salman Rushdie's latest book.' A letter signed by 21 prominent arbiters led by Dom Moraes and Adil Jussawala was sent to the Prime Minister of India, Rajiv Gandhi, on 20 October 1988.

15 The details of the case and the reactions world over have been extensively discussed in Appignanesi and Maitland (1989) and Pipes (1998).

16 Shahbuddin said, 'If to seek redress of a religious grievance from the government which is the custodian of the dignity of all our people is fundamentalism in your lexicon, so be it.' See 'You Did This with Satanic Forethought, Mr. Rushdie', *The Times of India*, 13 October 1988. He applauded the responsiveness of the government and claimed that it signified that the government was not 'insensitive to the religious sentiments of the people'. See 'Ban Welcomed', *The Times of India*, 9 October 1988.

17 Syed Sahabuddin, 'No, Mr. Rushdie, You Acted with Satanic Forethought', *Muslim India*, November 1988.

18 As quoted in '"A Senseless Step", says Rushdie', *The Times of India*, 8 October 1988.

19 'A Riot Has Been Averted: Khuswant Singh', *The Times of India*, 30 October 1988. Reports suggested that such fears were not completely unfounded. After Khomeini's fatwa riots broke out in parts of western India, and 12 people were reported dead in police firings in Mumbai. Similar riots were also reported from Kashmir. It was indicative of the possible situation if the book was not proscribed. See 'Freedom of Information and Expression in India', *Article 19*, October 1990, republished in the *PUCL Bulletin of April 1991*. Also see 'Uneasy Calm in Riot Hit Areas', *The Times of India*, 26 February 1989.

20 As quoted in Kumar (1997: 202). Similarly, Shahbuddin maintained that indecent remarks about 'the Prophet's wife violated the Indian Penal Code, which prohibited any writing that hurt the religious sentiments of the people and were in bad taste'. Here Khurshid and Shahbuddin were referring to the laws within IPC like sections 295(A), and 153(A). 'Ban Welcomed', *The Times of India*, 9 October 1988.

21 'Ban Welcomed', *The Times of India*, 9 October 1988.

22 'You Did This with Satanic Forethought, Mr. Rushdie', *The Times of India*, 13 October 1988.

23 Nasreen had used terms like 'ruthless murderer', 'rapist' and 'scoundrel' for the Prophet and criticized Islam for its treatment of women as slaves.

24 'Bengal Bans Taslima's Book', *Statesman*, 29 November 2003.

25 The position was reiterated in the party organ of CPI(M), *People's Democracy*, on 7 November 2003 (Vol. XXVII, No. 49). It said: "The Bengal left front government has decided to ban Bangladeshi author Taslima Nasreen's latest book, Dwikhandito because it was feared that the book would incite communal violence."

26 See Ghosh (2004: 447–454).

27 As quoted in an interview published in *Frontline* on 31 January 2004.

28 See Ansari (2008: 15–19).

29 *Sujato Bhadra*, 39 A.I.R. 239. Unless mentioned, all the references related to the case remain the same.

30 However, some commentators believed that it was a planned strategy of MIM for publicity. It was argued that MIM was losing its Muslim base in Hyderabad because of the left's increasing popularity in the Muslim pockets of the city. Hence its legislators felt the need to rekindle its image as the authentic protector of Muslim rights. Saba Naqvi, 'No Orchids for Miss Nasreen', *Outlook*, 27 August 2007.

31 The immediate reasons for the protest and attacks were different. In this background appeared an unsigned article in the CPI(M)-backed journal *Pathasanket* which endorsed Nasreen's views on Islam and the Quran. The article argued that Nasreen's hitting out at fundamentalists from a rational and scientific point of view could not be treated as an offence. It further compared her with Galileo and even made a vitriolic attack on the Prophet over his marital life. The article shocked the Muslim community and was construed as an attack on Islam. The Muslim groups, especially the AIMF, led by Idris Ali, took strong exception to it. AIMF demanded a ban on the magazine and seizure of all copies in the market. The Muslim organizations also demanded that Nasreen's visa be revoked and that she should be sent out from India as she had time and again created communal tensions here. The state government promptly banned the autumn issue of the magazine, but the decision over her visa did not fall under its jurisdiction. However, by this time, violence had erupted again in Nandigram, where, it was alleged, the CPI(M) cadres had opened fire killing around 30 villagers. Prominent anti-left Muslim organizations, including AIMF, Jamiat Ullema-e-Hind and Furfura Sharif Muzadeedia Ananth Foundation, came together to protest against violence in Nandigram and unethical refuge to Taslima Nasreen in order to expose the government on 21 November 2007. The protests turned violent and soon took the shape of riots. The army was called in to manage the public-order situation. See 'Left Magazine's Autumn Number Banned', *The Times of India*, 9 November 2007.

32 Though there were obvious links between attacks in Hyderabad and her deportation from Kolkata owing to the similarity of the issues raised and the nature of the opposition, the immediate reasons that forced government to act were different. It was a period of intense political instability in West Bengal, owing to violence at Nandigram and Singur, where land acquisition by government for industrial expansion was being opposed by villagers. The government took a strong stand, and opposition witnessed extremes of police brutality. Nandigram was a Muslim majority area, and it took no time for violence to develop a communal logic. Government was further cornered after the controversy generated by the case of Rizwanur Rehman, who was allegedly murdered for marrying a Hindu girl belonging to a reputed trading family. His death saw a heavy backlash from Muslims in Kolkata, and a difficult law-and-order situation developed in late September. Such incidents had alienated the Muslims, and the West Bengal government was already on the defensive. See 'Exiled to the Vote Bank', *India Today*, 30 November 2007.

33 Minister Abdus Suttar, as quoted in *The Times of India*, 29 December 2007.

34 'Basu: Taslima, Welcome to Kolkata', *The Times of India*, 21 December 2007.

35 This statement was made in both houses of Parliament.

36 'Taslima Removes Controversial Lines from Book', *The Hindustan Times*, 30 November 2007.

37 This included Muslim organizations such as AIMF, Jamiat Ullema-e-Hind and Furfura Sharif Muzadeedia Ananth Foundation and political parties like AIMIM, the Congress Party and CPI(M).

38 'Taslima Withdraws Controversial Lines from *Dwikhandito*', *The Financial Express*, 1 December 2007.
39 "Taslima Can Return to Kolkata, says Basu," *Hindu*, 26 December 2007.
40 "Taslima's Surrender on 'Dwikhandito' a Great Setback: Intellectuals," *DNA*, 9 December 2007.
41 Raipur formed a part of the state of Madhya Pradesh, but after state reorganization in the year 2000, it became the capital of the newly formed state of Chhattisgarh.
42 Started by Acharya Tulsi under the *Anuvrat* movement.
43 *Chaturmasa* is a holy period of four months in the Jain tradition dedicated to simple living.
44 The wife of Rama according to revered Hindu mythology Ramayana.
45 'Anuvrat Leader to Quit RaIpur after Furor over Book', *The Times of India*, 29 September 1970.
46 A section under the IPC which when evoked makes assemblies and gatherings unlawful.
47 'Anuvrat Leader to Quit Rampur after Furor over Book', *The Times of India*, 29 September 1970.
48 Justice Singh, in *Ramlal Puri*, AIR 1971 MP 252.
49 Justice Tare, in *Ramlal Puri*, AIR 1971 MP 252.
50 'Order on Muni's Book Set Aside', *The Times of India*, 25 December 1970. The author later claimed that as a monk his primary commitment was to the ideals of non-violence and therefore he withdrew the book from circulation even after the Madhya Pradesh court had ruled in his favor. For reference, see the book co-authored by Anuvrat Anushasta Tulsi and Acharya Mahaprajna, titled *Non-violence and World Peace* (Ladnun: Jain Visva Bharti), available at http://www.jainworld.com/book/nvoilence/primarylessons.asp (last accessed on 20 July 2022).
51 The controversy attached to this text and the case has been discussed in detail in Chapter 4.
52 The demand was initiated by the BJP and supported by Mulayam Singh, the leader of the opposition Samajwadi Party on the floor of the Legislative Assembly. See 'Periyar Ramayana Arouse Flak', *Deccan Herald*, 6 November 2007. The ruling BSP was accused of supporting the book and allowing its sale in the state. The state's Parliamentary Affairs minister Lalji Verma assured that the government was not aware that the book was on sale in UP. The accusations of the opposition did not affect the government, which was, as it claimed, ignorant of the book and had nothing to do with it. He also cited that the Supreme Court had in the past found nothing objectionable with the book and therefore it would not be possible technically for the government to ban it. See, 'UP Oppn. Wants Periyar's Ramayan Banned, but Not a Copy to Buy in State', *The Indian Express*, 8 November 2007.
53 This phenomenon, its growth during anti-colonial movement and its role during electoral politics have all been discussed in Chapter 2.
54 There were protests against Ambedkar's *Riddles in Hinduism* in 1989, which were led by the Shiv Sena and its legislators. See, 'Parts of Riddles to Be Dropped', *The Times of India*, 17 November 1987.
55 In 2012, when Rushdie was to appear at the Jaipur Literature Festival, the Muslim organizations protested against his appearance on the pretext that he should apologize for his book *Satanic Verses*. 'Oppose Rushdie's Arrival', *Radiance Newsweekly* XLIX, no. 42, 21 January 2012. Most prominent Muslim organizations in India like Jamaat-i-Islami Hind, All India Imam Council, All India Milli Council, and Muslim Forum jointly addressed a press conference in Jaipur reiterating the demand. See 'Muslim Groups Oppose Rushdie's Visit to Jaipur Fest', *The Hindu*, 14 January 2012.

56 The pressure exerted on Oxford University Press to remove Ramanujan's essay *Three Hundred Ramayana*. See 'When a Department Let the University Down', *The Hindu*, 3 November 2011.
57 See 'BJP Workers Burnt Copies of Sachchi Ramayana', 30 October 2007, available at http://news.webindia123.com/news/articles/India/20071030/808600.html (last accessed on 18 July 2018).
58 The attack on Taslima Nasreen is a clear example of this.
59 The Shiromani Gurudwara Prabhandak Committee (SGPC) not only became furious at alternative interpretations of Guru Granth Sahib, but also announced punishment for the authors. See, 'SGPC Takes Exception to Book on Scriptures', *The Times of India*, 17 December 1992. Also see Singh (1996).
60 As discussed in Chapter 3 in the case of the book *Living Biographies of Religious Leaders*.
61 It is to be noted that the controversy over *Living Biographies of Religious Leaders* occurred in 1956, and violent protests were led by members of Muslim community. Similarly, the controversy over *Agnipariksha* occurred in 1970 and saw clashes between members of Hindu and Jain communities, who had different views about the book. See, 'Raipur under 24 Hour Curfew', *The Times of India*, 8 November 1970.
62 This aspect is clearly evident in the writings of Bose (2006), Ghosh (2004, 2016) and Liang (2004, 2016).
63 See for example, the writings of Kapur (1996), Rajeev Dhavan (2008) and Noorani (1995, 1999, 2008).
64 This aspect has been extensively discussed in Chapter 4.
65 The court used the absence of 'ground of opinion' in the notification as the reason to dismiss the order for forfeiture in cases like *Harnam Das*, A.I.R 1662 and *Lalai Singh Yadav*, 1977 AIR 202 only because it was held that there was no way in which the court could assess whether the official had reached a conclusion to act against publication based on rational grounds.
66 The details of this case have been discussed earlier, in Chapter 3.
67 Other than being the Governor of the state of Uttar Pradesh, where the controversy took shape, K. M. Munshi was also one of the editors of Bharatiya Vidya Bhawan, the publishers of the book.
68 See Nehru (1990: 436).
69 This aspect of the law has been discussed in greater details in Chapter 4.
70 This aspect has been discussed earlier in the present chapter.
71 Chapter VIII of the IPC deals with *Offences against Public Tranquility*, and Chapter XII of the IPC deals with the subject of *Criminal Intimidation, Insult and Annoyance*.
72 The court has observed this in various judgements like *S. Rangrajan v. P. Jagjivan Ram*, 1989 2 SCC 574; *M/S Prakash Jha Productions v. Union of India*, Writ Petition (Civil) No. 345 of 2011.
73 *S. Rangrajan*, 2 SCC 574.
74 *M/S Prakash Jha Productions*, Writ Petition (Civil) No. 345 of 2011.
75 This case and its different aspects have been discussed in detail in Chapter 1. For judgement see *S. Tamilselvan*, W.P. No. 1215 of 2015.
76 This kind of argument has been raised variously by scholars like Liang (2004) and Ghosh (2004).
77 In the Indian context, the form that such grievances could take is reflected in violence that followed the publication of *The Satanic Verses*, even after the book was banned in India.
78 Examples of this kind can be found in the case of the Maharashtra government's intervention in the *Riddles in Hinduism* case. The controversy was about the government's decision to publish this essay written by Ambedkar, which was

essentially targeting the Hindu gods Ram and Krishna. Details of the controversy are discussed in Purandare (2002: 306–314).

79 *Viswaroopam* was a 2013 film produced and directed by popular actor Kamal Hasan. The movie had acquired required certificates from authorities. But before release it was caught in a controversy where Muslim groups argued that the representation of Muslims in the film had hurt Muslim sentiments. The actor took the issue to the court, but before the court could give its final verdict, the Chief Minister of the State intervened and helped the two parties reach an amicable solution, which included deletion of some scenes and muting some portions. The film later was released. See 'Muslim Organizations Demand Ban on *Viswaroopam*', *The Indian Express* (Online Ed.), 23 January 2013, http://www.indianexpress.com/news/muslim-organisations-demand-ban-on-vishwaroopam/1063259/ (last accessed on 30 July 2018); 'Amicably Settle *Vishwaroopam* Row', *The New Indian Express* (Online Ed.), 29 January 2013, http://newindianexpress.com/states/tamilnadu/article1440303.ece (last accessed on 30 July 2018).

CONCLUSION

In the last few decades, two incidents – publication of Salman Rushdie's *The Satanic Verses* (1989) and publication of cartoons of Prophet Muhammad by Denmark based Jyllands-Posten (2005) – became the subjects of intense debate regarding freedom of expression and the issue of religious offence. These publications were repeatedly criticized for offending the religious sensibilities of Muslims and creating debate as to whether legal sanctions were justified in cases related to religiously offensive speech acts. These cases were very similar in most respects, and in fact critical discussions that followed the cartoon controversy were framed very much like those during the Rushdie affair, even drawing explicit parallels with and analogies from the latter. However, here I primarily deal with debates surrounding legal aspects attached with such controversies. Some important questions that became the subject of intense deliberation among academicians and scholars were: Can legal sanctions be invoked in the name of protecting religious sentiments in multicultural and multi-religious societies? Is the state justified in restricting freedom of speech and expression in order to prevent religious offence or to diffuse the threat to law-and-order situations that could follow such incidents? Is there any provision for a 'right not to be offended' within the liberal discourse? The opinions of scholars of law, politics and anthropology were deeply divided. Both incidents witnessed protests from members of the Muslim community all over world. It was claimed that the publications desecrated their deeply cherished religious values (Emon 2007: 303–321), offended their religious feelings (Hoarsher 2008: 1225–1253), and discriminated against Muslims, which was unacceptable (Laegaard 2007: 481–498; Modood 2006). Some commentators argued that Rushdie and Jyllands-Posten had only exercised their freedom of expression, and the call for restriction was unwarranted, no matter how much they may have disturbed or offended a particular community. Posing religion as a matter of public interest, commentators held that in a democracy, every aspect of religion should be open to scrutiny in all possible forms (Dworkin 2006; Post 2007). It was also argued that incidents like the 'Rushdie affair' tested the toleration of the community that claimed religious offence, and therefore was a good thing (Waldron 1993: 134–142). Even if it was agreed

DOI: 10.4324/9781003369257-7

that hurting religious sensibilities, as claimed in the two cases, was morally wrong and that the argument about respecting other's religious sensibilities had strong moral appeal, it could not justify the use of law in these cases.[1] Legal philosopher Ronald Dworkin opined that legal sanctions were also not justified because the claims about religious offence were sentimental and subjective and, hence, not eligible for legal protection. He further asserted that 'in a democracy no one, however powerful or important, can have a right not to be insulted or offended' (Dworkin 2006: 53). On the question about legal sanctions against freedom of speech and expression, in cases such as that of Rushdie and Jyllands-Posten, where members of one religious group were demanding such sanctions in the name of religious offence, it was argued that any such protection could lead to a slippery slope. Preventing religious groups from hurt in such cases, as free speech scholar Eric Barendt (2011) feared, could become a thin disguise for protecting religious beliefs and truths, which had been resisted during the debates against blasphemy laws.

Some scholars raised reservations about the way the debate was being posed as a binary between objection to blasphemy and free speech, and it was argued that in the name of liberal discourse, commentators often ignored and rendered unintelligible the kind of injury involved in religiously offensive speech, particularly that which vilified the sacred (Asad 2009; Mahmood 2009). Questioning those who opined that religious offence was subjective and sentimental in nature, Saba Mahmood (2009) and Talal Asad (2009) argued that religion was something that was inherited and naturalized, which got manifested in one's practices and lived social realities. Without understanding this aspect of religion, they argued, it was not possible to debate the harm caused by religious offence. However, on the question whether legal protection to religious feelings was justified, both Asad and Mahmood differed. Asad held that if 'modern secular societies do have legal constraints on communication' such as copyrights, patents and others, questions should not be raised if restrictions on free speech are advocated to prevent religious offence, even if they lead to blasphemy laws (2011: 283). Mahmood, on the other hand, believed that laws do not have capacity to provide remedy for harm suffered due to religious offense, and so she suggested that legal recourse cannot be a valid or appropriate demand on the part of the communities who protest against such offenses (2009: 82–83). A similar view was articulated by Tariq Modood (2005), who viewed it as a problem of multiculturalism, and argued that religious beliefs form the self-definition of a group, and incidents such as the Rushdie affair and cartoon controversy have a deep impact in the group's participation in society. He opined that legal restrictions might not be the most appropriate solution, and societies need to develop alternate mechanisms to ensure that oppression caused due to such incidents is avoided, but he insisted that freedom of expression could be curtailed to protect vulnerable groups and individuals from attack on their deeply held beliefs (Modood 2005: 121).

Though these scholars believed that debate around free speech should be sensitive to the sentimentalities of communities that claimed religious offence, they had different views on whether legal sanctions could really help in the situation.

An alternative view was represented by political philosophers Charles Taylor (1989) and Bhikhu Parekh (2012), who maintained that the question of restricting free speech would depend on the context in which it is being dealt. They are of a view that free speech should be balanced with other rights and values that are cherished in a society. However, 'there is no "true" way of reconciling them; it all depends', Parekh says, 'on the history, traditions, political circumstances, and so on of a society' (2000: 320). This view advocates a context-sensitive approach to the understanding of religious offence. The diversity of legal provisions and restrictions regarding freedom of speech and expression in different countries is representative of the point that Parekh and Taylor stress.

Take, for example, the legality involved in the above-mentioned cases in countries which became centres of the controversy: Britain in the case of Rushdie affair and Denmark in the case of the cartoon controversy.[2] *The Satanic Verses* was prohibited on legal grounds in numerous Muslim countries, including Saudi Arabia, Somalia, Bangladesh, Sudan, Malaysia, among others. In Britain a case was filed by Abdal Hussain Choudhury, on behalf of the British Muslim Action Front,[3] to the Chief Metropolitan Stipendiary Magistrate to issue a summons against Rushdie and his publishers for alleged blasphemous libel. When the appeal was rejected, he appealed to the Queen's Bench Division of the High Court. The High Court upheld the decision of the Metropolitan Magistrate and commented that even if the publication was religiously offensive to the sensibilities of Muslims, blasphemy law in Britain was applied only to the protection of Christian religion, and the same could not be extended to protect any other religion.[4] Choudhury took the appeal to the ECtHR. In *Choudhury v. United Kingdom*, the appellant contended that English law was prejudiced against Islam. However, the appeal was declared inadmissible by the commission as it held that there was no positive obligation on states under ECtHR laws to protect all religious sensibilities.[5] The central claim made by the appellant in these cases was that the law of blasphemy should be extended to protect all religious groups in the country and could not be limited to the protection of only the religion of the majority. Though the law at the time could not be invoked in the case, it built a larger consensus on the subject, which was also reflected in the abolition of the blasphemy law[6] and its replacement by the more egalitarian and inclusive Religious and Racial Hatred Act 2006.

In the cartoon controversy, although complaints were filed, the editors or publishers were never taken to court since the Danish Public Prosecutor decided that the cartoons did not violate any law. Danish Penal Code makes it a criminal offence 'to publicly mock or degrade the religious beliefs or worship of any legal religious community' (Penal Code 140). It also considers it an offence to utter things that are 'threatening, insulting or degrading to a group of persons due to their race, skin colour, national or ethnic origin, faith or sexual orientation' (Penal Code 266b). However, the Regional Public Prosecutor in Viborg, who was entrusted with the investigation in the cartoon case, maintained that though some cartoons had the capacity to ridicule or express disdain for Muslims' religious beliefs, as protected under the blasphemy clause, it did not constitute an infringement of the clause.[7] It further exempted it from violation of the racism clause as it only depicted an individual and could not be held to mean against the whole community. Though the Public Prosecutor maintained that freedom of expression had to be exercised with respect for other human rights, he argued that the journalists responsible for the publication of the cartoons could not be held to be in violation of the legal codes.[8] The legal question in the cartoon controversy was whether the publication of cartoons qualified as acts punishable within the Penal Codes of Denmark, and the Public Prosecutor provided a wide interpretation of law claiming exemption of such acts from law under the guise of editorial freedom. As is visible, legal provisions in Britain and Denmark differed on how to treat blasphemous libel. Britain had a law against blasphemy, but it only protected Christian religion, and although courts agreed that the novel was religiously offensive, the limitations of the blasphemy law became the justification for the courts to reject a case against Rushdie and the publishers of the novel. In Denmark, on the other hand, there existed provisions within its Penal Codes that defined religious offence in clear terms, and was applicable to all religious communities, but the Public Prosecutor did not find the law applicable to the kind of offence in the cartoon controversy. On these bases, the governments in the respective countries decided not to act legally against the publications.

Contrast this with the response to the same publications in India. As shown in Chapter 5, the Indian government pronounced a ban on the import of *The Satanic Verses* under the Customs Act, citing it as a 'pre-emptive step' to avoid public-order problems. The Customs Act used for the purpose cannot be challenged in the judiciary and hence no formidable case law followed on the subject. However, regardless of the blanket ban, communal disturbances including violence were reported from different places in India, where Muslims took to the street to protest the book and its author, Rushdie. In the case of the cartoon controversy, a few newspapers in India reprinted the controversial cartoons published by Jyllands-Posten, which included the Patna edition of *The Times of India* (Khanduri 2014). Government reacted immediately against the initial publishers, and this prevented large-scale reprints. Publishers were arrested under section 295(A) and 153(A) of the IPC, which are meant to prevent religious offence and incitement of hate. Moreover, in an official release, the Indian government made its position clear: government was 'deeply concerned about the growing controversy over the publication of cartoons that offend the Muslim community worldwide' and it was 'incumbent on all of us to be sensitive to the beliefs and sentiments of others and avoid all actions that cause hurt to them'.[9] Government was concerned in the way the protests against the cartoons had turned violent and converted to riots in different cities like Srinagar, Patna and Lucknow. Fearing strong protest and demonstrations, the Central Government also cancelled the proposed state visit by Danish Prime Minister Rasmussen.[10] The Indian government indicated that it was not satisfied with the way Denmark had handled the situation, especially refusing legal actions against Jyllands-Posten. At the same time, it had also signalled that if any one reprinted or published such cartoons, it would be dealt with strongly under the available laws.

The legal means available with the Indian government are primarily the statutory laws like section 295(A) and 153(A) of the IPC, and section 95 of the CrPC. Section 295(A) and 153(A) are punitive in nature, where violation of section 295(A) can amount to arrest of publishers or authors who are found to be deliberately engaged in outraging religious feelings or insulting religion or religious beliefs of any class, and violation of section 153(A) can lead to similar punishments for those who are found to be spreading disharmony, ill feeling or hatred between different religious groups. Section 95 of CrPC, on the other hand, is preventive in nature and pertains to seizure and forfeiture of publications in case such publications are found violating section 295(A) and 153(A) of the IPC. Indian laws, in that sense, do not just protect the enraged communities from religious hurt, but also provide strong protection to religion and religious beliefs of different communities from insults. This provides a wide net for the government authorities to act in cases where a publication is found religiously offensive and contentious. In cases of proscription and forfeiture, the only legal reprieve is section 96 of the CrPC, which allows the aggrieved party to approach the court against government's action. However, law is so framed that rather than government defending its act of seizure/forfeiture in the court, the onus of proving innocence falls on the author/publisher, where they are expected to justify that their acts do not fall under the category of offence as defined by the above-mentioned statutory laws.[11] Legal scholars opine that such laws not only make it very difficult for the advocates/defenders of freedom of speech and expression but also pave way for the executive to respond to claims of hurt sentiments, without serious examination of either the scope of the law or substantive principles laid down by various courts in such cases (Liang 2016: 823). The above discussions reflect the context-specific nature of laws and their implementation for similar cases in different societies. In every society, the nature of laws to restrict freedom of expression corresponds to the needs and challenges that led to the creation of such laws and allow its existence. In the UK, for example, a need was realized, according to changing demography and nature of society, to abolish blasphemy laws and replace them with a different set of laws that protected all religious and racial communities. In the case of India, the creations of the statutory laws bore a colonial legacy and were created to respond to a specific set of issues dominant in Indian society – to curb the tendency to ignite communal hatred that led to violence. Subsequently these laws were amended, as and when required, according to the demands of the context.

Governing Freedom of Speech and Expression in India

The British approach to laws governing freedom of speech and expression was strictly guided by an instrumental logic to serve the colonial interests. At the same time, Indians had a dubious attitude towards freedom of speech and expression in the colonial context. So, they were demanding extensive freedom of expression in order to criticize the government, an argument derived from the consequentialist theories of free speech, which claimed that free speech was necessary to arrive closer to the truth and was beneficial for governance. However, where such liberty was seen as leading to religious offence, Indians not only demanded censorship from the government, but also participated actively in the legislatures to ensure successful promulgation of new laws. In the post-Independence period, particularistic concerns like partition and the communal violence that it accompanied inspired constitution makers to severely limit fundamental rights promised under article 19(1)(a) by adding a number of caveats under article 19(2). In this split manufactured between article 19(1)(a) and 19(2), there was also an inherent dichotomy. Article 19(1)(a) imagined citizens as rational subjects capable of exercising complete autonomy in speech acts, whereas article 19(2) reflected the challenges of an affective public sphere, where citizens were seen as corruptible and prone to outrage and provocation (Liang 2016: 818). This same imagination about the majority of Indian citizens being emotional beings, who lacked 'maturity', particularly on matters related to religion, also became the rallying point for the introduction of significant amendments to the constitution and other statutory laws. Lawmakers took it as their duty to provide a safety net in order to protect common people from the misuse of freedom of speech and expression, and law was also seen as a medium to discipline citizens and inculcate values of toleration.

This overemphasis on public tranquillity and order also guided the proactive role of government agencies in censoring or forfeiting publications or arresting authors/publishers when controversies related to such publications surfaced. The underlying assumption that Indian citizens lacked the capacity to handle hurtful speech, and could easily be swayed by passions if the subject under discussion was religion, allows, as Pratap Bhanu Mehta argues, for a paternalistic role of state, where state takes part in the controversy only as protector of public order, and not as defender of free speech (2008: 330–332). This is ably reflected in the IPC, which uses language of 'outrage', 'disgust' and 'pain' to regulate speech, and also in the fact that most statutory laws regulating religiously offensive speech acts are cognizable offences[12] and are non-bailable[13] in nature. The effectiveness of these laws is further buttressed by the legal defence such laws enjoy under the aegis of article 19(2) of constitution, which represents 'reasonable restrictions' for freedom of speech and expression. Consequently, laws governing freedom of speech and expression in India have allowed a wide net for executive control, and authorities deem it prudent to play it over-safe whenever they sense a threat to law and order. The general approach is to ban publication or proscribe it and/or arrest the author/publisher at the slightest controversy where the claim of religious offence is involved. They maintain that the aggrieved person has every right to approach the relevant court and obtain a judicial verdict in his/her favour. It also helps officials to temporarily pacify the prevalent law-and-order situation, and if there is any breach of peace following the judgement from the court, the responsibility can be placed on the judgement. Authorities can thereby disclaim the responsibility of incumbent situation by citing their alertness at the earlier instance.[14]

Freedom of Speech and Expression and 'Reasonable Restrictions'

One of the central questions with which I began this book was: how have the courts in India interpreted laws and defined 'reasonable restrictions' concerning freedom of speech and expression vis-à-vis the claims of religious offence? This begs an assessment of the grounds on which the courts allow restrictions of freedom of speech and expression when the claim of religious offence is raised against a publication. Firstly, it should be pointed out that in various cases, courts in general, and the Supreme Court in particular, have upheld the constitutionality of statutory laws that the executives use to restrict freedom of speech and expression.[15] As of now, courts have taken a position that these laws fall well within the definition of 'reasonable restrictions' as provided under article 19(2). Further, primary justifications used by courts for upholding the restrictions over freedom of speech and expression include: (1) a threat to public order posed by the publication and (2) protection of values of secularism and religious pluralism. The former is primarily based on an assumption that an aggravated form of insult targeted against any religion or incitement of religious hatred would invariably lead to a problem of maintaining public order, and the authorities must take prompt action in such situation. However, courts have also evolved certain balancing and protective mechanisms with regard to executive action. For example, it has been made mandatory by the court that a notification mentioning the reasons for action should be issued by the concerned authority before any publication is seized or forfeited. Similarly, in case of an arrest of an author/publisher, authority needs to prove in the court that the act was carried out with deliberate and malicious intent. The problem with these balancing mechanisms, however, is that either of these – proving intentions of the arrested individual or the question of validity of the notification issued before forfeiture – can only be tested on the floor of the courts, which can only happen at a later stage. So, broadly it can be said that government officials can act in these cases based on their own judgement of the situation, which is often guided by the instrumental logic of acting against such publication and its author/publisher, against whom the charges of causing religious offence is made in order to maintain public tranquillity. The second argument for restricting freedom of speech and expression is that, though important, freedom of speech and expression does not enjoy any special status in the Indian context,[16] and needs to be balanced against competing fundamental rights. The doctrine of proportionality[17] reigns supreme in such cases, and courts have maintained that the right to profess, practice and propagate one's religion guaranteed under article 25 is one such provision, with which the right to free speech needs to be balanced. Other than this, courts also stress that in a multicultural secular country, like India, it is the duty of the state to protect religious interests of all citizens. This argument has been extended to protection of religious principles, religious texts and even religious personages from attack. Courts also try to construct a distinction between criticizing religious practices or rituals, and insulting its principles or symbols, by putting the former under the category of permissible speech. This distinction, however, as free speech scholars like Peter Jones (1980) and Eric Barendt (2011) have shown in another context, is very difficult to maintain and prone to dissolve, which would mean that authorities could act against any criticism of religion.

The above discussions reflects two prominent aspects about the courts' position on the subject of religious offence committed by a publication. First, courts appear to provide legal patronage to state actions through an expansive interpretation of statutory laws and constitutional limitations;[18] and second, courts practice legal paternalism, whereby it guides the citizens regarding what to say, how to say it and how much to say.[19] Together with this, the language of statutory laws provides a sense of immunity to religions from criticism. This also has deep impact on historical analysis and other scholarship related to religion. In a way, any critical publication on the subject of religion or a literary piece like a novel on the subject of religion automatically becomes subject to potential controversy, which restrains the scope for freedom of speech and expression.

The aspects of law and legal process discussed above also contribute to strengthening the role of non-state actors in censorship. These non-state actors, who primarily claim to be representing the offended community, use the language of law to justify their grievances. It is also reflected in the way law and legal process is used by the non-state actors to express their grievances. This can either be in the form of writ petitions (both civil as well as criminal) filed in the courts against the publication and its author/publisher or as a justificatory means to exert pressure on government authorities to act against the publication and its author/publisher, or it is also used as a legitimate strategic tool to create public opinion in their favour.[20] The long legal process, which could be tiring and costly, and ambiguity in legal interpretations produces an environment where the author/publisher is forced to impose self-censorship – a phenomenon that Cook and Heilmann call 'public self-censorship'. This can either result in the amendment of the original text including significant exclusions or the deletion of controversial portions or even pulping or withdrawing the publication in controversy. This undoubtedly poses the most serious threat to the scope of freedom of speech and expression in independent India.

Notes

1 Jones held that if people are offended, they are liable to express their protest, and the advocates of free speech should have no problems with that. See Jones (1993: 118). This argument has also been endorsed by Dworkin and Waldron.

2 The legal dimensions of the cases have been discussed in detail in the following books, among others. See Hunt (2002: 187–188); Langer (2014: 50–90).

3 British Muslim Action Front was a group organized to protest against the religious offence caused by the publication of *Satanic Verses*.

4 As discussed in detail in *R. v. Chief Metropolitan Stipendiary Magistrate, exp. Choudhury* (Queen's Bench Division) (1991) 1 QB 429 (1990).

5 *Choudhury v. United Kingdom* (1991) Application No. 17439/90, ECommHR.

6 The common-law offences of blasphemy and blasphemous libel in the UK were abolished by the Criminal Justice and Immigration Act, 2008.

7 *Rigsadvokaten (Director of Public Prosecutions)* (2006) J. Nr. RA-2006-41-0151.

8 Summarized in *Rigsadvokaten*, J. Nr. RA-2006-41-0151; *Kasem Said Ahmad and Asmaa Abdol-hamid v. Denmark* (2008) Communication no. 1487/2006, CCPR. The response of the Danish law in the controversy has also been presented effectively in Lagoutte (2008: 379–404).

9 There was a lot of pressure on the government to take some position, which is also reflected in the debates of the Parliament, particularly in the Rajya Sabha, where the top leaders of the opposition party like Sushma Swaraj and Ravi Shankar Prasad questioned the position of the government and criticized its inability to contain violence in different parts. See *Rajya Sabha Debates*, 20 February 2006, pp. 171–179; 8 March 2006, p. 100. The official press release is available at the website of the Prime Minister's office, 'Govt. Expresses Concern over Publication of Cartoons That Offend Religious Sentiments', available at http://archivepmo.nic.in/drmanmohansingh/ content_print.php?nodeid=389&nodetype=1 (last accessed on 30 August 2018).

10 'Cartoon Row Kills Danish PM's Visit', *The Hindustan Times*, 18 March 2006.

11 This interpretation of law has been defended by the Supreme Court in various cases like *Lalai Singh Yadav*, 1977 AIR 202; *Sri Baragur Ramachandrappa*, 5 S.C.C. 11.

12 Cognizable offence is one where the police do not require prior approval either from the state government or any warrant from the court. It can act *suo motu* in such cases.

13 Non-bailable means that the accused cannot be granted bail with the case being heard in a court of law.

14 See Dhavan (2008: 145). He calls this a 'problem solving' politics used by government authorities to counter threats on public order in such cases.

15 The constitutionality of sections 295(A) and 153(A) of the IPC and section 95 of the CrPC have been respectively upheld in *Ramji Lal Modi*, 1957 AIR 620; *Babu Rao Patel*, 1980 A.I.R. 763; and *N. Veerabrahmam*, A.I.R. 1959 A.P. 572.

16 This position is reflected among the scholars in relation to the First Amendment in the US, like Dworkin and C. Edwin Baker, among others. This view has, however, been effectively questioned, even in the context of the US; for example, see Fish (1994); Waldron (2012).

17 The doctrine of proportionality broadly means that the application of a given law should not be unreasonable in its reciprocal relationship and a sense of proportion must exist between the ends desired and the means employed. In case of competing fundamental rights, it is also used to weigh the impact of a decision by authorities whether the use of law in a case has adverse effects upon the liberties of a person. For an analysis of the complexities involved in the doctrine of proportionality in relation to human rights, see Tsakyrakis (2009: 468–493). Madhav Khosla's response to this article is equally important (2010: 298–306).

18 It is not to say that this patronage is uncritical, as exhibited in many judgements, but the overall reading gives a sense that on most occasions, courts seem to justify the state's response profoundly when there is a threat to law and order.

19 The courts' approach in using 'matter-manner' together in analysis of publications, and particularly its suggestion about precaution against language that vilifies. For example, in *Sri Baragur Ramachandrappa*, the court reminds us that 'it cannot be ignored that India is [a] country with vast disparities in language, culture and religion and unwarranted and malicious criticism or interference in the faith of others cannot be accepted'.

20 Legal opinion becomes one of the important rallying points to create public opinion in such cases.

REFERENCES

Acharya, Bhairav. 2015. 'Free Speech in India: Still Plagued by Pre-modern Laws', *Media Asia*, vol. 42, no. 3–4, pp. 157–160.

Ahmed, Asad Ali. 2009. 'Spectre of Macaulay: Blasphemy, the Indian Penal Code and Pakistan's Postcolonial Predicament'. In Raminder Kaur and William Mazzarella (eds.), *Censorship in South Asia: Cultural Regulation from Sedition to Seduction*, pp. 172–205. Bloomington, Indianapolis: Indiana University Press.

Anderson, Benedict. 1983. *Imagined Communities: Reflections on the Origin and Spread of Nationalism*. London: Verso.

Ansari, Iqbal A. 2008. 'Free Speech – Hate Speech – The Taslima Nasreen Case', *Economic and Political Weekly*, vol. 43, no.8, pp. 15–19.

Appignanesi, Lisa Maitland, and Sara Maitland (eds.). 1989. *The Rushdie File*. London: Fourth Estate.

Asad, Talal. 1999. *The Indian Constitution: Cornerstone of a Nation*. New Delhi: Oxford University Press.

———. 2009. 'Free Speech, Blasphemy and Secular Criticism'. In Wendy Brown, Judith Butler, Saba Mahmood and Talal Asad (eds.), *Is Critique Secular? Blasphemy, Injury and Free Speech*, pp. 14–57. Berkeley: The Townsend Center for the Humanities, University of California.

———. 2011. 'Freedom of Speech and Religious Limitations'. In Craig Calhoun, Mark Juergensmeyer and Jonathan VanAntwerpen (eds.), *Rethinking Secularism*, pp. 282–298. Oxford: Oxford University Press.

Austin, Granville. 2003. *Working a Democratic Constitution: A History of the Indian Experience*. New Delhi: Oxford University Press.

———. 1997. *The Indian Constitution: Cornerstone of a Nation*. New Delhi: Oxford University Press.

Bajpai, Rochana. 2010. 'Cultural Rights of Minorities during Constitution-Making: A Re-reading'. In Gurpreet Mahajan and S. Jodhka (eds.), *Religion, Community and Development: Changing Contours of Politics and Policy in India*, pp. 282–300. New Delhi: Routledge.

———. 2011. *Debating Difference: Group Rights and Liberal Democracy in India*. Oxford: Oxford University Press.

Baker, Edwin. 1989. *Human Liberty and Freedom of Speech*. Oxford: Oxford University Press.

Barendt, Eric. 2011. 'Religious Hatred Laws: Protecting Groups or Beliefs', *Res Publica*, vol. 17, no. 1, pp. 41–53.

Barrier, N. G. 1974. *Banned: Controversial Literature and Political Control in British India, 1907–1947*. Columbia: University of Missouri Press.

———. 1992. 'Vernacular Publishing and Sikh Public Life in the Punjab, 1880–1910'. In Kenneth W. Jones (ed.), *Religious Controversy in British India: Dialogues in South Asian Languages*, pp. 200–228. New York: State University of New York Press.

Bayly, C. A. 2009. 'The Indian Ecumene: An Indigenous Public Sphere'. In Arvind Rajagopal (ed.), *The Indian Public Sphere: Readings in Media History*, pp. 49–64. New Delhi: Oxford University Press.

———. 2010. 'Rammohan Roy and the Advent of Constitutional Liberalism in India'. In Shruti Kapila (ed.), *An Intellectual History for India*, pp. 18–34. New Delhi: Cambridge University Press.

———. 2012. *Recovering Liberties: Indian Thought in the Age of Liberalism and Empire*. New Delhi: Cambridge University Press.

Bhargava, Rajeev. 1999. 'Democratic Vision of a New Republic: India, 1950'. In Francine R. Frankel, Zoya Hasan, Rajeev Bhargava and Balveer Arora (eds.), *Transforming India: Social and Political Dynamics of Democracy*, pp. 26–59. New Delhi: Oxford University Press.

———. 2012. *What Is Political Theory and Why Do We Need It?* New Delhi: Oxford University Press.

Bhatia, Gautam. 2016. *Offend, Shock or Disturb: Free Speech under the Indian Constitution*. New Delhi: Oxford University Press.

Bhatia, Nandi. 2010. 'Censorship, Social Reform and Mythological Drama in Colonial India'. In Diana Dimitrova (ed.), *Religion in Literature and Film in South Asia*, pp. 191–211. New York: Palgrave Macmillan.

Bhatia, S. 1997. *Freedom of Press: Politico-Legal Aspects of Press Legislation in India*. New Delhi: Rawat Publications.

Bhattacharya, Neeladri. 2005. 'Notes towards a Conception of the Colonial Public'. In Rajeev Bhargava and Helmut Reifeld (eds.), *Civil Society, Public Sphere and Citizenship: Dialogues and Perceptions*, pp. 130–156. New Delhi: Sage.

Bhowmik, Someswar. 2003. 'From Coercion to Power Relations: Film Censorship in Post-colonial India', *Economic and Political Weekly*, vol. 38, no. 3, pp. 3148–3152.

———. 2009. *Cinema and Censorship: The Politics of Control in India*. New Delhi: Orient Blackswan.

Blom, Hansen Thomas. 2004. 'Politics as Permanent Performance: The Production of Political Authority in Locality'. In John Zavos, Andrew Wyatt and Vernon Hewitt (eds.), *The Politics of Cultural Mobilization in India*, pp. 19–36. New Delhi: Oxford University Press.

Bollinger, Lee C. 1988. *The Tolerant Society: Freedom of Speech and Extremist Speech in America*. New York: Oxford University Press.

Bose, Brinda (ed.). 2006. *Gender and Censorship*. New Delhi: Kali for Women.

Brass, Paul. 2003. *The Production of Hindu-Muslim Violence in Contemporary India*. Seattle: University of Washington Press.

Buckland, C. E. 1976. *Bengal under the Lieutenant Governors: Being a Narrative of the Principal Events and Public Measures during Their Periods of Office from 1854–1898*, vol. 2. New Delhi: Deep Publications.

Burt, Richard. 1994. *The Administration of Aesthetics: Censorship, Political Criticism and Public Sphere*. Minnepolis and London: University of Minnesota.

Butler, Judith. 1997. *Excitable Speech: A Politics of the Performative*. New York and London: Routledge.

Chandoke, Neera. 2005. 'Individual and Group Rights: A View from India'. In Zoya Hasan, E. Sridharan and R. Sudharshan (eds.), *India's Living Constitution: Ideas, Practices, Controversies*, pp. 207–241. London: Anthem Press.

Chandra, Bipan. 1990. 'Communalism and the State: Some Issues in India', *Social Scientist*, vol. 18, no. 6–7, pp. 38–47.

Chandrachud, Abhinav. 2011. 'An Empirical Study of the Supreme Court's Composition', *Economic and Political Weekly*, vol. 46, no. 1, pp. 71–78.

———. 2012. 'Speech, Structure and Behavior on the Supreme Court of India', *Columbia Journal of Asian Law*, vol. 25, no. 2, pp. 222–274.

Chatterjee, Partha. 1993. *The Nation and Its Fragments: Colonial and Postcolonial Histories*. Princeton: Princeton University Press.

Chaudhuri, Reba. 1955. 'The Story of the Indian Press', *Economic and Political Weekly*, vol. 7, no. 9, pp. 291–292.

Cohen-Almagor, Raphael. 2005. *The Scope of Tolerance: Studies on the Cost of Freedom of Expression and Freedom of the Press*. Abingdon: Routledge.

Collini, Stefan. 2010. *That's Offensive: Criticism, Identity, Respect*. London: Seagull Books.

Collini, Stephen, Donald Winch and John Burrow. 1984. *That Noble Science of Politics: A Study in Nineteenth-Century Intellectual History*. Cambridge: Cambridge University Press.

Cook, Philip, and Conrad Heilmann. 2013. 'Two Types of Self-Censorship: Public and Private', *Political Studies*, vol. 61, no. 1, pp. 178–196.

Darnton, Robert. 2001. 'Literary Surveillance in the British Raj: The Contradictions of Liberal Imperialism', *Book History*, vol. 4, pp. 133–176.

———. 2002. 'Book Production in British India, 1850–1900', *Book History*, vol. 5, pp. 239–262.

De, Rohit. 2012. 'Emasculating the Executive: The Federal Court and Civil Liberties in Late Colonial India, 1942–1944'. In Terence C. Halliday, Lucien Karpik and Malcolm M. Feeley (eds.), *Fates of Political Liberalism in the British Post-Colony: The Politics of the Legal Complex*, pp. 59–90. Cambridge and New York: Cambridge University Press.

Department of Law, University of Toronto, and PEN International and International Human Rights Program (IHRP), n.d. *Imposing Silence: The Use of India's Laws to Supress Free Speech*. Available at www.pen-international.org/wp-content/uploads/2015/05/Imposing-Silence--FINAL.pdf (last accessed on 14 July 2015).

Devlin, Patrick. 1965. *The Enforcement of Morals*. London: Oxford University Press.

Dhavan, Rajeev. 2008. *Publish and Be Damned: Censorship and Intolerance in India*. New Delhi: Tulika Books.

Donough, Walter Russell. 1911. *A Treatise on the Law of Sedition and Cognate Offences in British India*. Kolkata: Thackel Spink & Co.

Dworkin, Ronald. 2006. 'The Right to Ridicule', *The New York Review of Books*. Available at http://www.nybooks.com/articles/2006/03/23/the-right-to-ridicule/ (last accessed on 27 September 2018).

———. 2009. 'Foreword'. In Ivan Hare and James Weinstein (eds.), *Extreme Speech and Democracy*. Oxford: Oxford University Press.

Emerson, Thomas I. 1966. *Towards a General Theory of the First Amendment*. New York: Random House.

Emon, Anver M. 2007. 'On the Pope, Cartoons and Apostates, Sharia', *Journal of Law and Religion*, vol. 22, no. 2, pp. 303–321.

Eswaran, Venkat. 1992. 'Advocacy of National, Racial and Religious Hatred: The Indian Experience'. In Sandra Colliver (ed.), *Striking a Balance: Hate Speech, Freedom of Expression and Non-discrimination*, pp. 171–181. Human Rights Centre, University of Essex, London: Article 19, International Centre Against Censorship.

Feinberg, Joel. 1973. 'Harmless Immoralities and Offensive Nuisances: Reply'. In Norman S. Care and Thomas K. Trelogan (eds.), *Issues in Law and Morality: Proceedings*, pp. 111–126. Cleveland and London: Case Western Reserve University Press.

———. 1985. *Offense to Others*. New York: Oxford University Press.

Fish, Stanley. 1994. *There Is No Such Thing as Free Speech: And It's a Good Thing Too*. Oxford: Oxford University Press.

Freitag, Sandria B. 1989. *Collective Action and Community: Public Arenas and the Emergence of Communalism in North India*. Berkeley and Oxford: University of California Press.

———. 1996. 'Contesting in Public: Colonial Legacies and Contemporary Communalism'. In David Ludden (ed.), *Contesting the Nation: Religion, Community and the Politics of Democracy in India*, pp. 211–234. Philadelphia: University of Pennsylvania Press.

Gandhi, M. K. 1967. *The Collected Works of Mahatma Gandhi*, 100 vols. New Delhi: Publications Division, Ministry of Information and Broadcasting.

Ghosh, Sohini. 1991. 'Democracy, Nationalism and the Public: A Speculation on Colonial Muslim Politics', *Journal of South Asian Studies*, vol. 14, no. 1, pp. 123–140.

———. 2004. 'Censorship Myths and Imagined Harms', *Sarai Reader*, vol. 4, pp. 447–454. Available at http://archive.sarai.net/files/original/755257fc6fa5744ae93c402cd54bc039.pdf (last accessed 17 June 2020).

———. 2016. 'The Alchemy of Hate and Hurt'. In Rina Ramdev, S. D. Nambiar and D. Bhattacharya (eds.), *Sentiment, Politics, Censorship: The State of Hurt*, pp. 55–70. New Delhi: Sage.

Gilmartin, David. 1998. 'Partition, Pakistan and South Asian History: In Search of a Narrative', *The Journal of Asian Studies*, vol. 57, no. 4, pp. 1068–1095.

———. 1991. 'Democracy, Nationalism and the Public: A Speculation on Colonial Muslim Politics', *Journal of South Asian Studies*, vol. 14, no. 1, pp. 123–140.

Gopal, S. (ed.). 1991. *Selected Works of Jawaharlal Nehru*. New Delhi: Oxford University Press.

Guha, Ranajit. 1977. *Dominance without Hegemony: History and Power in Colonial India*. New Delhi: Oxford University Press.

———. 2009. 'Transmission'. In Arvind Rajagopal (ed.), *The Indian Public Sphere: Readings in Media History*, pp. 31–48. New Delhi: Oxford University Press.

Gupta, Nand Lal. 2006. *Jawaharlal Nehru on Communalism*. New Delhi: Hope India.

Habermas, J. 1992. *The Structural Transformation of the Public Sphere: An Inquiry into a Category of Bourgeois Society*. Trans. Thomas Burger. Cambridge: Polity.

———. 1996. 'Between Facts and Norms', *Journal of Philosophy*, vol. 93, no. 6, pp. 307–315.

———. 2001. 'Constitutional Democracy: A Paradoxical Union of Contradictory Principles', trans. William Rehg, *Political Theory*, vol. 29, no. 6, pp. 766–781.

Hantman, Daniel. 2014. 'Shaking Fists and Simmering Craniums: India's Tolerance for Restricting Socially Offensive and Emotionally Harmful Speech', *Indonesian Journal of International and Comparative Law*, vol. 1, no. 1, pp. 73–104.

Hart, H. L. A. 1963. *Law, Liberty and Morality*. London: Oxford University Press.

Heyman, Steven J. 2002. 'Spheres of Autonomy: Reforming the Content Neutrality Doctrine in First Amendment Jurisprudence', *William & Mary Bill of Rights*, vol. 10, no. 3, pp. 649–716.

Hoarsher, Guys. 2008. 'Rhetoric and Its Abuses: How to Oppose Liberal Democracy while Speaking Its Language', *Chicago-Kent Law Review*, vol. 83, no. 3, pp. 1225–1253.

Holquist, Michael, 1994. 'Corrupt Originals: The Paradox of Censorship', *PMLA*, vol. 9, no. 1, pp. 14–25.

Hunt, Murray. 2002. *Using Human Rights Law in English Courts*. Oxford: Hart Publishing.

Huttmann, G. H. 1837. *A Penal Code Prepared by the Indian Law Commissioners*. Kolkata: Bengal Military Orphan Press.

Iyer, R. (ed.). 1986. *The Moral and Political Writings of Mahatma Gandhi*, vol. 1. New Delhi: Oxford University Press.

Jaffrelot, Christophe. 1999. *The Hindu Nationalist Movement and Indian Politics*. Delhi: Penguin.

———. 2010. *Religion, Caste and Politics in India*. New Delhi: Primus Books.

Jaffrelot, Christophe, L. Gayer and M. Maheshwari. 2010. 'Cultural Policing in South Asia'. In Helmut Anheir and Yudhishthir Raj Isar (eds.), *Cultural Expression, Creativity and Innovation*, pp. 148–158. Los Angeles: Sage Publications.

Jalal, Ayesha. 2000. *Self and Sovereignty: Individual and Community in South Asian Islam since 1850*. London and New York: Routledge.

Jansen, Sue Curry. 1991. *Censorship: The Knot That Binds Power and Knowledge*. New York: Oxford University Press.

Jones, Peter. 1980. 'Blasphemy, Offensiveness and Law', *British Journal of Political Science*, vol. 10, no. 2, pp. 129–148.

———. 1993. 'Respecting Beliefs and Rebuking Rushdie'. In J. Horton (ed.), *Liberalism, Multiculturalism and Toleration*, pp. 114–138. Basingstoke: Macmillan.

Kapur, Ratna. 1996. 'Who Draws the Line? Feminist Reflections on Speech and Censorship', *Economic and Political Weekly*, vol. 31, no. 16/17, pp. 15–30.

Kaur, Reminder. 2003. *Performative Politics and the Cultures of Hinduism: Public Uses of Religion in Western India*. London: Anthem Press.

Kaviraj, Sudipta. 2010. *The Imaginary Institution of India*. New Delhi: Permanent Black.

———. 2011. *The Enchantment of Democracy and India: Politics and Ideas*. New Delhi: Permanent Black.

Khanduri, Ritu Gairola. 2014. *Caricaturing Culture in India: Cartoons and History in the Modern World*. Cambridge: Cambridge University Press.

Khilnani, Sunil. 2015. 'The Indian Constitution and Democracy'. In Zoya Hasan Esridharan, and R. Sudarshan (eds.), *India's Living Constitution: Ideas, Practices, Controversies*, pp. 64–82. London: Anthem Press.

Khosla, Madhav. 2010. 'Proportionality: An Assault on Human Rights? A Reply', *International Journal of Constitutional Law*, vol. 7, no. 3, pp. 298–306.

King, Christopher R. 1992. 'Images of Virtue and Vice: The Hindi-Urdu Controversy in Two Nineteenth-Century Hindi Plays'. In Kenneth W. Jones (ed.), *Religious Controversy in British India: Dialogues in South Asian Languages*, pp. 124–147. New York: State University of New York Press.

Kolsky, Elizabeth. 2005. 'Codification and the Rule of Colonial Difference: Criminal Procedure in British India', *Law and History Review*, vol. 23, no. 3, pp. 640.
Kumar, Girja. 1990. *Censorship in India: With Special Reference to 'Satanic Verses'*. New Delhi: Har-Anand.
———. 1997. *The Book on Trial: Fundamentalism and Censorship in India*. New Delhi: Har Anand.
Laegaard, Sune. 2007. 'The Cartoon Controversy: Offense, Identity, Oppression', *Political Studies*, vol. 55, no. 3, pp. 481–98.
Lagoutte, Stephanie. 2008. 'The Cartoon Controversy in Context: Analyzing the Decisions Not to Prosecute under Danish Law', *Brooklyn Journal of International Law*, vol. 33, no. 2, pp. 379–404.
LaMarche, Gara. 1991. 'Some Thoughts on Chilling Effect', *Art Journal*, vol. 50, no. 4, pp. 56–58.
Langer, Lorenz. 2014. *Religious Offence and Human Rights: The Implications of Defamation of Religions*. Cambridge: Cambridge University Press.
Lee, Simon. 1990. *The Cost of Free Speech*. London and Boston: Faber and Faber.
Letsas, George. 2012. 'Is There a Right Not to Be Offended in One's Religious Beliefs?' In Lorenzo Zucca and Camil Ungureanu (eds.), *Law, State and Religion in the New Europe: Debates and Dilemmas*, pp. 239–260. Cambridge: Cambridge University Press.
Liang, Lawrence. 2004. 'Reasonable Restrictions and Unreasonable Speech', *Sarai Reader*, vol. 04, pp. 434–440. Available at http://archive.sarai.net/files/original/e8cc962416f0a1f2da6bc009347fa387.pdf (last accessed on 7 June 2020).
———. 2012. 'Love Language or Hate Speech', *Tehelka*, vol. 09, no. 3. Available at http://archive.tehelka.com/story_main51.asp?filename=hub030312love.asp (last accessed on 10 July 2020).
———. 2016. 'Free Speech and Expression'. In Sujit Choudhary, Madhav Khosla and Pratap Bhanu Mehta (eds.), *The Oxford Handbook of The Indian Constitution*, pp. 814–833. New Delhi: Oxford University Press.
Low, D. A. 1973. *Lion Rampant: Essays in the Study of British Imperialism*. London: Routledge.
Macaulay, T. B. 1837. *A Penal Code Prepared by the Indian Law Commissioners*. Kolkata: Bengal Military Orphan Press.
———. 1866. 'Introductory Report upon the Indian Penal Code (IPC)'. In Lady Trevlyn (ed.), *The Works of Lord Macaulay*, vol. VII. London: Longmans, Green, and Co.
———. 1898. *The Complete Works of Lord Macaulay*, Albany Edition, 12 vols. Lady Trevlyn (ed.). London: Longmans, Green, and Co.
Mackinnon, Catherine. 1996. *Only Words*. Cambridge, MA: Harvard University Press.
Madok, Bal Raj. 2001. *Portrait of a Martyr: Biography of Dr. Shyama Prasad Mookerjee*. New Delhi: Rupa.
Mahajan, Gurpreet. 1998. *Identities and Rights: Aspects of Liberal Democracy in India*. New Delhi: Oxford University Press.
———. 2008. 'Religion and the Indian Constitution: Questions of Separation and Equality', In Rajeev Bhargava (ed.), *Politics and Ethics of the Indian Constitution*, pp. 297–310. New Delhi: Oxford University Press, 2008.
———. 2013. *India: Political Ideas and the Making of a Democratic Discourse*. New York and London: Zed Books.

Maheshwari, Malvika. 2011. 'Violent Regulation and Artists in India: The Transformation of Freedom of Expression', PhD diss., Institut d'Etudes Politiques de Paris, Sciences Po.

Mahmood, Saba. 2009. 'Religious Reason and Secular Affect: An Incommensurable Divide?' In Wendy Brown, Judith Butler, Talal Asad and Saba Mahmood (eds.), *Is Critique Secular? Blasphemy, Injury and Free Speech*, pp. 58–94. Berkeley: The Townsend Center for the Humanities, University of California.

Maine, H. S. 1876. *Village Communities in the East and West*. London: John Murray.

Mantena, Karuna. 2009. *Alibis of Empire: Henry Maine and the Ends of Liberal Imperialism*. Princeton and Oxford: Princeton University Press.

Mayne, J. D. 1862. *Commentaries on Indian Penal Code*. Chennai: J. Higgenbotham.

Mehta, Pratap Bhanu. 2005. 'India's Judiciary: The Promise of Uncertainty'. In Devesh Kapur and Self (eds.), *Public Institutions in India: Performance and Design*, pp. 158–193. New Delhi: Oxford University Press.

———. 2008. 'Passion and Constraint: Courts and the Regulation of Religious Meaning'. In Rajeev Bhargava (ed.), *Politics and Ethics of the Indian Constitution*, pp. 311–338. New Delhi: Oxford University Press.

Mehta, Uday Singh. 1999. *Liberalism and Empire: A Study in Nineteenth-Century British Liberal Thought*. Chicago and London: University of Chicago Press.

———. 2011. 'Constitutionalism'. In Niraja Gopal Jayal and Pratap Bhanu Mehta (eds.), *The Oxford Companion to Politics in India*, pp. 14–27. New Delhi: Oxford University Press.

Mehta, V. R., & Thomas Pantham (eds.). 2006. *Political Ideas in Modern India: Thematic Explorations*. New Delhi: Sage.

Meiklejohn, Alexander. 1966. 'Freedom of Speech'. In Peter Radcliff (ed.), *Limits of Liberty: Studies of Mill's 'On Liberty'*, pp. 18–26. Belmont, CA: Wadsworth Publishing Co.

Melville, Casper. 2009. *Taking Offence*. London: Seagull Books.

Metcalf, Barbara D. 1992. 'Imagining Community: Polemical Debates in Colonial India'. In Kenneth W. Jones (ed.), *Religious Controversy in British India: Dialogues in South Asian Languages*, pp. 229–240. New York: State University of New York Press.

Metcalf, Barbara D., & Thomas R. Metcalf. 2012. *A Concise History of Modern India*. New York: Cambridge University Press.

Metcalf, Thomas. 1994. *Ideologies of the Raj*. Cambridge: Cambridge University Press.

Michelman, Frank. 1996. 'Between Facts and Norms by Jurgen Habermas', *Journal of Philosophy*, vol. 93, no. 6, pp. 307–315.

———. 1998. 'Constitutional Authorship'. In Larry Alexander (ed.), *Constitutionalism: Philosophical Foundations*, pp. 64–98. New York: Cambridge University Press.

Mill, J. S. 1978. *On Liberty*. Indianapolis: Hackett Publishing Press.

Modood, Tariq. 2005. *Multicultural Politics: Racism, Ethnicity and Muslims in Britain*. Edinburgh: Edinburgh University Press.

———. 2006. 'The Liberal Dilemma: Integration or Vilification?' *Open Democracy*, 8 February 2006. Available at http://www.opendemocracy.net/content/articles/PDF/3249.pdf (last accessed on 19 September 2018).

Muller, Beate (ed.). 2004. *Censorship and Cultural Regulation in the Modern Age*. Amsterdam: Editions Rodopi.

Nair, Neeti. 2013. 'Beyond the 'Communal' 1920s: The Problem of Intention, Legislative Pragmatism and the Making of Section 295A of the Indian Penal Code', *Indian Economic and Social History Review*, vol. 50, no. 3, pp. 317–340.

Narrain, Siddharth. 2016a. 'The Harm in Hate Speech Laws: Examining the Origins of Hate Speech Legislation in India'. In Rina Ramdev, S. D. Nambiar, and D. Bhattacharya (eds.), *Sentiment, Politics, Censorship: The State of Hurt*, pp. 39–54. New Delhi: Sage.

———. 2016b. 'Hate Speech, Hurt Sentiment and the (Im)Possibility of Free Speech', *Economic and Political Weekly*, vol. 51, no. 17, pp. 119–126.

Nehru, Jawaharlal, 1990. *Letters to Chief Ministers*, 5 vols. G. Parthasarathi (ed.). New Delhi: Oxford University Press.

Noorani, A. G. 1995. 'Informal Censorship', *Economic and Political Weekly*, vol. 30, no. 40, p. 2472.

———. 1999. 'Free Speech and Provocation', *Economic and Political Weekly*, vol. 34, no. 41, p. 2898.

———. 2008. 'Films and Free Speech', *Economic and Political Weekly*, vol. 43, no. 18, pp. 11–12.

O'Dowd, T. John. 2013. 'Pilate's Paramount Duty: Constitutional Reasonableness and the Restriction of Freedom of Expression and Assembly'. In Sunil Khilnani, Vikram Raghavan and Arun K. Thiruvengadam (eds.), *Comparative Constitutionalism in South Asia*, pp. 267–302. New Delhi: Oxford University Press.

Pamment, Claire. 2009. 'The Police of Pig and Sheep: Representations of the White Sahib and the Construction of Theatre Censorship in Colonial India', *South Asian Popular Culture*, vol. 7, no. 3, pp. 233–245.

Parekh, Bhikhu. 1994. 'Superior People: The Narrowness of Liberalism from Mill to Rawls', *Times Literary Supplement*, February 25, pp. 11–13.

———. 2000. *Rethinking Multiculturalism: Cultural Diversity and Political Theory*. Cambridge, MA: Harvard University Press.

———. 2008. 'The Constitution as a Statement of Indian Identity'. In Rajeev Bhargava (ed.), *Politics and Ethics of the Indian Constitution*, pp. 43–58. New Delhi: Oxford University Press.

———. 2012. 'Is There a Case for Banning Hate Speech?' In Michael Herz and Peter Molnar (eds.), *The Content and Context of Hate Speech*, pp. 37–56. New York: Cambridge University Press.

Patel, Vallabhbhai. 1972. *Sardar Patel's Correspondence*, 10 vols. Durga Das (ed.). Ahmedabad: Navjivan Publishing House.

Peel, Lawrence. 1848. *Observations on the Indian Penal Code*. Kolkata: Military Orphan Press.

Philips, C. H., H. L. Singh & B. N. Pandey (eds.). 1962. *The Evolution of India and Pakistan, 1858 and 1947: Select Documents*. London: Oxford University Press.

Pinney, Christopher. 1997. 'The Nation (Un)Pictured? Chromolithography and "Popular" Politics in India, 1878–1995', *Critical Inquiry*, vol. 23, no. 4, pp. 834–867.

———. 2009. 'Iatrogenic Religion and Politics'. In Raminder Kaur and William Mazzarella (eds.), *Censorship in South Asia: Cultural Regulation from Sedition to Seduction*, pp. 29–62. Bloomington and Indianapolis: Indiana University Press.

Pipes, Daniel. 1998. *The Rushdie Affair: The Novel, the Ayatollah and the West*. New Delhi: Voice of India.

Post, Robert. 1988. 'Cultural Heterogeneity and Law: Pornography, Blasphemy and the First Amendment', *California Law Review*, vol. 76, no. 2, pp. 297–335.

———. (ed.). 1998. *Censorship and Silencing: Practices of Cultural Regulation*. Los Angeles: Getty Publications.

———. (ed.). 2007. 'Religion and Freedom of Speech: Portraits of Muhammad', *Constellations*, vol. 14, no. 1, pp. 72–90.

Purandare, Vaibhav. 2002. *The Sena Story*. Mumbai: Business Publications Inc.

Rao, B Shiva. 1966–1968. *The Framing of India's Constitution: Select Documents*, 5 vols. New Delhi: Indian Institute of Public Administration.

Richman, Paula (ed.). 1991. *Many Ramayanas: The Diversity of a Narrative Tradition in South Asia*. Berkeley and Los Angeles: University of California Press.

Robinson, Nick, et al. 2011. 'Interpreting the Constitution: Supreme Court Constitution Benches since Independence', *Economic and Political Weekly*, vol. 46, no. 9, pp. 27–31.

Rosenfeld, M. 2012. 'Hate Speech in Constitutional Jurisprudence: A Comparative Analysis'. In Michael Herz and Peter Molnar (eds.), *The Content and Context of Hate Speech: Rethinking Regulation and Responses*, pp. 242–289. Cambridge: Cambridge University Press.

Roy, Rammohan. 1925. *Raja Ram Mohun Roy: His Life, Writings and Speeches*. Madras: G. A. Natesan.

Said, Edward. 1978. *Orientalism*. London: Routledge and Kegan Paul.

Sapru, Sir Tej Bahadur. 1945. *Constitutional Proposals of the Sapru Committee*, The Sapru Report. Bombay: Padma Prakashan.

Sarkar, Sumit. 1983. *Modern India*. New Delhi: Macmillan.

Seal, Anil. 1968. *The Emergence of Indian Nationalism: Competition and Collaboration in the Late Nineteenth Century*. London: Cambridge University Press.

Setalvad, Teesta. 2011. 'When Hate Speech and Writing Infiltrate Public Discourse Segregation and Discrimination Become the Norm and Rape and War can Always Be Incited in the Name of That Hatred.' Paper presented at *the Expert Workshop for the Asia Pacific organized by the United Nations High Commissioner for Human Rights (OHCHR)*, 6–7 July. Available at http://www.ohchr.org/Documents/Issues/Expression/ICCPR/Bangkok/TeestaSetalvad.pdf (last accessed on 17 June 2018).

Sethi, Aarti, & Shuddhabrata Sengupta. 2014. 'Towards a Readers' Uprising: Reflections in the Wake of Assaults on Books and Authors in Today's India', *India Review*, vol. 13, no. 3, pp. 290–299.

Singh, Piar. 1996. *Gatha Sri Adi Granth and the Controversy*. Grand Ledge: Anant Education and Rural Development Foundation.

Smith, K. J. M. 1991. 'Macaulay's 'Utilitarian' Indian Penal Code: An Illustration of the Accidental Function of Time, Place and Personalities in Law Making'. In W. M. Gordon and T. D. Fergus (ed.), *Legal History in the Making: Proceedings of the Ninth British Legal History Conference, Glasgow, 1989*, pp. 145–164. London: Hambledon Press.

———. 1988. *James Fitzjames Stephen: Portrait of a Victorian Rationalist*. Cambridge: Cambridge University Press.

Sorabjee, Soli J. 1994. 'Freedom of Expression and Censorship: Some Aspects of the Indian Experience,' *Northern Ireland Legal Quarterly*, vol. 45, no. 4, pp. 327–342.

———. 1976. *Law of Press Censorship in India*. Bombay: N. M. Tripathi.
Sridharan, Eswaran, and Anthony Cerulli. 2014. 'Editor's Introduction to the Roundtable on Intellectual Freedom, Vigilantism and Censorship in India', *India Review*, vol. 13, no. 3, pp. 274–276.
Stephen, J. F. 1967. *Liberty, Equality and Fraternity*. Cambridge: Cambridge University Press.
———. 1883. *A History of Criminal Law of England*, vol. III. London: Macmillan and Co.
Stephen, L. 1895. *Life of Sir James Fitzjames Stephen*, 2nd ed. London: Smith, Elder & Co.
Stephens, Julia. 2014. 'The Politics of Muslim Rage: Secular Law and Religious Sentiment in Late Colonial India', *History Workshop Journal*, vol. 77, no. 1, pp. 45–64.
Stokes, Eric. 1959. *English Utilitarians and India*. Oxford: Clarendon Press.
Taylor, Charles. 1989. 'The Rushdie Controversy', *Public Culture*, vol. 2, no. 1, pp. 118–121.
———. 2012. *The Harm in Hate Speech*. London: Harvard University Press.
Thiruvengadam, Arun K. 2013. 'The Evolution of the Constitutional Right to Free Speech in India (1800–1950): The Interplay of Universal and Particular Rationales." University of Washington Trans-Pacific Comparative Constitutional Roundtable, Centre for Asian Legal Studies, National University of Singapore, Working Paper Series. Available at http://papers.ssrn.com/sol3/papers.cfm?abstract_id=2470905 (last accessed on 23 August 2020).
Thursby, G. R. 1975. *Hindu-Muslim Relations in British India*. Leiden: E. J. Brill.
Tsakyrakis, Stavros. 2009. 'Proportionality: An Assault on Human Rights', *International Journal of Constitutional Law*, vol. 7, no. 3, pp. 468–493.
Waldron, Jeremy. 1993. *Liberal Rights*. New York: Cambridge University Press.
———. 2010. 'Dignity and Defamation: The Visibility of Hate, 2009 Oliver Wendell Holmes Lectures', *Harvard Law Review*, vol 123, no. 7, pp. 1596–1657.
———. 2012. *The Harm in Hate Speech*. London: Harvard University Press.
Walker, Samuel. 1994. *Hate Speech: The History of an American Controversy*. London: University of Nebraska Press.
Wilkinson, Steven I. 2005. *Religious Politics and Communal Violence*. Oxford: Oxford University Press.
Wright, Barry. 2011. 'Macaulay's Indian Penal Code: Historical Context and Originating Principles'. In Stanley Yeo Self and Wing-Cheong Chan (ed.), *Codification, Macaulay and The Indian Penal Code: The Legacies and Modern Challenges of Criminal Law Reforms*, pp. 19–55. Surrey: Ashgate.

Government Publications

Constituent Assembly Debates, 12 vols.
Gazette of India (1927)
Lok Sabha Debates (1961, 1969, 2004, 2007)
Parliamentary Debates (1951)
UP State Assembly Debates (1969, 2005)
Rajya Sabha Debates (1961, 1969, 1988, 2006, 2007)

INDEX

Pages in **bold** refer to tables.

For Product Safety Concerns and Information please contact our EU
representative GPSR@taylorandfrancis.com
Taylor & Francis Verlag GmbH, Kaufingerstraße 24, 80331 München, Germany

www.ingramcontent.com/pod-product-compliance
Ingram Content Group UK Ltd.
Pitfield, Milton Keynes, MK11 3LW, UK
UKHW020139200926
475702UK00005B/818
9781032384993